# QUICK SPANISH for Law Enforcement

## Essential Words and Phrases for Police Officers and Law Enforcement Personnel

DAVID B. DEES

McGraw-Hill

New York Chicago San Francisco Lisbon London Madrid Mexico City
Milan New Delhi San Juan Seoul Singapore Sydney Toronto

The McGraw-Hill Companies

**Library of Congress Cataloging-in-Publication Data**

Dees, David B.
Quick Spanish for law enforcement / by David B. Dees.
p. cm.
ISBN 0-07-146017-9

1. Spanish language—Conversation and phrase books (for police). I. Title.

PC4120.P64D44 2005
468.3′421′0243632—dc22 2005047935



6 7 8 9 0 FGR/FGR 0 9

ISBN 0-07-146017-9

McGraw-Hill books are available at special quantity discounts to use as premiums and sales promotions, or for use in corporate training programs. For more information, please write to the Director of Special Sales, Professional Publishing, McGraw-Hill, Two Penn Plaza, New York, NY 10121-2298. Or contact your local bookstore.

This book is printed on acid-free paper.

*To the memory of my loving wife and soul mate,*

Colette Joly Dees

*For the past 16 years, we have taught police officers, firefighters, and cadets. Colette was always enthusiastic about training cops and firefighters! God has kept her in my heart as my guardian angel and co-instructor!*

# Contents



## 1
## Basic Spanish Vocabulary 1

# 2
# Law Enforcement Vocabulary 63

# 4

# 5

## Culture and Survival Tips 258



# 6

## Quick Reference 279

# Acknowledgments

For administrative, language, and scenario support, I thank Ventura County Sheriff Bob Brooks; former students Commanders Linda Oksner and Dennis Carpenter and Sergeants Tim Hagel, Joe Galante, and Derek West; Fillmore P.D. Detectives Luis de Anda and Taurino Almazán; Thousand Oaks P.D. Detective P. J. Dain; Ventura County Sheriff's and Fire Department Dispatcher Supervisors Danita Crombach and Debra Zinskey; Oxnard P.D. Officer Jeff Miller and his Spanish-speaking wife, Lidia; and Sister Maria Socorro Roman, S. de M. (Sister didn't see the list of dirty words!). I am also grateful to McGraw-Hill Editor Karen S. Young and the McGraw-Hill editorial/production staff.

# Introduction

**¡Hola y bienvenidos!** Hello and welcome!

## What Is This Book?

*Quick Spanish for Law Enforcement* is an on-scene survival guide for law enforcement personnel; it is intended for use during routine calls and emergencies.

## Who Should Use This Book?

This book is primarily for patrol officers and sheriff's deputies. However, detectives, investigators, and cadets, as well as corrections, probation, parole, highway patrol, and fish and game officers, have similar communication needs and will find this book helpful.

## How Is This Book Organized?

*Quick Spanish for Law Enforcement* has six chapters: basic vocabulary, law enforcement vocabulary, commands and key terms, law enforcement scenarios, culture and survival tips, and a mini-dictionary of commands, key questions, and statements. Sections are developed in a logical progression, and communication terms are linked among sections for easy reference.

Throughout the book, **Ojo** ("Watch out!") boxes explain tricky points in using Spanish: errors to avoid and idiomatic expressions to make you look good. Overly academic terms are generally avoided, but we use a few basic grammatical terms in parentheses, like *verbs* and *prepositions.*

## How Is This Book Useful?

Let's say you're on patrol and you want to question a suspected Spanish-speaking drug pusher—but you know little or no Spanish. Prepare ahead!

First, you become familiar with basic Spanish (Chapter 1); you identify the pusher in "Criminals" and learn field interview vocabulary (Chapter 2); you learn commands, key questions, and statements (Chapter 3); and finally, you arrest him in a pedestrian stop scenario (Chapter 4).

You can also pick up Latino culture and survival tips, along with Spanglish and street Spanish (Chapter 5).

## What Kind of Spanish Am I Learning?

We use generic Latin American Spanish, with a sprinkling of regional terms. This book will help you speak with and understand the majority of Latinos in North America. *Quick Spanish for Law Enforcement* is an emerging tool that helps you enforce the law and serve citizens who are primarily from Mexico and Central America. Although we focus on everyday Spanish spoken in the Southwest, especially in Arizona and California, this book will help you communicate with most Spanish speakers throughout the United States and Canada.

## How Is This Book Different?

This book has been prepared *just for cops.* The content of this book is California P.O.S.T. certified for use in Spanish-language academy and in-service officer/deputy training programs. It has been prepared to help cops break through the language barrier quickly and effectively.

The Spanish in this book is not "proper" school Spanish. Boring and useless words have been eliminated. We emphasize conversation: speaking and understanding Spanish, not reading and writing it. We occasionally use Spanglish and street language, and we focus on practical questions and commands. We keep things simple and we use everyday language like **sheriff**, **troque**, and **tíquete**, words that Latinos use. As a special feature, we include the phonetic pronunciation for the first three chapters.

## How Do I Use This Book?

This book might save your life! Use it as a weapon. Put it in your pocket right after you strap on your gun, and take it with you on all calls. As a police officer, you call the shots, so take charge. Take this book with you and use it regularly; this will build your confidence as it increases your effectiveness!

First, leaf through the vocabulary and select words you may need. Then turn to the scenarios, which list the most common phrases and sentences that you hear and say. You can create your own scenarios—even make up cheat-sheet scenarios! Practice the material until you can say it in your sleep. Your sergeant will be delighted, and your chief will reward you!

## What If I'm Only a Rookie Spanish Speaker?

You need to get your feet wet *en español.* Spanish is easier to pronounce than English, and the two languages share many sounds. Keep it simple! Use words that are similar to English words. Use "quickie" commands and ask bottom-line questions.

Don't worry if you sound like a gringo at first, or if you get blank stares when you ask questions. Keep working at it. Keep your confidence up. After all, you're making the effort to learn their language. Spanish speakers are generally very nice, cooperative people; they will appreciate your efforts and will try to meet you halfway. Use simple words, along with hand and face gestures. If everything else fails, point to the Spanish translation in this book!

## What's the Best Way to Ask Questions?

The easiest are bottom-line questions with yes-or-no (**sí o no**) answers. For personal information, you can often use one-word questions: "Name?" (**¿Nombre?**) "Address?" (**¿Dirección?**). You can also ask complete questions: "What is your name?" (**¿Cómo se llama?**). For more information, use fill-in-the-blank questions, using words that we provide: "Was he tall or short?" (**¿Era alto o bajo?**) "Did they take your money? Wallet? Credit card?" (**¿Le llevaron su dinero? ¿Cartera? ¿Tarjeta de crédito?**). Generally, you should try to avoid open-ended questions that could get you in trouble. In scenarios, we often give both complete and shortened forms of questions: "(When was) the last time you ate?" (**¿(Cuándo fue) la última vez que comió?**).

## How Can This Book Help Me Down the Road?

Keep up your skills with periodic review of *Quick Spanish for Law Enforcement.* Listen to, watch, and read Spanish-language media. Talk with native-Spanish-speaking officers and form a Spanish club. Expand your skills by taking a Spanish class. Then, spend your next vacation south of the border. **Dos Equis, por favor.**

## Who Is the Author of This Book?

I'm David B. Dees, owner and director of Dees Multilingual Services, providing language services in Spanish, French, and Russian. In 1989, my wife and I started emergency Spanish classes with the Santa Monica Fire Department. Since 1996, we have been instructors of Spanish for Law Enforcement in California P.O.S.T.-certified classes for the Ventura County Sheriff's Department, and for the Tri-County Criminal Justice Training Center. Over the past 16 years, we have also taught Spanish to cops and firefighters in fire science/public safety courses at community colleges and in fire departments—more than 2,000 students in all!

I majored in Russian and Spanish at Emporia State University, and I earned an M.A. in Russian at the University of Wisconsin and an equivalent M.A. in Spanish at Marquette University. I did Ph.D. coursework at the University of Pittsburgh. I have traveled extensively and have lived in Latin America and Europe, including seven years' residence in Spain teaching English. I have taught in elementary and secondary schools and in colleges, including exclusive private schools. I hold a California life teaching credential; I have published articles in trade magazines and I have addressed language topics at police, fire, and paramedic conferences.

## Do You Have Other Books or Materials?

We have developed lots of police and fire/paramedic Spanish-language training materials, including beginning, intermediate, and advanced student and instructor textbooks, booklets, and CDs, for self-study or classroom instruction. Our company, Dees Multilingual Services, can be found on the Internet at **www.spanishforpoliceandfire.com**; to contact us, send an e-mail to **info@spanishforpoliceandfire.com** or call us at 805-984-3201. Through McGraw-Hill, we have also published a book targeted specifically for firefighters, paramedics, and EMTs: *Quick Spanish for Emergency Responders*.

We hope you will find this book useful.

**Buena suerte con tus estudios.**
Good luck with your studies.

# Basic Spanish Vocabulary

Welcome to our book! We begin with the Spanish alphabet and pronunciation. Spanish is much easier to pronounce than English. Plus, the two languages share many sounds. Let's get to it! **¡Vamos!**

## SPANISH ALPHABET
El alfabeto español

| LETTER | SOUNDS LIKE/EXAMPLE |
| --- | --- |
| A [ah] | "a" in "mama"<br>**ayuda** [ah-YOO-thah] **(help)** |
| ai [ay] | "i" in "ire"<br>**aire** [AY-reh] **(air)** |
| B [beh] | "b" in "boy"<br>**bombero** [bohm-BEH-roh] **(firefighter)** |
| C [seh] | |
| ce [seh] | "ce" in "cent"<br>**incendio** [een-SEHN-dyoh] **(fire)** |
| ci [see] | "see" in "seen"<br>**policía** [poh-lee-SEE-ah] **(police)** |
| ca [kah] | "co" in "cop"<br>**rescate** [reh-SKAH-teh] **(rescue)** |
| co [koh] | "co" in "cold"<br>**corra** [KOH-rrah] **(run)** |
| cu [koo] | "coo" in "cool"<br>**culpable** [kool-PAH-bleh] **(guilty)** |
| cu + *vowel* [kw] | "qu" in "queen"<br>**cuello** [KWEH-yoh] **(collar)** |
| c + *consonant* [k] | "c" in "clap"<br>**clase** [KLAH-seh] **(class)** |
| cc [ks] | "cc" in "access"<br>**accidente** [ahk-see-THEHN-teh] (accident) |

| LETTER | SOUNDS LIKE/EXAMPLE |
|---|---|
| CH [cheh] | "ch" in "cheese"<br>**escuche** [eh-SKOO-cheh] **(listen)** |
| D [deh] | |
| d (*at beginning*) [d] | "d" in "dare"<br>**dolor** [doh-LOHR] **(pain)** |
| d (*between vowels*) [th] | "th" in "father"<br>**nada** [NAH-thah] **(nothing)** |
| d (*at end*) [th] | "th" in "father"<br>**ciudad** [see-oo-THAHTH] **(city)** |
| E [eh] | "e" in "bet"<br>**enfermo** [ehn-FEHR-moh] **(sick)** |
| F [EH-feh] | "f" in "father"<br>**foto** [FOH-toh] **(photo)** |
| G [heh] | |
| ge [heh] | "he" in "help"<br>**gente** [HEHN-teh] **(people)** |
| gi [hee] | "he" in "hero"<br>**gigante** [hee-GAHN-teh] **(giant)** |
| ga [gah] | "ga" in "garage"<br>**garaje** [gah-RAH-heh] **(garage)** |
| go [goh] | "go" in "go"<br>**golpe** [GOHL-peh] **(blow)** |
| gu [goo] | "goo" in "goose"<br>**gusano** [goo-SAH-noh] **(worm)** |
| gue [geh] | "gue" in "guess"<br>**guerra** [GEH-rrah] **(war)** |
| gui [gee] | "gee" in "geese"<br>**guitarra** [gee-TAH-rrah] **(guitar)** |
| g + *consonant* [g] | "g" in "grab"<br>**gracias** [GRAH-syahs] **(thanks)** |
| H [AH-cheh] | silent<br>**hombre** [OHM-breh] **(man)** |
| I [ee] | "e" in "be"<br>**inglés** [een-GLEHS] **(English)** |
| ia [yah] | "ya" in "yacht"<br>**estudiante** [eh-stoo-DYAHN-teh] **(student)** |
| ie [yeh] | "ye" in "yet"<br>**quien** [kyehn] **(who)** |

| LETTER | SOUNDS LIKE/EXAMPLE |
|---|---|
| io [yoh] | "yo" in "yoga"<br>**nación** [nah-SYOHN] **(nation)** |
| J [HOH-tah] | "h" in "hot"<br>**ojo** [OH-hoh] **(eye)** |
| K [kah] (*found only in foreign words*) | "k" in "kite"<br>**kilo** [KEE-loh] **(kilo)** |
| L [EH-leh] | "l" in "lip"<br>**luz** [loos] **(light)** |
| LL [EH-yeh] | "y" in "yes"<br>**llamo** [YAH-moh] **(I call)** |
| M [EH-meh] | "m" in "map"<br>**mano** [MAH-noh] **(hand)** |
| N [EH-neh] | "n" in "net"<br>**nombre** [NOHM-breh] **(name)** |
| Ñ [EH-nyeh] | "ny" in "canyon"<br>**niño** [NEE-nyoh] **(child)** |
| O [oh] | "o" in "open"<br>**oreja** [oh-REH-hah] **(ear)** |
| P [peh] | "p" in "pin"<br>**pie** [pyeh] **(foot)** |
| Q [koo] | |
| qu [k] | "k" in "key"<br>**aquí** [ah-KEE] **(here)** |
| R [EH-reh] | trilled "r"<br>**gracias** [GRAH-syahs] **(thanks)** |
| r (*at beginning*) [EH-reh] | very trilled "rr"<br>**rojo** [RROH-hoh] **(red)** |

The Spanish **R** has no direct equivalent in English. It is always trilled in Spanish.

| LETTER | SOUNDS LIKE/EXAMPLE |
|---|---|
| RR [EH-rreh] | very trilled "rr"<br>**perro** [PEH-rroh] **(dog)** |
| S [EH-seh] | "s" in "see"<br>**señor** [seh-NYOHR] **(sir)** |
| s *before* m [z] | "s" in "trees"<br>**mismo** [MEEZ-moh] **(same)** |

| LETTER | SOUNDS LIKE/EXAMPLE |
|---|---|
| s *before* d [z] | "s" in "trees"<br>**desde** [DEHZ-deh] **(since)** |
| T [teh] | "t" in "tooth"<br>**tráfico** [TRAH-fee-koh] **(traffic)** |
| U [oo] | "oo" in "boot"<br>**tú** [too] **(you)** |
| ua [wah] | "wa" in "wad"<br>**guapo** [GWAH-poh] **(handsome)** |
| ue [weh] | "we" in "wet"<br>**cuerpo** [KWEHR-poh] **(body)** |
| ui [wee] | "wee" in "weed"<br>**cuidado** [kwee-THAH-thoh] **([be] careful)** |
| uo [woh] | "wo" in "woke"<br>**cuota** [KWOH-tah] **(quota)** |
| V [beh] | "b" in "boy"<br>**víctima** [BEEK-tee-mah] **(victim)** |
| W [DOH-bleh oo] | "w" in "win"<br>**whisky** [WEE-skee] **(whiskey)** |
| X [EH-kees] | "ks" in "books"<br>**sexto** [SEHKS-toh] **(sixth)** |
| Y [ee gree-EH-gah] | |
| y (*as consonant*) | "y" in "yes"<br>**ya** [yah] **(already, now)** |
| y (*as vowel*) | "ee" in "heel"<br>**whisky** [WEE-skee] **(whiskey)** |
| Z [SEH-tah] | "s" in "see"<br>**comenzar** [koh-mehn-SAHR] **(to begin)** |

## SPANISH PRONUNCIATION

### La pronunciación española

Your goal is to make yourself understood. If you sound like a gringo, that's okay. If you can't roll your **R**s, that's okay too.

This book provides the phonetic pronunciation of most words and phrases in the first three chapters. Syllables within words are separated by a hyphen, and the stressed syllable appears in CAPITAL letters. Where two vowels are pronounced together in the same syllable (as in **cuerpo** ("body") [KWEHR-poh]), the vowels are represented phonetically by a consonant-plus-vowel combination. [KWEHR] is pronounced as one syllable and is stressed. The second, unstressed syllable is [poh]. Read the phonetic pronunciations aloud, pronouncing each syllable separately and stressing the syllable in capital letters. Exaggerate your pronunciation.

As you pronounce whole phrases and sentences, run the words together, squeezing little words (like **el** and **la**) into big words (for instance, **el libro** → **ellibro**) without pauses. Pay very close attention to vowel sounds:

A [ah], pronounced like "a" in English "mama":
**mañana** [mah-NYAH-nah] (tomorrow)

E [eh], pronounced like "e" in English "bet":
**teléfono** [teh-LEH-foh-noh] (phone)

I [ee], pronounced like "e" in English "be":
**víctima** [BEEK-tee-mah] (victim)

O [oh], pronounced like "o" in English "open":
**otro** [OH-troh] (other)

U [oo], pronounced like "oo" in English "boot":
**número** [NOO-meh-roh] (number)

## Hard Sounds to Pronounce

### Los sonidos difíciles para pronunciar

Let's practice Spanish sounds that are hard for gringos to pronounce. You'll often need to use the following words:

**apellido** [ah-peh-YEE-thoh] (last name)

The **ll** is pronounced "y," and the **d** between vowels is pronounced "th," as in "father." Don't use a hard "d" sound.

**azul** [ah-SOOL] (blue)

The **z** is pronounced "s."

**cabeza** [kah-BEH-sah] (head)

The **z** has a clear "s" sound—not "z."

**cicatriz** [see-kah-TREES] (scar)

Even at the end of a word, **z** is pronounced "s."

**ciudad** [see-oo-THAHTH] (city)

Both **ds** are pronounced "th," as in "father."

**domicilio** [doh-mee-SEE-lee-oh] (address)

The **ci** sounds like "see."

**estación** [eh-stah-SYOHN] (station)

There is no "sh" sound in **ción**.

**fuego** [FWEH-goh] (fire)

**investigador** [een-beh-stee-gah-THOHR] (investigator)

**izquierda** [ees-KYEHR-thah] (left)

The **z** is pronounced "s," and the **qu** is pronounced "k."

**licencia** [lee-SEHN-syah] (license)

The **li** is pronounced "lee."

**nacionalidad** [nah-syoh-nah-lee-THAHTH] (nationality)

Slowly pronounce all the syllables, stressing the last one.

**persona** [pehr-SOH-nah] (person)

The **e** is pronounced like the "e" in "bet."

**pie** [pyeh] (foot)

The **ie** is pronounced like the "ye" in "yet," not like its sound in American "pie."

**policía** [poh-lee-SEE-ah] (police officer)

There is no "sh" sound in **cía**.

**profesión** [proh-feh-SYOHN] (profession)

The **sión** is pronounced just like **ción**; there is no "sh" sound.

**que** [keh] (what, that)

The **qu** is pronounced like "k" in "Kay"; it is always a hard sound.

**qui** [kee] (who)

The **qu** is pronounced like "k" in "key"; it is always a hard sound.

**quince** [KEEN-seh] (fifteen)

The **qu** is pronounced hard like "k" in "keen."

**suelo** [SWEH-loh] (ground, floor)

The **sue** sounds like "swea" in "sweater."

**tatuaje** [tah-TWAH-heh] (tattoo)

The Spanish **j** is always pronounced like English "h."

**voltéese** [bohl-TEH-eh-seh] (turn around)

Pronounce all four syllables, stressing [TEH].

## DAYS OF THE WEEK
Los días de la semana

| | |
|---|---|
| Sunday | **domingo**<br>doh-MEEN-goh |
| Monday | **lunes**<br>LOO-nehs |
| Tuesday | **martes**<br>MAHR-tehs |
| Wednesday | **miércoles**<br>MYEHR-koh-lehs |
| Thursday | **jueves**<br>HWEH-behs |
| Friday | **viernes**<br>BYEHR-nehs |
| Saturday | **sábado**<br>SAH-bah-thoh |

## MONTHS OF THE YEAR
Los meses del año

| | |
|---|---|
| January | **enero**<br>eh-NEH-roh |
| February | **febrero**<br>feh-BREH-roh |
| March | **marzo**<br>MAHR-soh |
| April | **abril**<br>ah-BREEL |
| May | **mayo**<br>MAH-yoh |
| June | **junio**<br>HOO-nee-oh |
| July | **julio**<br>HOO-lee-oh |
| August | **agosto**<br>ah-GOH-stoh |
| September | **septiembre**<br>sehp-TYEHM-breh |
| October | **octubre**<br>ohk-TOO-breh |

| | |
|---|---|
| November | **noviembre**<br>noh-BYEHM-breh |
| December | **diciembre**<br>dee-SYEHM-breh |

## SEASONS
Las estaciones

| | |
|---|---|
| spring | **la primavera**<br>pree-mah-BEH-rah |
| summer | **el verano**<br>beh-RAH-noh |
| fall | **el otoño**<br>oh-TOH-nyoh |
| winter | **el invierno**<br>een-BYEHR-noh |

## WEATHER
El tiempo

Here are useful words and phrases about the weather.

| | |
|---|---|
| How's the weather? | **¿Qué tiempo hace?**<br>keh TYEHM-poh AH-seh |
| air | **el aire**<br>AY-reh |
| clear | **despejado**<br>deh-speh-HAH-thoh |
| It's clear. | **Está despejado.**<br>eh-STAH deh-speh-HAH-thoh |
| climate | **el clima**<br>KLEE-mah |
| cloud(s) | **la(s) nube(s)**<br>NOO-beh(s) |
| It's cloudy. | **Está nublado.**<br>eh-STAH noo-BLAH-thoh |
| cold | **frío**<br>FREE-oh |
| It's cold. | **Hace frío.**<br>AH-seh FREE-oh |

| | |
|---|---|
| I'm cold. | **Tengo frío.**<br>TEHN-goh FREE-oh |
| cool | **fresco**<br>FREH-skoh |
| It's cool. | **Hace fresco.**<br>AH-seh FREH-skoh |
| dark | **oscuro**<br>oh-SKOO-roh |
| It's dark. | **Está oscuro.**<br>eh-STAH oh-SKOO-roh |
| drizzle | **lloviznar**<br>yoh-beez-NAHR |
| It's drizzling. | **Está lloviznando.**<br>eh-STAH yoh-beez-NAHN-doh |
| earthquake | **el terremoto**<br>teh-rreh-MOH-toh |
| flood | **la inundación**<br>een-oon-dah-SYOHN |
| fog | **la niebla**<br>NYEH-blah |
| It's foggy. | **Hay niebla.**<br>ay NYEH-blah |
| frost | **la escarcha**<br>eh-SKAHR-chah |
| frozen | **helado**<br>eh-LAH-thoh |
| I'm freezing. | **Estoy helado[a].**<br>eh-STOY eh-LAH-thoh[-thah] |
| hail | **el granizo**<br>grah-NEE-soh |

If a Spanish word has a masculine form ending in **-o** and a feminine form ending in **-a**, the feminine ending is shown as **[a]** after the masculine word. If you're talking about more than one, add **-s**.

| | |
|---|---|
| frozen | **helado[a]**<br>**helados[as]** |

| | |
|---|---|
| heat | **el calor**<br>kah-LOHR |
| It's hot. | **Hace calor.**<br>AH-seh kah-LOHR |
| I'm hot. | **Tengo calor.**<br>TEHN-goh kah-LOHR |

Be careful with "hot."

| | |
|---|---|
| It's hot (weather). | **Hace calor.** |
| It's hot (to touch). | **Está caliente.** |
| It's hot (spicy food). | **Está picante.** |

| | |
|---|---|
| humidity | **la humedad**<br>oo-meh-THAHTH |
| hurricane | **el huracán**<br>oo-rah-KAHN |
| ice | **el hielo**<br>YEH-loh |
| lightning | **el relámpago**<br>rreh-LAHM-pah-goh |
| mist | **la neblina**<br>neh-BLEE-nah |
| moon | **la luna**<br>LOO-nah |

If an English expression has two or more equivalent forms in Spanish, they are separated by a "~".

| | |
|---|---|
| It's snowing. | **Nieva. ~ Está nevando.** |

| | |
|---|---|
| rain | **la lluvia**<br>YOO-byah |
| It's raining. | **Llueve. ~ Está lloviendo.**<br>YWEH-beh ~<br>eh-STAH yoh-BYEHN-doh |

| | |
|---|---|
| sky | **el cielo**<br>SYEH-loh |
| snow | **la nieve**<br>NYEH-beh |
| It's snowing. | **Nieva. ~ Está nevando.**<br>NYEH-bah ~<br>eh-STAH neh-BAHN-doh |
| star(s) | **la(s) estrella(s)**<br>eh-STREH-yah(s) |
| storm | **la tormenta**<br>tohr-MEHN-tah |
| sun | **el sol**<br>sohl |
| It's sunny. | **Hace sol.**<br>AH-seh sohl |
| thunder | **el trueno**<br>troo-EH-noh |
| tornado | **el tornado**<br>tohr-NAH-thoh |
| weather | **el tiempo**<br>TYEHM-poh |
| It's bad weather. | **Hace mal tiempo.**<br>AH-seh mahl TYEHM-poh |
| It's good weather. | **Hace buen tiempo.**<br>AH-seh bwehn TYEHM-poh |
| wind | **el viento**<br>BYEHN-toh |
| It's windy. | **Hace viento.**<br>AH-seh BYEHN-toh |

## NUMBERS
Los números

| | |
|---|---|
| 0 | **cero**<br>SEH-roh |
| 1 | **uno**<br>OO-noh |
| 2 | **dos**<br>dohs |
| 3 | **tres**<br>trehs |

| | |
|---|---|
| 4 | **cuatro**<br>KWAH-troh |
| 5 | **cinco**<br>SEEN-koh |
| 6 | **seis**<br>sehs |
| 7 | **siete**<br>SYEH-teh |
| 8 | **ocho**<br>OH-choh |
| 9 | **nueve**<br>NWEH-beh |
| 10 | **diez**<br>dyehs |
| 11 | **once**<br>OHN-seh |
| 12 | **doce**<br>DOH-seh |
| 13 | **trece**<br>TREH-seh |
| 14 | **catorce**<br>kah-TOHR-seh |
| 15 | **quince**<br>KEEN-seh |
| 16 | **dieciséis**<br>dyehs-ee-SEHS |
| 17 | **diecisiete**<br>dyehs-ee-SYEH-teh |
| 18 | **dieciocho**<br>dyehs-ee-OH-choh |
| 19 | **diecinueve**<br>dyehs-ee-NWEH-beh |
| 20 | **veinte**<br>BEHN-teh |
| 21 | **veintiuno**<br>behn-tee-OO-noh |
| 22 | **veintidós**<br>behn-tee-DOHS |
| 30 | **treinta**<br>TREHN-tah |

| | |
|---|---|
| 33 | **treinta y tres**<br>TREHN-tah ee trehs |
| 40 | **cuarenta**<br>kwah-REHN-tah |
| 44 | **cuarenta y cuatro**<br>kwah-REHN-tah ee KWAH-troh |
| 50 | **cincuenta**<br>seen-KWEHN-tah |
| 55 | **cincuenta y cinco**<br>seen-KWEHN-tah ee SEEN-koh |
| 60 | **sesenta**<br>seh-SEHN-tah |
| 66 | **sesenta y seis**<br>seh-SEHN-tah ee sehs |
| 70 | **setenta**<br>seh-TEHN-tah |
| 77 | **setenta y siete**<br>seh-TEHN-tah ee SYEH-teh |
| 80 | **ochenta**<br>oh-CHEHN-tah |
| 88 | **ochenta y ocho**<br>oh-CHEHN-tah ee OH-choh |
| 90 | **noventa**<br>noh-BEHN-tah |
| 99 | **noventa y nueve**<br>noh-BEHN-tah ee NWEH-beh |
| 100 | **ciento / cien**<br>SYEHN-toh / syehn |
| 101 | **ciento uno**<br>SYEHN-toh OO-noh |
| 200 | **doscientos[as]**<br>dohs-SYEHN-tohs[-tahs] |
| 300 | **trescientos[as]**<br>trehs-SYEHN-tohs[-tahs] |
| 400 | **cuatrocientos[as]**<br>kwah-troh-SYEHN-tohs[-tahs] |
| 500 | **quinientos[as]**<br>kee-NYEHN-tohs[-tahs] |
| 600 | **seiscientos[as]**<br>sehs-SYEHN-tohs[-tahs] |

If a Spanish word has a masculine form ending in **-o** and a feminine form ending in **-a**, the feminine ending is shown as **[a]** after the masculine word. If you're talking about more than one, add **-s**.

| | |
|---|---|
| first (one) | **primero[a]** |
| first (ones) | **primeros[as]** |

| | |
|---|---|
| 700 | **setecientos[as]**<br>seh-teh-SYEHN-tohs[-tahs] |
| 800 | **ochocientos[as]**<br>oh-choh-SYEHN-tohs[-tahs] |
| 900 | **novecientos[as]**<br>noh-beh-SYEHN-tohs[-tahs] |
| 1,000 | **mil**<br>meel |
| 2,000 | **dos mil**<br>dohs meel |
| 1,000,000 | **un millón**<br>oon mee-YOHN |
| 2,000,000 | **dos millones**<br>dohs mee-YOH-nehs |
| first | **primer / primero[a]**<br>pree-MEHR/<br>pree-MEH-roh[-rah] |
| second | **segundo[a]**<br>seh-GOON-doh[-dah] |
| third | **tercer / tercero[a]**<br>tehr-SEHR/tehr-SEH-roh[-rah] |
| fourth | **cuarto[a]**<br>KWAHR-toh[-tah] |
| fifth | **quinto[a]**<br>KEEN-toh[-tah] |
| sixth | **sexto[a]**<br>SEHKS-toh[-tah] |
| seventh | **séptimo[a]**<br>SEHP-tee-moh[-mah] |

| | |
|---|---|
| eighth | **octavo[a]**<br>ohk-TAH-boh[-bah] |
| ninth | **noveno[a]**<br>noh-BEH-noh[-nah] |
| tenth | **décimo[a]**<br>DEH-see-moh[-mah] |

## DATES
Las fechas

| | |
|---|---|
| What's the date? | **¿Cuál es la fecha?**<br>kwahl ehs lah FEH-chah |
| Today's the first of October. | **Hoy es el primero de octubre.**<br>oy ehs ehl pree-MEH-roh deh ohk-TOO-breh |
| What year? | **¿Qué año?**<br>keh AH-nyoh |
| 1999 | **mil novecientos noventa y nueve**<br>meel noh-beh-SYEHN-tohs noh-BEHN-tah ee NWEH-beh |
| 2000 | **dos mil**<br>dohs meel |
| September 8, 2006 | **el ocho de septiembre, dos mil seis**<br>ehl OH-choh deh sehp-TYEHM-breh dohs meel sehs |

The first day of the month is **el primero (del mes)**. The second is **el dos**, the third is **el tres**, and so on.

## TIME EXPRESSIONS
### Las expresiones del tiempo

Time expressions indicate when events take place.

What time is it? **¿Qué hora es?** keh OH-rah ehs

It's one o'clock. **Es la una.** ehs lah OO-nah

It's two thirty. **Son las dos y media.** sohn lahs dohs ee MEH-dyah

At three fifteen. **A las tres y cuarto.** ah lahs trehs ee KWAHR-toh

For one o'clock, **es la** is used for "it's" and **a la** for "at." For two o'clock, three o'clock, and so on, use **son las** and **a las**.

after (*a given time*) **después de** dehs-PWEHS deh

afternoon **la tarde** TAHR-theh

this afternoon **esta tarde** EH-stah TAHR-theh

already **ya** yah

always **siempre** SYEHM-preh

before (*a given time*) **antes de** AHN-tehs deh

dawn **el amanecer** ah-mah-neh-SEHR

at dawn **al amanecer** ahl ah-mah-neh-SEHR

day **el día** DEE-ah

all day **todo el día** toh-thoh ehl DEE-ah

| | |
|---|---|
| every day | **todos los días**<br>toh-thohs lohs DEE-ahs |
| in a day | **en un día**<br>ehn oon DEE-ah |
| evening | **la noche**<br>NOH-cheh |
| this evening | **esta noche**<br>EH-stah NOH-cheh |
| fast | **pronto**<br>PROHN-toh |
| from time to time | **de vez en cuando**<br>deh vehs ehn KWAHN-doh |
| hour | **la hora**<br>OH-rah |
| in half an hour | **en media hora**<br>ehn MEH-dyah OH-rah |
| in an hour | **en una hora**<br>ehn OO-nah OH-rah |
| an hour ago | **hace una hora**<br>AH-seh OO-nah OH-rah |
| half an hour ago | **hace media hora**<br>AH-seh MEH-dyah OH-rah |
| minute | **el minuto**<br>mee-NOO-toh |
| in a minute | **en un minuto**<br>ehn oon mee-NOO-toh |
| a minute ago | **hace un minuto**<br>AH-seh oon mee-NOO-toh |
| month | **el mes**<br>mehs |
| in a month | **en un mes**<br>ehn oon mehs |
| last month | **el mes pasado**<br>mehs pah-SAH-thoh |
| morning | **la mañana**<br>mah-NYAH-nah |
| in the morning | **en la mañana**<br>ehn lah mah-NYAH-nah<br>**por la mañana**<br>pohr lah mah-NYAH-nah |

| | |
|---|---|
| (at ten) in the morning | **(a las diez) de la mañana**<br>(ah lahs dyehs) deh lah mah-NYAH-nah |
| this morning | **esta mañana**<br>EH-stah mah-NYAH-nah |
| never | **nunca**<br>NOON-kah |
| almost never | **casi nunca**<br>KAH-see NOON-kah |
| next to the last | **el penúltimo / la penúltima**<br>peh-NOOL-tee-moh / peh-NOOL-tee-mah |
| night | **la noche**<br>NOH-cheh |
| last night | **anoche**<br>ah-NOH-cheh |
| the night before last | **anteanoche**<br>ahn-teh-ah-NOH-cheh |
| tonight | **esta noche**<br>EH-stah NOH-cheh |
| now | **ahora**<br>ah-OH-rah |
| now (already) | **ya**<br>yah |
| right now | **ahorita ~ ahora mismo**<br>ah-oh-REE-tah ~ ah-OH-rah MEEZ-moh |
| often | **a menudo**<br>ah meh-NOO-thoh |
| seldom | **casi nunca**<br>KAH-see NOON-kah |
| sometimes/at times | **a veces**<br>ah BEH-sehs |
| soon | **pronto**<br>PROHN-toh |
| time | **la hora**<br>OH-rah |
| (At) what time ...? | **¿A qué hora...?**<br>ah keh OH-rah |
| the first time | **la primera vez**<br>pree-MEH-rah behs |

Note that **tiempo** means both "weather" and "time."

| | |
|---|---|
| It's nice weather. | **Hace buen tiempo.** |
| He never arrives on time. | **Nunca llega a tiempo.** |

| | |
|---|---|
| the only time | **la única vez**<br>OO-nee-kah behs |
| time | **el tiempo**<br>TYEHM-poh |
| today | **hoy**<br>oy |
| tomorrow | **mañana**<br>mah-NYAH-nah |
| week | **la semana**<br>seh-MAH-nah |
| in a week | **en una semana**<br>ehn OO-nah seh-MAH-nah |
| last week | **la semana pasada**<br>seh-MAH-nah pah-SAH-thah |
| (a) while | **un rato**<br>oon RRAH-toh |
| in a while | **en un rato**<br>ehn oon RRAH-toh |
| year | **el año**<br>AH-nyoh |
| last year | **el año pasado**<br>AH-nyoh pah-SAH-thoh |
| in two years | **en dos años**<br>ehn dohs AH-nyohs |
| yesterday | **ayer**<br>ah-YEHR |

## LOCATION WORDS—PREPOSITIONS AND ADVERBS

### Las palabras de lugar—las preposiciones y los adverbios

Prepositions and adverbs help you locate people and things and tell you where events take place.

| | |
|---|---|
| above | **encima**<br>ehn-SEE-mah |
| around | **alrededor**<br>ahl-reh-theh-THOHR |
| at/in | **en**<br>ehn |
| at the bottom | **en el fondo**<br>ehn ehl FOHN-doh |
| before | **delante**<br>deh-LAHN-teh |
| behind | **detrás ~ atrás**<br>deh-TRAHS ~ ah-TRAHS |
| below | **abajo ~ debajo**<br>ah-BAH-hoh ~ deh-BAH-hoh |
| between | **entre**<br>EHN-treh |
| down | **abajo**<br>ah-BAH-hoh |
| far | **lejos**<br>LEH-hohs |
| from | **de**<br>deh |
| front | **frente**<br>FREHN-teh |
| in front (of) | **enfrente (de)**<br>ehn-FREHN-teh (deh) |
| in/inside | **en**<br>ehn |
| inside | **adentro**<br>ah-DEHN-troh |
| left | **izquierda**<br>ees-KYEHR-thah |

| | |
|---|---|
| at/to the left | **a la izquierda**<br>ah lah ees-KYEHR-thah |
| near | **cerca**<br>SEHR-kah |
| next to | **al lado (de)**<br>ahl LAH-thoh (deh) |
| of | **de**<br>deh |
| on | **en**<br>ehn |
| on top of | **encima de**<br>ehn-SEE-mah deh |
| opposite | **enfrente**<br>ehn-FREHN-teh |
| outside | **afuera**<br>ah-FWEH-rah |
| over | **sobre**<br>SOH-breh |
| over there | **por allá ~ allí**<br>pohr ah-YAH ~ ah-YEE |
| right | **derecha**<br>deh-REH-chah |
| to the right | **a la derecha**<br>ah lah deh-REH-chah |
| through | **por**<br>pohr |
| to/toward | **hacia**<br>AH-syah |
| under | **abajo ~ debajo**<br>ah-BAH-hoh ~ deh-BAH-hoh |
| up | **arriba**<br>ah-RREE-bah |
| with | **con**<br>kohn |
| without | **sin**<br>seen |

## QUESTION WORDS
### Las palabras para hacer preguntas

These question words are one-liners—like Sergeant Friday said, "Just the facts, ma'am."

| | |
|---|---|
| Who? (*singular*) | **¿Quién?**<br>kyehn |
| Who? (*plural*) | **¿Quiénes?**<br>KYEH-nehs |
| Whom? To whom? | **¿A quién?**<br>ah kyehn |
| With whom? | **¿Con quién?**<br>kohn kyehn |
| Whose? | **¿De quién?**<br>deh kyehn |
| What? | **¿Cuál? ~ ¿Qué?**<br>kwahl ~ keh |

Don't confuse **cuál** and **qué**.
**¿Cuál?** asks for identification, as in a field interview.
**¿Qué?** asks for information, as in "What's going on?"

| | |
|---|---|
| What is your name? | **¿Cuál es su nombre?** |
| What are you doing here? | **¿Qué hace aquí?** |

| | |
|---|---|
| What for? | **¿Para qué?**<br>PAH-rah keh |
| Which one? | **¿Cuál?**<br>kwahl |
| Which ones? | **¿Cuáles?**<br>KWAH-lehs |
| How much? | **¿Cuánto[a]?**<br>KWAHN-toh[-tah] |
| How many? | **¿Cuántos[as]?**<br>KWAHN-tohs[-tahs] |
| Where? | **¿Dónde?**<br>DOHN-deh |
| (To) where? | **¿Adónde?**<br>ah-DOHN-deh |

| | |
|---|---|
| From where? | **¿De dónde?**<br>deh DOHN-deh |
| How? | **¿Cómo?**<br>KOH-moh |
| When? | **¿Cuándo?**<br>KWAHN-doh |
| (At) what time? | **¿A qué hora?**<br>ah keh OH-rah |
| Why? | **¿Por qué?**<br>pohr keh |

**¿Cuándo?** asks for time in general.
**¿A qué hora?** asks for a specific time.

**¿Por que?** ("Why?") is pronounced with rising intonation. **Porque** ("because") is pronounced with falling intonation.

## COLORS
Los colores

Most descriptive words (adjectives) that describe males or masculine things end in **-o**. You change the **-o** to **-a** when you're describing females or feminine things.

| | |
|---|---|
| He's white.<br>She's white. | **(Él) es blanco.**<br>**(Ella) es blanca.** |
| The coat is red.<br>The jacket is red. | **El abrigo es rojo.**<br>**La chaqueta es roja.** |

| | |
|---|---|
| beige | **beige**<br>behzh |
| black | **negro[a]**<br>NEH-groh[-grah] |

|  |  |
|---|---|
| blond | **rubio[a]**<br>RROO-byoh[-byah] |
| blond hair | **pelo rubio ~ cabello rubio**<br>PEH-loh RROO-byoh ~<br>kah-BEH-yoh RROO-byoh |
| blond guy/gal | **güero[a]** (*in Mexico*)<br>GWEH-roh[-rah] |
| blue | **azul**<br>ah-SOOL |
| brown | **café ~ castaño[a] ~ pardo[a]**<br>kah-FEH ~<br>kah-STAH-nyoh[-nyah] ~<br>PAHR-thoh[-thah] |
| light brown hair | **pelo castaño ~<br>cabello castaño**<br>PEH-loh kah-STAH-nyoh ~<br>kah-BEH-yoh kah-STAH-nyoh |
| dark brown hair | **pelo café ~ cabello café**<br>PEH-loh kah-FEH ~<br>kah-BEH-yoh kah-FEH |
| clear/light | **claro[a]**<br>KLAH-roh[-rah] |
| copper | **cobre**<br>KOH-breh |
| cream | **color crema**<br>koh-LOHR KREH-mah |
| dark | **oscuro[a]**<br>oh-SKOO-roh[-rah] |
| of dark complexion | **moreno[a]**<br>moh-REH-noh[-nah] |
| gold | **el color de oro**<br>koh-LOHR deh OH-roh |
| golden | **dorado[a]**<br>doh-RAH-thoh[-thah] |
| gray | **gris**<br>grees |
| green | **verde**<br>BEHR-theh |
| light/clear | **claro[a]**<br>KLAH-roh[-rah] |
| maroon | **marrón**<br>mah-RROHN |

olive — **oliva**
oh-LEE-bah

orange — **naranja**
nah-RAHN-hah

pink — **rosado[a] ~ rosa**
rroh-SAH-thoh[-thah] ~ RROH-sah

purple — **morado[a]**
moh-RAH-thoh[-thah]

red — **rojo[a]**
RROH-hoh[-hah]

red hair — **pelo rojo**
PEH-loh RROH-hoh

redhead — **pelirrojo[a]**
peh-lee-RROH-hoh[-hah]

silver — **plateado[a]**
plah-teh-AH-thoh[-thah]

tan — **café claro**
kah-FEH KLAH-roh

turquoise — **turquesa**
toor-KEH-sah

violet — **violeta**
bee-oh-LEH-tah

white — **blanco[a]**
BLAHN-koh[-kah]

yellow — **amarillo[a]**
ah-mah-REE-yoh[-yah]

## CLOTHING
La ropa

What clothes is he/she wearing? — **¿Qué ropa lleva?**
keh RROH-pah YEH-bah

What clothes does he have on? — **¿Qué ropa tiene puesto (él)?**
keh RROH-pah TYEH-neh PWEH-stoh (ehl)

What clothes does she have on? — **¿Qué ropa tiene puesta (ella)?**
keh RROH-pah TYEH-neh PWEH-stah (EH-yah)

| | |
|---|---|
| Can you identify the clothes? | **¿Puede identificar la ropa?** PWEH-theh ee-dehn-tee-fee-KAHR lah RROH-pah |
| Can you describe the clothes? | **¿Puede describir la ropa?** PWEH-theh deh-skree-BEER lah RROH-pah |
| He's wearing ... | **(Él) lleva...** (ehl) YEH-bah |
| She's wearing ... | **(Ella) lleva...** (EH-yah) YEH-bah |
| He has on ... | **(Él) tiene puesto...** (ehl) TYEH-neh PWEH-stoh |
| She has on ... | **(Ella) tiene puesta...** (EH-yah) TYEH-neh PWEH-stah |

The following words and phrases can be used to complete the sentences above and describe clothing in general.

| | |
|---|---|
| bandana | **el pañuelo** pah-NWEH-loh |
| bathing suit | **el traje de baño** TRAH-heh deh BAH-nyoh |
| bathrobe | **la bata** BAH-tah |
| belt | **el cinturón ~ el cinto** seen-too-ROHN ~ SEEN-toh |
| blouse | **la blusa** BLOO-sah |
| boots | **las botas** BOH-tahs |
| bra | **el sostén ~ el brazier** soh-STEHN ~ brah-SYEHR |
| bracelet | **la pulsera** pool-SEH-rah |
| buckle | **la hebilla** eh-BEE-yah |
| button | **el botón** boh-TOHN |
| cap | **la gorra ~ el gorro ~ la cachucha** (*slang*) GOH-rrah ~ GOH-rroh ~ kah-CHOO-chah |

To make a Spanish word ending in a vowel plural, add **-s**. For words ending in a consonant (anything but a vowel), add **-es**. For plural words (things and people), **el** changes to **los** and **la** changes to **las**.

**el zapato → los zapatos**
**la blusa → las blusas**
**el suéter → los suéteres**

| | |
|---|---|
| coat/overcoat | **el abrigo**<br>ah-BREE-goh |
| collar | **el cuello**<br>KWEH-yoh |
| cuff | **el puño**<br>POO-nyoh |
| dress | **el vestido**<br>beh-STEE-thoh |
| girdle | **la faja**<br>FAH-hah |
| gloves | **los guantes**<br>GWAHN-tehs |
| hairnet | **la red de pelo**<br>rrehth deh PEH-loh |
| handkerchief | **el pañuelo**<br>pah-NWEH-loh |
| hat | **el sombrero**<br>sohm-BREH-roh |
| jacket | **la chaqueta ~ el saco**<br>chah-KEH-tah ~ SAH-koh |
| mask | **la máscara**<br>MAH-skah-rah |
| overcoat/coat | **el abrigo**<br>ah-BREE-goh |
| pajamas | **la pijama**<br>pee-HAH-mah |
| panties | **las pantaletas**<br>pahn-tah-LEH-tahs |
| pants | **los pantalones**<br>pahn-tah-LOH-nehs |

| | |
|---|---|
| He's wearing … | **(Él) lleva…**<br>(ehl) YEH-bah |
| She's wearing … | **(Ella) lleva…**<br>(EH-yah) YEH-bah |
| He has on … | **(Él) tiene puesto…**<br>(ehl) TYEH-neh PWEH-stoh |
| She has on … | **(Ella) tiene puesta…**<br>(EH-yah) TYEH-neh PWEH-stah |
| panty hose | **las medias**<br>MEH-dyahs |
| pocket | **el bolsillo ~ el bolso**<br>bohl-SEE-yoh ~ BOHL-soh |
| raincoat | **el impermeable**<br>eem-pehr-meh-AH-bleh |
| sandals | **las sandalias ~ los huaraches**<br>sahn-DAH-lee-ahs ~<br>wah-RAH-chehs |
| scarf | **la bufanda**<br>boo-FAHN-dah |
| shirt | **la camisa**<br>kah-MEE-sah |
| shoes | **los zapatos**<br>sah-PAH-tohs |
| shorts | **los pantalones cortos ~**<br>**los chorts**<br>pahn-tah-LOH-nehs<br>KOHR-tohs ~ chohrts |
| skirt | **la falda**<br>FAHL-dah |
| sleeve | **la manga**<br>MAHN-gah |
| slip | **la combinación**<br>kohm-bee-nah-SYOHN |
| slippers | **las pantuflas**<br>pahn-TOO-flahs |
| socks | **los calcetines**<br>kahl-seh-TEE-nehs |
| sports coat | **la chamarra**<br>chah-MAH-rrah |
| stockings | **las medias**<br>MEH-dyahs |

When referring to clothing or parts of the body, possessives ("my," "your," etc.) are expressed by **el, la, los,** and **las**.

Take off your shirt. **Quítese la camisa.**

| | |
|---|---|
| strap | **la correa**<br>koh-RREH-ah |
| suit | **el traje**<br>TRAH-heh |
| sweater | **el suéter**<br>SWEH-tehr |
| sweatshirt | **la sudadera**<br>soo-thah-THEH-rah |
| T-shirt | **la camiseta**<br>kah-mee-SEH-tah |
| tennis shoes | **los (zapatos de) tenis**<br>(sah-PAH-tohs deh) TEH-nees |
| tie | **la corbata**<br>kohr-BAH-tah |
| umbrella | **el paraguas**<br>pah-RAH-gwahs |
| underwear | **la ropa interior ~ los chones (*slang*)**<br>RROH-pah een-teh-ree-OHR ~ CHOH-nehs |
| uniform | **el uniforme**<br>oo-nee-FOHR-meh |
| vest | **el chaleco**<br>chah-LEH-koh |
| zipper | **el cierre**<br>SYEH-rreh |

## PEOPLE AND FAMILY
La gente y la familia

| | |
|---|---|
| adolescent | **el / la adolescente**<br>ah-doh-leh-SEHN-teh |
| adopted child | **el niño adoptado**<br>NEE-nyoh ah-dohp-TAH-thoh |
| adult | **el adulto / la adulta**<br>ah-DOOL-toh / ah-DOOL-tah |
| aunt | **la tía**<br>TEE-ah |
| baby | **el bebé ~ el nene**<br>beh-BEH ~ NEH-neh |
| bachelor | **el soltero**<br>sohl-TEH-roh |
| boss/employer | **el jefe / la jefa**<br>HEH-feh / HEH-fah |
| | **el patrón / la patrona**<br>pah-TROHN / pah-TROH-nah |
| boy | **el muchacho**<br>moo-CHAH-choh |
| young boy | **el muchacho ~ el niño**<br>moo-CHAH-choh ~ NEE-nyoh |
| boyfriend | **el novio**<br>NOH-byoh |
| bride | **la novia**<br>NOH-byah |
| brother | **el hermano**<br>ehr-MAH-noh |
| brother-in-law | **el cuñado**<br>koo-NYAH-thoh |
| buddy | **el compañero**<br>kohm-pah-NYEH-roh |
| child | **el niño / la niña**<br>NEE-nyoh / NEE-nyah |
| civilian | **el ciudadano / la ciudadana**<br>see-oo-thah-THAH-noh /<br>see-oo-thah-THAH-nah |
| cousin | **el primo / la prima**<br>PREE-moh / PREE-mah |

| | |
|---|---|
| customer | **el / la cliente**<br>klee-EHN-teh |
| daddy | **el papá ~ el papi**<br>pah-PAH ~ PAH-pee |
| daughter | **la hija**<br>EE-hah |
| daughter-in-law | **la nuera**<br>NWEH-rah |
| dependent | **el / la dependiente**<br>deh-pehn-DYEHN-teh |
| divorced | **divorciado[a]**<br>dee-bohr-SYAH-thoh[-thah] |
| elderly person | **el anciano / la anciana**<br>ahn-SYAH-noh / ahn-SYAH-nah |
| elderly person (*male or female*) | **la persona mayor**<br>pehr-SOH-nah mah-YOHR |
| employee | **el empleado / la empleada**<br>ehm-pleh-AH-thoh / ehm-pleh-AH-thah |
| father | **el padre**<br>PAH-dreh |
| father-in-law | **el suegro**<br>SWEH-groh |
| fiancé (*male*) | **el prometido**<br>proh-meh-TEE-thoh |
| fiancée (*female*) | **la prometida**<br>proh-meh-TEE-thah |
| foster child | **el ahijado / la ahijada**<br>ah-ee-HAH-thoh / ah-ee-HAH-thah |
| friend | **el amigo / la amiga**<br>ah-MEE-goh / ah-MEE-gah |
| gentleman | **el señor ~ el caballero**<br>seh-NYOHR ~ kah-bah-YEH-roh |
| girl | **la muchacha ~ la niña**<br>moo-CHAH-chah ~ NEE-nyah |
| girlfriend | **la novia**<br>NOH-byah |
| godfather | **el padrino**<br>pah-DREE-noh |

| | |
|---|---|
| godmother | **la madrina**<br>mah-DREE-nah |
| granddaughter | **la nieta**<br>NYEH-tah |
| grandfather | **el abuelo**<br>ah-BWEH-loh |
| grandmother | **la abuela**<br>ah-BWEH-lah |
| grandson | **el nieto**<br>NYEH-toh |
| groom | **el novio**<br>NOH-byoh |
| guardian | **el guardián ~ el tutor**<br>gwahr-DYAHN ~ too-TOHR |
| husband | **el marido ~ el esposo**<br>mah-REE-thoh ~ eh-SPOH-soh |
| immigrant | **el / la inmigrante**<br>een-mee-GRAHN-teh |
| lady | **la señora ~ la dama ~ la mujer**<br>seh-NYOH-rah ~ DAH-mah ~ moo-HEHR |
| landlord | **el propietario / la propietaria**<br>proh-pyeh-TAH-ree-oh / proh-pyeh-TAH-ree-ah<br>**el dueño / la dueña**<br>DWEH-nyoh / DWEH-nyah |
| Ma'am | **Señora**<br>seh-NYOH-rah |
| man | **el hombre**<br>OHM-breh |
| manager | **el / la gerente**<br>heh-REHN-teh |
| married | **casado[a]**<br>kah-SAH-thoh[-thah] |
| minor | **el / la menor de edad**<br>meh-NOHR deh eh-THAHTH |
| Miss | **Señorita**<br>seh-nyoh-REE-tah |

Don't confuse **los padres** ("parents") with **los parientes** ("the relatives").

| | |
|---|---|
| mommy | **la mamá ~ la mami**<br>mah-MAH ~ MAH-mee |
| mother | **la madre**<br>MAH-dreh |
| mother-in-law | **la suegra**<br>SWEH-grah |
| Mr. | **Señor**<br>seh-NYOHR |
| Mrs. | **Señora**<br>seh-NYOH-rah |
| neighbor | **el vecino / la vecina**<br>beh-SEE-noh / beh-SEE-nah |
| nephew | **el sobrino / la sobrina**<br>soh-BREE-noh / soh-BREE-nah |
| next of kin (closest relatives) | **los parientes más próximos**<br>pah-ree-EHN-tehs mahs PROHK-see-mohs |
| owner | **el dueño / la dueña**<br>DWEH-nyoh / DWEH-nyah |
| parents | **los padres**<br>PAH-drehs |
| partner | **el socio / la socia**<br>SOH-syoh / SOH-syah |
| passenger | **el pasajero / la pasajera**<br>pah-sah-HEH-roh / pah-sah-HEH-rah |
| patient | **el / la paciente**<br>pah-SYEHN-teh |
| pedestrian | **el peatón / la peatona**<br>peh-ah-TOHN / peh-ah-TOH-nah |
| priest | **el padre**<br>PAH-dreh |
| relatives | **los parientes**<br>pah-ree-EHN-tehs |

| | |
|---|---|
| renter/tenant | **el inquilino / la inquilina**<br>een-kee-LEE-noh / een-kee-LEE-nah |
| resident | **el / la residente**<br>rreh-see-THEHN-teh |
| responsible party | **el guardián ~ el tutor**<br>gwahr-DYAHN ~ too-TOHR |
| single | **soltero[a]**<br>sohl-TEH-roh[-rah] |
| Sir | **Señor**<br>seh-NYOHR |
| sister | **la hermana**<br>ehr-MAH-nah |
| sister (religious) | **la religiosa ~ la hermana**<br>rreh-lee-hee-OH-sah ~ ehr-MAH-nah |
| sister-in-law | **la cuñada**<br>koo-NYAH-thah |
| son | **el hijo**<br>EE-hoh |
| son-in-law | **el yerno**<br>YEHR-noh |
| stepdaughter | **la hijastra**<br>ee-HAH-strah |
| stepfather | **el padrastro**<br>pah-DRAH-stroh |
| stepmother | **la madrastra**<br>mah-DRAH-strah |
| stepson | **el hijastro**<br>ee-HAH-stroh |
| stranger | **el desconocido / la desconocida**<br>dehs-koh-noh-SEE-thoh / dehs-koh-noh-SEE-thah |
| teenagers/youths | **los muchachos ~ los jóvenes**<br>moo-CHAH-chohs ~ HOH-beh-nehs |
| tenant/renter | **el inquilino / la inquilina**<br>een-kee-LEE-noh / een-kee-LEE-nah |

| | |
|---|---|
| tourist | **el / la turista**<br>too-REE-stah |
| twin | **el gemelo / la gemela**<br>heh-MEH-loh / heh-MEH-lah |
| | **el / la cuate**<br>KWAH-teh |
| uncle | **el tío**<br>TEE-oh |
| vagrant | **el vagabundo / la vagabunda**<br>bah-gah-BOON-doh / bah-gah-BOON-dah |
| victim (*male or female*) | **la víctima**<br>BEEK-tee-mah |
| visitor | **el / la visitante**<br>bee-see-TAHN-teh |
| widow | **la viuda**<br>bee-OO-thah |
| widower | **el viudo**<br>bee-OO-thoh |
| wife | **la esposa ~ la mujer**<br>eh-SPOH-sah ~ moo-HEHR |
| witness | **el / la testigo**<br>teh-STEE-goh |
| woman | **la mujer ~ la señora ~ la dama**<br>moo-HEHR ~ seh-NYOH-rah ~ DAH-mah |
| youth | **el / la joven**<br>HOH-behn |

## PROFESSIONS
### Las profesiones

| | |
|---|---|
| What's your profession? | **¿Cuál es su profesión?**<br>kwahl ehs soo proh-feh-SYOHN |
| What's your job? | **¿Cuál es su trabajo?**<br>kwahl ehs soo trah-BAH-hoh |
| What kind of work do you do? | **¿Qué tipo de trabajo tiene?**<br>key TEE-poh deh trah-BAH-hoh TYEH-neh |

If the Spanish name for an occupation can be used for both males and females, it is shown with **el** and **la** separated by a "/".

| | |
|---|---|
| dentist | **el / la dentista** |

If the Spanish name for an occupation differs between male and female, both forms are given, the male form with **el** and the female form with **la**. The forms are separated by a "/".

| | |
|---|---|
| driver | **el conductor / la conductora** |

If an occupation has two or more equivalent forms in Spanish, they are separated by a "~".

| | |
|---|---|
| waitress | **la mesera ~ la camarera** |

| | |
|---|---|
| artist | **el / la artista**<br>ahr-TEE-stah |
| babysitter | **la niñera ~ la cuidaniños**<br>nee-NYEH-rah ~<br>kwee-dah-NEE-nyohs |
| barber | **el barbero / la barbera**<br>bahr-BEH-roh / bahr-BEH-rah |
| bellhop | **el / la botones**<br>boh-TOH-nehs |
| bus driver | **el conductor de autobús / la conductora de autobús**<br>kohn-dook-TOHR deh ah-oo-toh-BOOS / kohn-dook-TOH-rah deh ah-oo-toh-BOOS |
| | **el / la chofer de autobús**<br>choh-FEHR deh ah-oo-toh-BOOS |
| busboy | **el mozo**<br>MOH-soh |
| car wash attendant | **el / la lavacarros**<br>lah-bah-KAH-rrohs |

| | |
|---|---|
| carpenter | **el carpintero / la carpintera**<br>kahr-peen-TEH-roh / kahr-peen-TEH-rah |
| cashier | **el cajero / la cajera**<br>kah-HEH-roh / kah-HEH-rah |
| clerk | **el / la dependiente**<br>deh-pehn-DYEHN-teh |
| cook | **el cocinero / la cocinera**<br>koh-see-NEH-roh / koh-see-NEH-rah |
| cowboy | **el vaquero**<br>bah-KEH-roh |
| cowgirl | **la vaquera**<br>bah-KEH-rah |
| day laborer | **el jornalero / la jornalera**<br>hohr-nah-LEH-roh / hohr-nah-LEH-rah |
| dentist | **el / la dentista**<br>dehn-TEE-stah |
| dishwasher | **el / la lavaplatos**<br>lah-bah-PLAH-tohs |
| dressmaker | **el / la modista**<br>moh-THEE-stah |
| driver | **el conductor / la conductora**<br>kohn-dook-TOHR / kohn-dook-TOH-rah<br>**el / la chofer**<br>choh-FEHR |
| electrician | **el / la electricista**<br>eh-lehk-tree-SEE-stah |
| engineer | **el ingeniero / la ingeniera**<br>een-heh-NYEH-roh / een-heh-NYEH-rah |
| farmworker | **el labrador / la labradora**<br>lah-brah-THOHR / lah-brah-THOH-rah |
| farmer | **el granjero / la granjera**<br>grahn-HEH-roh / grahn-HEH-rah |
| field hand | **el campesino / la campesina**<br>kahm-peh-SEE-noh / kahm-peh-SEE-nah |

| | |
|---|---|
| fisherman | **el pescador**<br>peh-skah-THOHR |
| gardener | **el jardinero / la jardinera**<br>hahr-thee-NEH-roh/<br>hahr-thee-NEH-rah |
| gas station attendant | **el gasolinero / la gasolinera**<br>gah-soh-lee-NEH-roh/<br>gah-soh-lee-NEH-rah |
| guard | **el / la guardia**<br>GWAHR-dyah |
| hairdresser | **el peluquero / la peluquera**<br>peh-loo-KEH-roh/<br>peh-loo-KEH-rah |
| helper | **el / la ayudante**<br>ah-yoo-DAHN-teh |
| housecleaner | **el / la limpiacasas**<br>leem-pyah-KAH-sahs |
| housekeeper | **la empleada de casa**<br>ehm-pleh-AH-thah deh<br>KAH-sah |
| housewife | **la ama de casa**<br>AH-mah deh KAH-sah |
| ice cream vendor | **el paletero / la paletera**<br>pah-leh-TEH-roh/<br>pah-leh-TEH-rah |
| interpreter | **el / la intérprete**<br>een-TEHR-preh-teh |
| janitor | **el / la conserje**<br>kohn-SEHR-heh |
| jeweler | **el joyero / la joyera**<br>hoh-YEH-roh/hoh-YEH-rah |
| journalist | **el / la periodista**<br>peh-ree-oh-THEE-stah |
| junk dealer | **el trapero / la trapera**<br>trah-PEH-roh/trah-PEH-rah |
| lawyer | **el abogado / la abogada**<br>ah-boh-GAH-thoh/<br>ah-boh-GAH-thah |
| letter carrier | **el cartero / la cartera**<br>kahr-TEH-roh/kahr-TEH-rah |

| | |
|---|---|
| maid | **la criada**<br>kree-AH-thah |
| manager | **el / la gerente**<br>heh-REHN-teh |
| mason | **el / la albañil**<br>ahl-bah-NYEEL |
| mechanic | **el mecánico / la mecánica**<br>meh-KAH-nee-koh / meh-KAH-nee-kah |
| painter | **el pintor / la pintora**<br>peen-THOHR / peen-THOH-rah |
| plumber | **el plomero / la plomera**<br>ploh-MEH-roh / ploh-MEH-rah |
| priest | **el cura ~ el sacerdote**<br>KOO-rah ~ sah-sehr-THOH-teh |
| professor | **el profesor / la profesora**<br>proh-feh-SOHR / proh-feh-SOH-rah |
| prostitute | **la prostituta**<br>proh-stee-TOO-tah |
| ranch hand | **el ranchero / la ranchera**<br>rrahn-CHEH-roh / rrahn-CHEH-rah |
| | **el vaquero / la vaquera**<br>bah-KEH-roh / bah-KEH-rah |
| sailor | **el marinero / la marinera**<br>mah-ree-NEH-roh / mah-ree-NEH-rah |
| sales clerk | **el / la dependiente**<br>deh-pehn-DYEHN-teh |
| | **el vendedor / la vendedora**<br>behn-deh-THOHR / behn-deh-THOH-rah |
| seamstress | **la costurera**<br>koh-stoo-REH-rah |
| secretary | **el secretario / la secretaria**<br>seh-kreh-TAH-ree-oh / seh-kreh-TAH-ree-ah |
| shopkeeper | **el tendero / la tendera**<br>tehn-DEH-roh / tehn-DEH-rah |

| | |
|---|---|
| student | **el / la estudiante**<br>eh-stoo-DYAHN-teh |
| tailor | **el / la sastre**<br>SAH-streh |
| teacher | **el maestro / la maestra**<br>mah-EH-stroh / mah-EH-strah |
| translator | **el traductor / la traductora**<br>trah-thook-TOHR / trah-thook-TOH-rah |
| truck driver | **el camionero / la camionera**<br>kah-myoh-NEH-roh / kah-myoh-NEH-rah |
| | **el troquero / la troquera**<br>troh-KEH-roh / troh-KEH-rah |
| unemployed | **sin trabajo**<br>seen trah-BAH-hoh |
| | **desempleado[a]**<br>dehs-ehm-pleh-AH-thoh[-thah] |
| waiter | **el mesero ~ el camarero**<br>meh-SEH-roh ~ kah-mah-REH-roh |
| waitress | **la mesera ~ la camarera**<br>meh-SEH-rah ~ kah-mah-REH-rah |
| worker (factory) | **el obrero / la obrera**<br>oh-BREH-roh / oh-BREH-rah |
| worker (general) | **el trabajador / la trabajadora**<br>trah-bah-hah-THOHR / trah-bah-hah-THOH-rah |

# THE HOUSE, INSIDE AND OUTSIDE

La casa, adentro y afuera

You are a detective investigating a crime scene. You look everywhere—inside and outside—for evidence.

## Outside the House

Fuera de la casa

When you first arrive, you search the yard for clues—behind trees, under rocks, everywhere.

| | |
|---|---|
| balcony | **el balcón**<br>bahl-KOHN |
| bushes | **los arbustos**<br>ahr-BOOH-stohs |
| carport/garage | **el garaje ~ la cochera**<br>gah-RAH-heh ~<br>koh-CHEH-rah |
| corner (exterior) | **la esquina**<br>eh-SKEE-nah |
| street corner | **la esquina de la calle**<br>eh-SKEE-nah deh lah KAH-yeh |
| dirt | **la tierra**<br>TYEH-rrah |
| door | **la puerta**<br>PWEHR-tah |
| back door | **la puerta trasera**<br>PWEHR-tah trah-SEH-rah |
| front door | **la puerta principal**<br>PWEHR-tah preen-see-PAHL |
| security door | **la puerta de seguridad**<br>PWEHR-tah deh<br>seh-goo-ree-THAHTH |
| side door | **la puerta lateral**<br>PWEHR-tah lah-teh-RAHL |
| driveway | **la entrada para carros**<br>ehn-TRAH-thah PAH-rah<br>KAH-rrohs |
| fence | **el cerco ~ la cerca**<br>SEHR-koh ~ SEHR-kah |

| | |
|---|---|
| flowers | **las flores**<br>FLOH-rehs |
| garage/carport | **el garaje ~ la cochera**<br>gah-RAH-heh ~ koh-CHEH-rah |
| garden | **el jardín**<br>hahr-THEEN |
| gate | **el portón**<br>pohr-TOHN |
| lawn | **el césped**<br>SEH-spehth |
| leaves | **las hojas**<br>OH-hahs |
| mud | **el lodo ~ el barro**<br>LOH-thoh ~ BAH-rroh |
| porch | **el pórtico**<br>POHR-tee-koh |
| rocks | **las rocas**<br>RROH-kahs |
| roof | **el tejado ~ el techo**<br>teh-HAH-thoh ~ TEH-choh |
| sand | **la arena**<br>ah-REH-nah |
| sidewalk | **la acera ~ la banqueta**<br>ah-SEH-rah ~ bahn-KEH-tah |
| tree | **el árbol**<br>AHR-bohl |
| wall (exterior) | **el muro**<br>MOO-roh |
| window | **la ventana**<br>behn-TAH-nah |
| window bars | **las rejas en las ventanas**<br>RREH-hahs ehn lahs behn-TAH-nahs |
| yard | **la yarda**<br>YAHR-thah |
| front yard | **la yarda de enfrente**<br>YAHR-thah deh ehn-FREHN-teh |
| backyard | **la yarda de atrás**<br>YAHR-thah deh ah-TRAHS |

## Inside the House
Dentro de la casa

Then you enter the house to search for more clues.

| | |
|---|---|
| attic | **el ático ~ el desván**<br>AH-tee-koh ~ dehs-BAHN |
| basement | **el sótano**<br>SOH-tah-noh |
| bathroom | **el cuarto de baño ~ el baño**<br>KWAHR-toh deh BAH-nyoh ~ BAH-nyoh |
| bedroom | **el dormitorio ~ la recámara**<br>dohr-mee-TOH-ree-oh ~ rreh-KAH-mah-rah |
| ceiling | **el techo ~ el cielo**<br>TEH-choh ~ SYEH-loh |
| chimney | **la chimenea**<br>chee-meh-NEH-ah |
| closet | **el ropero ~ el armario**<br>rroh-PEH-roh ~ ahr-MAH-ree-oh |
| corner (interior) | **el rincón**<br>rreen-KOHN |
| den | **el estudio**<br>eh-STOO-dyoh |
| dining room | **el comedor**<br>koh-meh-THOR |
| door | **la puerta**<br>PWEHR-tah |
| entrance | **la entrada**<br>ehn-TRAH-thah |

An interior corner is **el rincón**.
An exterior corner is **la esquina**.
A street corner is **la esquina de la calle**.

An interior wall is **la pared**.
An exterior wall is **el muro**.

| | |
|---|---|
| exit | **la salida**<br>sah-LEE-thah |
| floor | **el piso ~ el suelo**<br>PEE-soh ~ SWEH-loh |
| hallway | **el pasillo**<br>pah-SEE-yoh |
| kitchen | **la cocina**<br>koh-SEE-nah |
| ladder/stairs | **la escalera**<br>eh-skah-LEH-rah |
| laundry room | **el cuarto de lavadora ~ el cuarto de lavar**<br>KWAHR-toh deh lah-bah-THOH-rah ~ KWAHR-toh deh lah-BAHR |
| living room | **la sala**<br>SAH-lah |
| room | **el cuarto**<br>KWAHR-toh |
| shower | **la ducha ~ la regadera**<br>DOO-chah ~ rreh-gah-THEH-rah |
| sink (kitchen) | **el fregadero**<br>freh-gah-THEH-roh |
| stairs/ladder | **la escalera**<br>eh-skah-LEH-rah |
| step | **el escalón**<br>eh-skah-LOHN |
| study | **el estudio**<br>eh-STOO-dyoh |
| toilet | **el retrete ~ el excusado**<br>rreh-TREH-teh ~ ehks-koo-SAH-thoh |
| wall (interior) | **la pared**<br>pah-REHTH |
| window | **la ventana**<br>behn-TAH-nah |

## Furniture and Electrical Appliances
Los muebles y los electrodomésticos

Once inside, you look for more clues in the furniture and appliances.

| | |
|---|---|
| air conditioner | **el aire (acondicionado)** AY-reh (ah-kohn-dee-syoh-NAH-thoh) |
| answering machine | **la grabadora telefónica** grah-bah-THOH-rah teh-leh-FOH-nee-kah |
| armchair | **el sillón** see-YOHN |
| bathtub | **la bañera ~ la tina** bah-NYEH-rah ~ TEE-nah |
| bed | **la cama** KAH-mah |
| bedside table | **la mesita** meh-SEE-tah |
| bookshelf | **el estante de libros** eh-STAHN-teh deh LEE-brohs |
| carpet | **la alfombra** ahl-FOHM-brah |
| chest of drawers | **la cómoda** KOH-moh-thah |
| clock | **el reloj** rreh-LOH |
| computer | **la computadora** kohm-poo-tah-THOH-rah |
| couch | **el sofá** soh-FAH |
| counter | **el mostrador** moh-strah-THOHR |
| curtain | **la cortina** kohr-TEE-nah |
| desk | **el escritorio** eh-skree-TOH-ree-oh |
| dishwasher | **el lavaplatos** lah-bah-PLAH-tohs |
| drawer | **el cajón** kah-HOHN |

Don't confuse **los muebles** (furniture) with **el mueble** (a piece of furniture).

| | |
|---|---|
| dryer | **la secadora**<br>seh-kah-THOH-rah |
| DVD | **el DVD**<br>dee-bee-DEE |
| electrical outlet | **el enchufe**<br>ehn-CHOO-feh |
| furniture (in general) | **los muebles**<br>MWEH-blehs |
| a piece of furniture | **el mueble**<br>MWEH-bleh |
| heater | **el calentador**<br>kah-lehn-tah-THOHR |
| lamp | **la lámpara**<br>LAHM-pah-rah |
| mattress | **el colchón**<br>kohl-CHOHN |
| medicine chest | **el botiquín**<br>boh-tee-KEEN |
| microwave (oven) | **el horno de microondas**<br>OHR-noh deh mee-kroh-OHN-dahs |
| oven | **el horno**<br>OHR-noh |
| piano | **el piano**<br>PYAH-noh |
| picture | **el cuadro**<br>KWAH-droh |
| refrigerator | **el refrigerador ~ la nevera**<br>rreh-free-heh-rah-THOHR ~ neh-BEH-rah |
| rug (small) | **el tapete**<br>tah-PEH-teh |
| security system | **el sistema de seguridad**<br>see-STEH-mah deh seh-goo-ree-THAHTH |

| | |
|---|---|
| sewing machine | **la máquina de coser** MAH-kee-nah deh koh-SEHR |
| sofa | **el sofá** soh-FAH |
| stereo | **el estéreo** eh-STEH-reh-oh |
| stove | **la estufa** eh-STOO-fah |
| table | **la mesa** MEH-sah |
| bedside table | **la mesita** meh-SEE-tah |
| TV set | **el televisor** teh-leh-bee-SOHR |
| vacuum cleaner | **la aspiradora** ah-spee-rah-THOH-rah |
| VCR | **el VCR** bee-see-AHR |
| video recorder | **la videograbadora** bee-deh-oh-grah-bah-THOH-rah |
| wash basin | **el lavabo** lah-BAH-boh |
| washing machine | **la lavadora** lah-bah-THOH-rah |

## Cloth and Building Materials
### La tela y los materiales de construcción

Finally, you search for clues in fabrics and building materials. We have omitted **el** and **la** since we're dealing with things made of cloth or other materials, for example, **hecho de madera** ("made of wood").

| | |
|---|---|
| What's it made of? | **¿De qué está hecho?** deh keh eh-STAH EH-choh |
| It's made of … | **Está hecho de…** eh-STAH EH-choh deh |
| asphalt | **asfalto** ahs-FAHL-toh |
| brass | **latón** lah-TOHN |

|  |  |
| --- | --- |
| It's made of ... | **Está hecho de...**<br>eh-STAH EH-choh deh |
| cardboard | **cartón**<br>kahr-TOHN |
| cement | **cemento**<br>seh-MEHN-toh |
| cloth | **tela**<br>TEH-lah |
| corduroy | **pana**<br>PAH-nah |
| cotton | **algodón**<br>ahl-goh-THOHN |
| denim | **tela de mono**<br>TEH-lah deh MOH-noh |
| glass | **vidrio**<br>BEE-dree-oh |
| glue | **pegamento**<br>peh-gah-MEHN-toh |
| iron | **hierro**<br>ee-EH-rroh |
| leather | **cuero**<br>KWEH-roh |
| material | **material**<br>mah-teh-ree-AHL |
| metal | **metal**<br>meh-TAHL |
| nylon | **nilón**<br>nee-LOHN |
| paper | **papel**<br>pah-PEHL |
| plastic | **plástico**<br>PLAH-stee-koh |
| rubber | **goma**<br>GOH-mah |
| satin | **satín**<br>sah-TEEN |
| silk | **seda**<br>SEH-thah |
| steel | **acero**<br>ah-SEH-roh |

| | |
|---|---|
| stone | **piedra** PYEH-drah |
| suede | **gamuza** gah-MOO-sah |
| wood | **madera** mah-THEH-rah |
| wool | **lana** LAH-nah |

## CITY BUILDINGS AND PLACES

### Los edificios y los lugares de la ciudad

These terms will help you get around town. As you drive to work, try to identify buildings and places you may need to describe.

| | |
|---|---|
| Where are you going? | **¿Adónde va?** ah-DOHN-deh bah |
| What direction are you going in? | **¿En qué dirección va?** ehn keh dee-rehk-SYOHN bah |
| He's/She's in/at the … | **Está en…** eh-STAH ehn |
| airport | **el aeropuerto** ah-eh-roh-PWEHR-toh |
| apartment | **el apartamento ~ el departamento** ah-pahr-tah-MEHN-toh ~ deh-pahr-tah-MEHN-toh |
| bakery | **la panadería** pah-nah-theh-REE-ah |
| bank | **el banco** BAHN-koh |
| bar | **el bar** bahr |
| bar (*rural*) | **la cantina** kahn-TEE-nah |
| barber shop | **la peluquería** peh-loo-keh-REE-ah |
| beach | **la playa** PLAH-yah |
| beauty salon | **el salón de belleza** sah-LOHN deh beh-YEH-sah |

| | |
|---|---|
| He's/She's in/at the ... | **Está en...**<br>eh-STAH ehn |
| bookstore | **la librería**<br>lee-breh-REE-ah |
| building | **el edificio**<br>eh-dee-FEE-syoh |
| cabin | **la cabaña**<br>kah-BAH-nyah |
| café | **el café**<br>kah-FEH |
| camp | **el campamento**<br>kahm-pah-MEHN-toh |
| carport/garage | **el garaje ~ la cochera**<br>gah-RAH-heh ~ koh-CHEH-rah |
| casino | **el casino**<br>kah-SEE-noh |
| clinic | **la clínica**<br>KLEE-nee-kah |
| college/university | **la universidad**<br>oo-nee-behr-see-THAHTH |
| condominium | **el condominio**<br>kohn-doh-MEE-nee-oh |
| courtyard | **el patio**<br>PAH-tyoh |
| dance | **el baile**<br>BAY-leh |
| department store | **el almacén**<br>ahl-mah-SEHN |
| downtown | **el centro**<br>SEHN-troh |
| drugstore | **la farmacia**<br>fahr-MAH-syah |
| dry cleaner | **la tintorería**<br>teen-toh-reh-REE-ah |
| factory | **la fábrica**<br>FAH-bree-kah |
| fair | **la feria**<br>FEH-ree-ah |
| fire station | **la estación de bomberos**<br>eh-stah-SYOHN deh bohm-BEH-rohs |

| | |
|---|---|
| flea market | **el remate**<br>rreh-MAH-teh |
| flower shop | **la florería**<br>floh-reh-REE-ah |
| garage/carport | **el garaje ~ la cochera**<br>gah-RAH-heh ~ koh-CHEH-rah |
| gas station | **la gasolinera ~ la estación de gasolina**<br>gah-soh-lee-NEH-rah ~ eh-stah-SYOHN deh gah-soh-LEE-nah |
| grocery store | **la bodega**<br>boh-THEH-gah |
| hardware store | **la ferretería**<br>feh-rreh-teh-REE-ah |
| high school | **el colegio**<br>koh-LEH-hee-oh |
| hospital | **el hospital**<br>oh-spee-TAHL |
| hotel | **el hotel**<br>oh-TEHL |
| house | **la casa**<br>KAH-sah |
| jail | **la cárcel**<br>KAHR-sehl |
| jewelry store | **la joyería**<br>hoh-yeh-REE-ah |
| laundromat | **la lavandería**<br>lah-bahn-deh-REE-ah |
| library | **la biblioteca**<br>bee-blee-oh-TEH-kah |
| liquor store | **licorería**<br>lee-koh-reh-REE-ah |
| market | **el mercado**<br>mehr-KAH-thoh |
| open-air market | **el mercado abierto**<br>mehr-KAH-thoh ah-BYEHR-toh |
| massage parlor | **la sala de masajes**<br>SAH-lah deh mah-SAH-hehs |

| | |
|---|---|
| He's/She's in/at the ... | **Está en...**<br>eh-STAH ehn |
| mobile home | **la casa móvil ~ el trailer**<br>KAH-sah MOH-beel ~ TRAY-lehr |
| motel | **el motel**<br>moh-TEHL |
| movies | **el cine**<br>SEE-neh |
| museum | **el museo**<br>moo-SEH-oh |
| neighborhood | **el vecindario**<br>beh-seen-DAH-ree-oh |
| nightclub | **el club de noche**<br>kloob deh NOH-cheh |
| office | **la oficina ~ el despacho**<br>oh-fee-SEE-nah ~ deh-SPAH-choh |
| park | **el parque**<br>PAHR-keh |
| party | **la fiesta**<br>FYEH-stah |
| pawnshop | **la casa de empeño**<br>kah-sah deh ehm-PEH-nyoh |
| pharmacy | **la farmacia**<br>fahr-MAH-syah |
| pier | **el muelle**<br>MWEH-yeh |
| police station | **la estación de policía**<br>eh-stah-SYOHN deh poh-lee-SEE-ah |
| pool (swimming) | **la piscina ~ la alberca**<br>pee-SEE-nah ~ ahl-BEHR-kah |
| pool hall | **la sala de biliar**<br>SAH-lah deh bee-lee-AHR |
| port | **el puerto**<br>PWEHR-toh |
| post office | **el correo ~ la oficina de correos**<br>koh-RREH-oh ~ oh-fee-SEE-nah deh koh-RREH-ohs |

| | |
|---|---|
| repair shop | **el taller mecánico**<br>tah-YEHR meh-KAH-nee-koh |
| restaurant | **el restaurante**<br>rreh-stah-oo-RAHN-teh |
| school | **la escuela**<br>eh-SKWEH-lah |
| elementary school | **la escuela primaria**<br>eh-SKWEH-lah pree-MAH-ree-ah |
| high school | **el colegio**<br>koh-LEH-hee-oh |
| shoe store | **la zapatería**<br>sah-pah-teh-REE-ah |
| sidewalk | **el banquete ~ la acera**<br>bahn-KEH-teh ~ ah-SEH-rah |
| skyscraper | **el rascacielos**<br>rrah-skah-SYEH-lohs |
| square | **la plaza**<br>PLAH-sah |
| stadium | **el estadio**<br>eh-STAH-dyoh |
| station | **la estación**<br>eh-stah-SYOHN |
| bus station | **la estación de autobús**<br>eh-stah-SYOHN deh ah-oo-toh-BOOS |
| subway station | **la estación de metro**<br>eh-stah-SYOHN deh MEH-troh |
| taxi station | **la estación de taxi**<br>eh-stah-SYOHN deh TAHK-see |
| train station | **la estación de tren**<br>eh-stah-SYOHN deh trehn |
| store | **la tienda**<br>TYEHN-dah |
| studio | **el estudio**<br>eh-STOO-dyoh |
| suburb | **el suburbio**<br>soo-BOOR-byoh |
| supermarket | **el supermercado**<br>soo-pehr-mehr-KAH-thoh |

| | |
|---|---|
| He's/She's in/at the ... | **Está en...**<br>eh-STAH ehn |
| swap meet | **el remate**<br>rreh-MAH-teh |
| theater | **el teatro**<br>teh-AH-troh |
| tower | **la torre**<br>TOH-rreh |
| trash bin | **el basurero**<br>bah-soo-REH-roh |
| trash can | **el bote de basura**<br>BOH-teh deh bah-SOO-rah |
| university | **la universidad**<br>oo-nee-behr-see-THAHTH |
| warehouse | **el almacén**<br>ahl-mah-SEHN |
| workshop | **el taller mecánico**<br>tah-YEHR meh-KAH-nee-koh |

## PARTS OF THE BODY

### Las partes del cuerpo

When referring to parts of the body, use your hands to point to your own body.

| | |
|---|---|
| Where does it hurt? | **¿Dónde le duele?**<br>DOHN-deh leh DWEH-leh |
| Touch (your) ... | **Toque... ~ Tóquese...**<br>TOH-keh ~ TOH-keh-seh |
| Show me your ... | **Enséñeme... ~ Muéstreme...**<br>ehn-SEH-nyeh-meh ~ MWEH-streh-meh |
| Move your ... | **Mueva... ~ Muévase...**<br>MWEH-bah ~ MWEH-bah-seh |
| Point to your ... | **Séñale...**<br>SEH-nyah-leh |
| abdomen | **el abdomen ~ el estómago**<br>ahb-DOH-mehn ~ eh-STOH-mah-goh |
| ankle | **el tobillo**<br>toh-BEE-yoh |

When referring to parts of the body, possessives ("my," "your," etc.) are expressed by **el**, **la**, **los**, and **las**.

Move your fingers. **Mueva los dedos.**

| | |
|---|---|
| arm | **el brazo**<br>BRAH-soh |
| back | **la espalda**<br>eh-SPAHL-dah |
| belly/stomach | **el estómago ~ el vientre**<br>eh-STOH-mah-goh ~ BYEHN-treh |
| bones | **los huesos**<br>WEH-sohs |
| brain | **el cerebro**<br>seh-REH-broh |
| breast | **el seno**<br>SEH-noh |
| buttocks/backside | **las nalgas ~ el trasero**<br>NAHL-gahs ~ trah-SEH-roh |
| cheek | **la mejilla ~ el cachete**<br>meh-HEE-yah ~ kah-CHEH-teh |
| chest | **el pecho**<br>PEH-choh |
| chin | **la barbilla ~ el mentón**<br>bahr-BEE-yah ~ mehn-TOHN |
| ear | **la oreja**<br>oh-REH-hah |
| inner ear | **el oído**<br>oh-EE-thoh |
| eye | **el ojo**<br>OH-hoh |
| face | **la cara**<br>KAH-rah |
| finger | **el dedo**<br>DEH-thoh |
| fist | **el puño**<br>POO-nyoh |

| | |
|---|---|
| Touch (your) … | **Toque… ~ Tóquese…**<br>TOH-keh ~ TOH-keh-seh |
| Show me your … | **Enséñeme… ~ Muéstreme…**<br>ehn-SEH-nyeh-meh ~ MWEH-streh-meh |
| Move your … | **Mueva… ~ Muévase…**<br>MWEH-bah ~ MWEH-bah-seh |
| Point to your … | **Séñale…**<br>SEH-nyah-leh |
| foot | **el pie**<br>pyeh |
| forehead | **la frente**<br>FREHN-teh |
| genitals | **los genitales**<br>heh-nee-TAH-lehs |
| groin | **el ingle**<br>EEN-gleh |
| hair | **el pelo ~ el cabello**<br>PEH-loh ~ kah-BEH-yoh |
| hand | **la mano**<br>MAH-noh |
| head | **la cabeza**<br>kah-BEH-sah |
| heart | **el corazón**<br>koh-rah-SOHN |
| heel | **el talón**<br>tah-LOHN |
| hip | **la cadera**<br>kah-THEH-rah |
| knee | **la rodilla**<br>rroh-THEE-yah |
| leg | **la pierna**<br>PYEHR-nah |
| lips | **los labios**<br>LAH-byohs |
| lung | **el pulmón**<br>pool-MOHN |
| mouth | **la boca**<br>BOH-kah |
| muscle | **el músculo**<br>MOO-skoo-loh |

To make a Spanish word ending in a vowel plural, add **-s**. For words ending in a consonant (anything but a vowel), add **-es**. For plural words (things and people), **el** changes to **los** and **la** changes to **las**.

**el dedo → los dedos**
**la pierna → las piernas**

| | |
|---|---|
| nape (back of neck) | **la nuca**<br>NOO-kah |
| neck | **el cuello**<br>KWEH-yoh |
| nose | **la nariz**<br>nah-REES |
| ribs | **las costillas**<br>koh-STEE-yahs |
| shoulder | **el hombro**<br>OHM-broh |
| side | **el costado ~ el lado**<br>koh-STAH-thoh ~ LAH-thoh |
| skin | **la piel**<br>pyehl |
| stomach/belly | **el estómago ~ el vientre**<br>eh-STOH-mah-goh ~ BYEHN-treh |
| throat | **la garganta**<br>gahr-GAHN-tah |
| thumb | **el pulgar**<br>pool-GAHR |
| toe | **el dedo del pie**<br>DEH-thoh dehl pyeh |
| tongue | **la lengua**<br>LEHN-gwah |
| tooth | **el diente**<br>DYEHN-teh |
| waist | **la cintura**<br>seen-TOO-rah |
| wrist | **la muñeca**<br>moon-YEH-kah |

## FOOD AND DRINK

La comida y las bebidas

As a detective, you can trap suspects' lies on what they ate or drank. And the next time you're at a restaurant, be sure to ask for Mexican food! For a list of alcoholic drinks, see p. 72 and the section on alcohol and drugs, pp. 141–147.

| | |
|---|---|
| What did you eat for …? | **¿Qué comió para…?** keh koh-MYOH PAH-rah |
| breakfast | **el desayuno** deh-sah-YOO-noh |
| lunch | **el almuerzo ~ el lonche** ahl-MWEHR-soh ~ LOHN-cheh |
| dinner | **la cena** SEH-nah |
| dessert | **el postre** POH-streh |
| What did you drink? | **¿Qué bebió?** keh beh-BYOH |
| coffee | **café** kah-FEH |
| beer | **cerveza** sehr-BEH-sah |
| water | **agua** AH-gwah |
| How did you eat your eggs? | **¿Cómo comió sus huevos?** KOH-moh koh-MYOH soos WEH-bohs |
| eggs | **los huevos** WEH-bohs |
| scrambled | **revueltos** rreh-BWEHL-tohs |
| sunny side up | **estrellados** eh-streh-YAH-thohs |
| How did you drink your coffee? | **¿Cómo tomó el café?** KOH-moh toh-MOH ehl kah-FEH |
| coffee | **café** kah-FEH |

| | |
|---|---|
| black | **solo**<br>SOH-loh |
| with cream | **con crema**<br>kohn KREH-mah |
| with milk | **con leche**<br>kohn LEH-cheh |
| with sugar | **con azúcar**<br>kohn ah-SOO-kahr |

## Mexican Food
La comida para mexicanos

| | |
|---|---|
| What kind of Mexican food did you eat? | **¿Qué tipo de comida mexicana comió?**<br>keh TEE-poh deh koh-MEE-thah meh-hee-KAH-nah koh-MYOH |
| flour tortillas with filling | **los burritos**<br>boo-RREE-tohs |
| grilled strips of beef | **la carne asada**<br>KAHR-neh ah-SAH-thah |
| roasted pork | **las carnitas**<br>kahr-NEE-tahs |
| chili with meat | **el chile con carne**<br>CHEE-leh kohn KAHR-neh |
| stuffed peppers | **el chile relleno**<br>CHEE-leh rreh-YEH-noh |
| rolled tortillas with cheese and sauce | **las enchiladas**<br>ehn-chee-LAH-thahs |
| eggs and hot sauce with tomatoes | **los huevos rancheros**<br>WEH-bohs rrahn-CHEH-rohs |
| tortilla with cheese | **la quesadilla**<br>keh-sah-THEE-yah |
| soft meat rolls | **los tacos**<br>TAH-kohs |
| corn dough with meat or chicken | **las tamales**<br>tah-MAH-lehs |
| corn tortilla with meat or chicken | **la tostada**<br>toh-STAH-thah |

## Gringo Food
La comida para gringos

| | |
|---|---|
| apple | **la manzana**<br>mahn-SAH-nah |
| banana | **la banana ~ el plátano**<br>bah-NAH-nah ~ PLAH-tah-noh |
| beans | **los frijoles**<br>free-HOH-lehs |
| bread | **el pan**<br>pahn |
| toast | **el pan tostado**<br>pahn toh-STAH-thoh |
| with butter | **con mantequilla**<br>kohn mahn-teh-KEE-yah |
| cake | **el pastel ~ la torta**<br>pah-STEHL ~ TOHR-tah |
| cheese | **el queso**<br>KEH-soh |
| chicken | **el pollo**<br>POH-yoh |
| broiled chicken | **el pollo asado**<br>POH-yoh ah-SAH-thoh |
| cookies | **las galletas**<br>gah-YEH-tahs |
| custard/pudding | **el flan**<br>flahn |
| fish | **el pescado**<br>peh-SKAH-thoh |
| fruit | **la fruta**<br>FROO-tah |
| grapes | **las uvas**<br>OO-bahs |
| ham | **el jamón**<br>hah-MOHN |
| hamburger | **la hamburguesa**<br>ahm-boor-GEH-sah |
| ice cream | **el helado ~ la nieve**<br>eh-LAH-thoh ~ NYEH-beh |
| juice | **el jugo ~ el zumo**<br>HOO-goh ~ SOO-moh |

To say "some" when referring to particular foods, omit the **el** or **la**.

I want some bread. **Quiero pan.**

To say "a" or "an," change the **el** to **un** or **la** to **una.**

a melon **un melón**
a beer **una cerveza**

| | |
|---|---|
| orange juice | **el jugo de naranja**<br>HOO-goh deh nah-RAHN-hah |
| tomato juice | **el jugo de tomate**<br>HOO-goh deh toh-MAH-teh |
| lamb chop | **la chuleta de cordero**<br>choo-LEH-tah deh kohr-THEH-roh |
| meat | **la carne**<br>KAHR-neh |
| melon | **el melón**<br>meh-LOHN |
| oil | **el aceite**<br>ah-SEH-teh |
| onion | **la cebolla**<br>seh-BOH-yah |
| pear | **la pera**<br>PEH-rah |
| pineapple | **la piña**<br>PEE-nyah |
| pizza | **la pizza**<br>PEET-sah |
| pork chop | **la chuleta de puerco**<br>choo-LEH-tah deh PWEHR-koh |
| potatoes | **las papas**<br>PAH-pahs |
| fried potatoes | **las papas fritas**<br>PAH-pahs FREE-tahs |
| mashed potatoes | **el puré de papas**<br>poo-REH deh PAH-pahs |

| | |
|---|---|
| pudding/custard | **el flan**<br>flahn |
| rice | **el arroz**<br>ah-RROHS |
| salad | **la ensalada**<br>ehn-sah-LAH-thah |
| fruit salad | **la ensalada de fruta**<br>ehn-sah-LAH-thah deh FROO-tah |
| tomato salad | **la ensalada de tomate**<br>ehn-sah-LAH-thah deh toh-MAH-teh |
| sandwich | **el sándwich**<br>SAHND-weech |
| cheese sandwich | **el sándwich de queso**<br>SAHND-weech deh KEH-soh |
| ham sandwich | **el sándwich de jamón**<br>SAHND-weech deh hah-MOHN |
| tuna sandwich | **el sándwich de atún**<br>SAHND-weech deh ah-TOON |
| soda | **la soda**<br>SOH-thah |
| soup | **la sopa**<br>SOH-pah |
| steak | **el bistec**<br>bee-STEHK |
| strawberries | **las fresas**<br>FREH-sahs |
| tea | **el té**<br>teh |
| vegetables (green) | **las verduras**<br>behr-THOO-rahs |
| vegetables (all) | **las legumbres**<br>leh-GOOM-brehs |
| water | **el agua**<br>AH-gwah |

# Law Enforcement Vocabulary

## EMERGENCY PROFESSIONS AND WORK SITES

Las profesiones de emergencia y los sitios de trabajo

We begin with the good guys and where they work. My name's Friday, and I'm a cop!

| | |
|---|---|
| animal control officer | **el / la oficial para el control de animales**<br>oh-fee-SYAHL PAH-rah ehl kohn-TROHL deh ah-nee-MAH-lehs |
| booking center | **el centro de fichar**<br>SEHN-troh deh fee-CHAHR |
| border patrol agent | **el / la agente de la patrulla de la frontera**<br>ah-HEHN-teh deh lah pah-TROO-yah deh lah frohn-TEH-rah |
| clinic | **la clínica**<br>KLEE-nee-kah |
| coast guard officer | **el / la guardacostas**<br>gwahr-thah-KOH-stahs |
| coroner | **el médico forense / la médica forense**<br>MEH-thee-koh foh-REHN-seh / MEH-thee-kah foh-REHN-seh |
| corrections officer | **el / la oficial de correcciones**<br>oh-fee-SYAHL deh koh-rrehk-SYOH-nehs |
| customs officer | **el aduanero / la aduanera**<br>ah-dwah-NEH-roh / ah-dwah-NEH-rah |

If the Spanish name for an occupation can be used for both males and females, it is shown with **el** and **la** separated by a "/".

detective **el / la detective**

If the Spanish name for an occupation differs between male and female, both forms are given, the male form with **el** and the female form with **la**. The forms are separated by a "/".

dispatcher **el despachador / la despachadora**

If an occupation has two or more equivalent forms in Spanish, they are separated by a "~".

waitress **la mesera ~ la camarera**

| | |
|---|---|
| deputy sheriff/ sheriff's deputy | **el / la oficial del sheriff**<br>oh-fee-SYAHL dehl SHEH-reef |
| detective | **el / la detective**<br>deh-tehk-TEE-beh |
| detective bureau | **el despacho de detectives**<br>deh-SPAH-choh deh deh-tehk-TEE-behs |
| | **la oficina de detectives**<br>oh-fee-SEE-nah deh deh-tehk-TEE-behs |
| dispatch center | **el centro de despacho**<br>SEHN-troh deh deh-SPAH-choh |
| dispatcher | **el despachador / la despachadora**<br>deh-spah-chah-THOHR / deh-spah-chah-THOH-rah |
| doctor | **el médico / la médica**<br>MEH-thee-koh / MEH-thee-kah |
| | **el doctor / la doctora**<br>dohk-TOHR / dohk-TOH-rah |

| | |
|---|---|
| emergency responder | **el personal de respuesta de emergencia**<br>pehr-soh-NAHL deh rreh-SPWEH-stah deh eh-mehr-HEHN-syah |
| FBI | **la Oficina Federal de Investigación**<br>oh-fee-SEE-nah feh-theh-RAHL deh een-beh-stee-gah-SYOHN |
| FBI agent | **el / la agente de la Oficina Federal de Investigación**<br>ah-HEHN-teh deh lah oh-fee-SEE-nah feh-theh-RAHL deh een-beh-stee-gah-SYOHN |
| fire department | **el departamento de bomberos**<br>deh-pahr-tah-MEHN-toh deh bohm-BEH-rohs |
| fire station | **la estación de bomberos**<br>eh-stah-SYOHN deh bohm-BEH-rohs |
| firefighter | **el bombero / la bombera**<br>bohm-BEH-roh / bohm-BEH-rah |
| first responder (*male*) | **el que responde primero en emergencias**<br>ehl keh rreh-SPOHN-deh pree-MEH-roh ehn eh-mehr-HEHN-syahs |
| first responder (*female*) | **la que responde primero en emergencias**<br>lah keh rreh-SPOHN-deh pree-MEH-roh ehn eh-mehr-HEHN-syahs |
| fish and game warden | **el / la agente de la pesca y la caza**<br>ah-HEHN-teh deh lah PEH-skah ee lah KAH-sah |
| forest ranger/park ranger | **el / la guardabosques**<br>gwahr-thah-BOH-skehs |
| guard | **el / la guardia**<br>GWAHR-dyah |

|  |  |
|---|---|
| harbor patrol officer | **el patrullero de puertos**<br>pah-troo-YEH-roh deh PWEHR-tohs |
| highway patrol officer | **el / la oficial de la patrulla de camino**<br>oh-fee-SYAHL deh lah pah-TROO-yah deh kah-MEE-noh |
| hospital | **el hospital**<br>oh-spee-TAHL |
| immigration officer | **el / la oficial de inmigración**<br>oh-fee-SYAHL deh een-mee-grah-SYOHN<br>**el / la oficial de la migra (*slang*)**<br>oh-fee-SYAHL deh lah MEE-grah |
| investigator | **el investigador / la investigadora**<br>een-beh-stee-gah-THOHR / een-beh-stee-gah-THOH-rah |
| jail | **la cárcel**<br>KAHR-sehl |
| jailer | **el carcelero / la carcelera**<br>kahr-seh-LEH-roh / kahr-seh-LEH-rah |
| juvenile division | **la división juvenil**<br>dee-bee-SYOHN hoo-beh-NEEL |
| juvenile hall | **la cárcel para menores**<br>KAHR-sehl PAH-rah meh-NOH-rehs |
| law enforcement officer | **el / la policía**<br>poh-lee-SEE-ah |
| lifeguard | **el / la salvavidas**<br>sahl-bah-BEE-thahs |
| nurse | **el enfermero / la enfermera**<br>ehn-fehr-MEH-roh / ehn-fehr-MEH-rah |
| officer | **el / la oficial**<br>oh-fee-SYAHL |

peace officer — **el / la oficial de orden público**
oh-fee-SYAHL deh OHR-thehn POO-blee-koh

operator — **el operador / la operadora**
oh-peh-rah-THOHR / oh-peh-rah-THOH-rah

**el / la telefonista**
teh-leh-foh-NEE-stah

paramedic — **el paramédico / la paramédica**
pah-rah-MEH-thee-koh / pah-rah-MEH-thee-kah

park ranger/forest ranger — **el / la guardabosques**
gwahr-thah-BOH-skehs

patrol officer — **el patrullero / la patrullera**
pah-troo-YEH-roh / pah-troo-YEH-rah

penitentiary — **la cárcel presidio**
KAHR-sehl preh-SEE-dyoh

police chief — **el jefe de policía / la jefa de policía**
HEH-feh deh poh-lee-SEE-ah / HEH-fah deh poh-lee-SEE-ah

**el / la comandante de policía**
koh-mahn-DAHN-teh deh poh-lee-SEE-ah

police department — **el departamento de policía**
deh-pahr-tah-MEHN-toh deh poh-lee-SEE-ah

police headquarters — **la comisaría**
koh-mee-sah-REE-ah

police officer — **el / la policía**
poh-lee-SEE-ah

police station — **la estación de policía**
eh-stah-SYOHN deh poh-lee-SEE-ah

prison — **la prisión**
pree-SYOHN

state prison — **la prisión del estado**
pree-SYOHN dehl eh-STAH-thoh

federal prison — **la prisión federal**
pree-SYOHN feh-theh-RAHL

|  |  |
|---|---|
| probation | **la probación**<br>proh-bah-SYOHN |
| county probation department | **el departamento de probación del condado**<br>deh-pahr-tah-MEHN-toh deh proh-bah-SYOHN dehl kohn-DAH-thoh |
| probation officer | **el / la oficial de probación**<br>oh-fee-SYAHL deh proh-bah-SYOHN |
| public health department | **el departamento de la salud del público**<br>deh-pahr-tah-MEHN-toh deh lah sah-LOOTH dehl POO-blee-koh |
| public safety department | **el departamento de la seguridad del público**<br>deh-pahr-tah-MEHN-toh deh lah seh-goo-ree-THAHTH dehl POO-blee-koh |
| robbery division | **la sección de robos**<br>sehk-SYOHN deh RROH-bohs |
| secret service agent | **el / la agente de servicio secreto**<br>ah-HEHN-teh deh sehr-BEE-syoh seh-KREH-toh |
| sheriff | **el / la sheriff**<br>SHEH-reef |
| county sheriff's department | **el departamento del sheriff del condado**<br>deh-pahr-tah-MEHN-toh dehl SHEH-reef dehl kohn-DAH-thoh |
| sheriff's deputy/ deputy sheriff | **el / la oficial del sheriff**<br>oh-fee-SYAHL dehl SHEH-reef |
| traffic division | **la sección de tráfico**<br>sehk-SYOHN deh TRAH-fee-koh |
| welfare | **el bienestar**<br>byehn-eh-STAHR |

county welfare department — **el departamento de bienestar del condado**
deh-pahr-tah-MEHN-toh deh byehn-eh-STAHR dehl kohn-DAH-thoh

welfare fraud investigator (*male*) — **el investigador contra el fraude de bienestar**
een-beh-stee-gah-THOHR kohn-trah ehl FRAH-oo-theh deh byehn-eh-STAHR

welfare fraud investigator (*female*) — **la investigadora contra el fraude de bienestar**
een-beh-stee-gah-THOH-rah kohn-trah ehl FRAH-oo-theh deh byehn-eh-STAHR

## CRIMINALS
### Los criminales

And now come the baddies!

accomplice — **el / la cómplice**
KOHM-plee-seh

addict — **el adicto / la adicta**
ah-DEEK-toh / ah-DEEK-tah

agitator — **el alborotador / la alborotadora**
ahl-boh-roh-tah-THOHR / ahl-boh-roh-tah-THOH-rah

arsonist — **el incendiario / la incendiaria**
een-sehn-DYAH-ree-oh / een-sehn-DYAH-ree-ah

assailant — **el / la asaltante**
ah-sahl-TAHN-teh

assassin — **el asesino / la asesina**
ah-seh-SEE-noh / ah-seh-SEE-nah

bank robber — **el atracador / la atracadora**
ah-trah-kah-THOHR / ah-trah-kah-THOH-rah

| | |
|---|---|
| bookie | **el corredor de apuestas / la corredora de apuestas**<br>koh-rreh-THOHR deh ah-PWEH-stahs/ koh-rreh-THOH-rah deh ah-PWEH-stahs |
| burglar | **el ladrón / la ladrona**<br>lah-DROHN/lah-DROH-nah |
| convict | **el condenado / la condenada**<br>kohn-deh-NAH-thoh/ kohn-deh-NAH-thah |
| criminal | **el / la criminal**<br>kree-mee-NAHL |
| delinquent | **el / la delincuente**<br>deh-leen-KWEHN-teh |
| drug dealer | **el / la narcotraficante**<br>nahr-koh-trah-fee-KAHN-teh |
| drunk | **el borracho / la borracha**<br>boh-RRAH-choh/ boh-RRAH-chah |
| escapee | **el fugitivo / la fugitiva**<br>foo-hee-TEE-boh/ foo-hee-TEE-bah |
| felon | **el felón / la felona**<br>feh-LOHN/feh-LOH-nah |
| fence (*male*) | **el corredor de cosas robadas**<br>koh-rreh-THOHR deh KOH-sahs rroh-BAH-thahs |
| fence (*female*) | **la corredora de cosas robadas**<br>koh-rreh-THOH-rah deh KOH-sahs rroh-BAH-thahs |
| forger | **el falsificador / la falsificadora**<br>fahl-see-fee-kah-THOHR/ fahl-see-fee-kah-THO-rah |
| fugitive | **el fugitivo / la fugitiva**<br>foo-hee-TEE-boh/ foo-hee-TEE-bah |
| gang member | **el pandillero / la pandillera**<br>pahn-dee-YEH-roh/ pahn-dee-YEH-rah |

| | |
|---|---|
| gang member (*male or female*) | **el miembro de una pandilla** MYEHM-broh deh OO-nah pahn-DEE-yah |
| homeless person (*male or female*) | **la persona sin hogar** pehr-SOH-nah seen oh-GAHR |
| | **la persona de la calle** pehr-SOH-nah deh lah KAH-yeh |
| inmate | **el preso / la presa** PREH-soh / PREH-sah |
| kidnapper | **el secuestrador / la secuestradora** seh-kweh-strah-THOHR / seh-kweh-strah-THOH-rah |
| killer | **el asesino / la asesina** ah-seh-SEE-noh / ah-seh-SEE-nah |
| mugger | **el / la asaltante** ah-sahl-TAHN-teh |
| murderer | **el asesino / la asesina** ah-seh-SEE-noh / ah-seh-SEE-nah |
| pickpocket/shoplifter | **el ratero / la ratera** rrah-TEH-roh / rrah-TEH-rah |
| pimp | **el chulo** CHOO-loh |
| prisoner | **el prisionero / la prisionera** pree-syoh-NEH-roh / pree-syoh-NEH-rah |
| | **el preso / la presa** PREH-soh / PREH-sah |
| prostitute | **la prostituta** proh-stee-TOO-tah |
| prowler | **el ladrón / la ladrona** lah-DROHN / lah-DROH-nah |
| rapist | **el violador / la violadora** bee-oh-lah-THOHR / bee-oh-lah-THOH-rah |
| shoplifter | **el ratero de tiendas / la ratera de tiendas** rrah-TEH-roh deh TYEHN-dahs / rrah-TEH-rah deh TYEHN-dahs |

smuggler — **el / la contrabandista**
kohn-trah-bahn-DEE-stah

suspect — **el sospechoso / la sospechosa**
soh-speh-CHOH-soh / soh-speh-CHOH-sah

swindler — **el estafador / la estafadora**
eh-stah-fah-THOHR / eh-stah-fah-THOH-rah

terrorist — **el / la terrorista**
teh-rroh-REE-stah

thief — **el ladrón / la ladrona**
lah-DROHN / lah-DROH-nah

transient/vagrant — **el vago / la vaga**
BAH-goh / BAH-gah

**el vagabundo / la vagabunda**
bah-gah-BOON-doh / bah-gah-BOON-dah

## WEIGHTS AND MEASURES
Los pesos y las medidas

### Liquids and Weight
Los líquidos y el peso

How much did you drink? — **¿Cuánto tomó?**
KWAHN-toh toh-MOH

a shot (glass) of tequila — **un tequilero (de tequila)**
oon teh-kee-LEH-roh (deh teh-KEE-lah)

(two) ounces of whiskey — **(dos) onzas de whisky**
(dohs) OHN-sahs deh WEE-skee

only a couple of beers — **solamente un par de cervezas**
soh-lah-MEHN-teh oon pahr deh sehr-BEH-sahs

a fifth of whiskey — **un quinto de un galón de whisky**
oon KEEN-toh deh oon gah-LOHN deh WEE-skee

a quart of milk — **un cuarto (de un galón) de leche**
oon KWAHR-toh (deh oon gah-LOHN) deh LEH-cheh

a gallon — **un galón**
oon gah-LOHN

How much does it weigh? — **¿Cuánto pesa?**
KWAHN-toh PEH-sah

in pounds — **en libras**
ehn LEE-brahs

in kilos — **en kilos**
ehn KEE-lohs

in tons — **en toneladas**
ehn-toh-neh-LAH-thahs

☞ For numbers, see pp. 11–15.

## Distance and Measure
La distancia y la medida

How tall are you? — **¿Cuánto mide?**
KWAHN-toh MEE-theh
**¿Qué estatura tiene?**
keh eh-stah-TOO-rah TYEHN-neh

in feet and inches — **en pies y pulgadas**
ehn pyehs ee pool-GAH-thahs

How fast were you driving? — **¿A qué velocidad manejaba?**
ah keh beh-loh-see-THAHTH mah-neh-HAH-bah

(60) miles an hour — **(sesenta) millas por hora**
(seh-SEHN-tah) MEE-yahs pohr OH-rah

How far did it/you go? — **¿A qué distancia fue?**
ah keh dee-STAHN-syah fweh

inches — **pulgadas**
pool-GAH-thahs

feet — **pies**
pyehs

yards — **yardas**
YAHR-thahs

What size? (*clothing and body*) — **¿Qué talla?**
keh TAH-yah
**¿Qué número?**
keh NOO-meh-roh
**¿Qué medida?**
keh meh-THEE-thah

size

- small — **pequeño[a] ~ chico[a]**
  peh-KEH-nyoh[-nyah] ~ CHEE-koh[-kah]
- medium — **medio[a] ~ mediano[a]**
  MEH-dyoh[-dyah] ~ meh-DYAH-noh[-nah]
- large — **grande**
  GRAHN-deh
- size (10) shoes — **zapatos número (10)**
  sah-PAH-tohs NOO-meh-roh (dyehs)
- waist size — **medida de cinta**
  meh-THEE-thah deh SEEN-tah

## FIELD INTERVIEW
### La entrevista

For the field interview, here are some one-liners that will get the job done. Keep it short and simple. Omit **el** and **la**.

name

- last name and first name — **apellido y nombre**
  ah-peh-YEE-thoh ee NOHM-breh
- first name and last name — **nombre y apellido**
  NOHM-breh ee ah-peh-YEE-thoh
- A.K.A. — **otros nombres**
  OH-trohs NOHM-brehs
- nickname — **apodo ~ sobrenombre**
  ah-POH-thoh ~ soh-breh-NOHM-breh

Latinos don't have middle names. For additional cultural information, see Chapter 5.

When giving a date, Latinos write the day first and the month second. For example, they write **10-01** for January 10 (not October 1); they write **30-07** for July 30.

| | |
|---|---|
| driver's license | **licencia de manejar**<br>lee-SEHN-syah deh mah-neh-HAHR |
| state | **estado**<br>eh-STAH-thoh |
| address | |
| home address | **dirección de casa ~ domicilio**<br>dee-rehk-SYOHN deh KAH-sah ~ doh-mee-SEE-lee-oh |
| work address | **dirección de trabajo ~ dirección de negocio**<br>dee-rehk-SYOHN deh trah-BAH-hoh ~ dee-rehk-SYOHN deh neh-GOH-syoh |
| number | **número**<br>NOO-meh-roh |
| street | **calle**<br>KAH-yeh |
| city | **ciudad**<br>see-oo-THAHTH |
| zip code | **zona postal ~ código postal**<br>SOH-nah poh-STAHL ~ KOH-thee-goh poh-STAHL |
| state | **estado**<br>eh-STAH-thoh |

| | |
|---|---|
| phone number with area code | **número de teléfono con área** NOO-meh-roh deh teh-LEH-foh-noh kohn AH-reh-ah |
| occupation | **ocupación** oh-koo-pah-SYOHN |
| business/work | **negocio ~ trabajo** neh-GOH-syoh ~ trah-BAH-hoh |
| school | **escuela** eh-SKWEH-lah |
| birthday | **cumpleaños** koom-pleh-AH-nyohs |
| date of birth | **fecha de nacimiento** FEH-chah deh nah-see-MYEHN-toh |
| month | **mes** mehs |
| day | **día** DEE-ah |
| year | **año** AH-nyoh |
| Social Security number | **número de seguro social** NOO-meh-roh deh seh-GOO-roh soh-SYAHL |
| race | **raza** RRAH-sah |
| Asian | **asiático[a]** ah-SYAH-tee-koh[-kah] |
| black | **negro[a]** NEH-groh[-grah] |
| Hispanic | **hispano[a]** ee-SPAH-noh[-nah] |
| Latino | **latino[a]** lah-TEE-noh[-nah] |
| Oriental | **oriental** oh-ree-ehn-TAHL |
| white | **blanco[a]** BLAHN-koh[-kah] |
| eyes | **ojos** OH-hohs |
| blue | **azules** ah-SOO-lehs |

Most descriptive words (adjectives) that describe males or masculine things end in **-o**. You change the **-o** to **-a** when you're describing females or feminine things.

He's white. — **(Él) es blanco.**
She's white. — **(Ella) es blanca.**

The coat is red. — **El abrigo es rojo.**
The jacket is red. — **La chaqueta es roja.**

| | |
|---|---|
| green | **verdes** BEHR-thehs |
| brown | **cafés** kah-FEHS |
| gray | **grises** GREE-sehs |
| civil state | **estado civil** eh-STAH-thoh see-BEEL |
| single | **soltero[a]** sohl-TEH-roh[-rah] |
| married | **casado[a]** kah-SAH-thoh[-thah] |
| divorced | **divorciado[a]** dee-bohr-SYAH-thoh[-thah] |
| separated | **separado[a]** seh-pah-RAH-thoh[-thah] |
| height (in feet and inches) | **estatura (en pies y pulgadas)** eh-stah-TOO-rah (ehn pyehs ee pool-GAH-thahs) |
| weight (in pounds) | **peso (en libras)** PEH-soh (ehn LEE-brahs) |
| U.S. citizen | **ciudadano de USA / ciudadana de USA** see-oo-thah-THAH-noh de oo EH-seh ah / see-oo-thah-THAH-nah de oo EH-seh ah |

| | |
|---|---|
| country | **país**<br>pah-EES |
| here since when | **desde cuando aquí**<br>DEHZ-deh KWAHN-doh ah-KEE |
| gang | **pandilla ~ ganga**<br>pahn-DEE-yah ~ GAHN-gah |
| associate | **asociado[a]**<br>ah-soh-SYAH-thoh[-thah] |
| name of gang/moniker | **nombre de pandilla**<br>NOHM-breh deh pahn-DEE-yah<br>**nombre de ganga**<br>NOHM-breh deh GAHN-gah |
| on probation | **en probación**<br>ehn proh-bah-SYOHN |
| probation officer | **oficial de probación**<br>oh-fee-SYAHL deh proh-bah-SYOHN |
| on parole | **en parole**<br>ehn pah-ROH-leh |
| parole officer | **oficial de parole**<br>oh-fee-SYAHL deh pah-ROH-leh |

## PHYSICAL CHARACTERISTICS

Las señas particulares

At a crime scene, you need detailed descriptions for reports, including physical characteristics.

### Hair

El pelo ~ el cabello

| | |
|---|---|
| Afro | **afro ~ natural**<br>AH-froh ~ nah-too-RAHL |
| bald | **calvo ~ pelón**<br>KAHL-boh ~ peh-LOHN |
| braided | **en trenzas**<br>ehn TREHN-sahs |

| | |
|---|---|
| bushy | **espeso**<br>eh-SPEH-soh |
| coarse | **grueso**<br>groo-EH-soh |
| color | |
| black | **negro**<br>NEH-groh |
| blond | **rubio**<br>RROO-byoh |
| brown (dark) | **café**<br>kah-FEH |
| brown (light) | **castaño**<br>kah-STAH-nyoh |
| brunette | **moreno**<br>moh-REH-noh |
| gray | **gris ~ canoso**<br>grees ~ kah-NOH-soh |
| red (hair) | **(pelo) rojo**<br>(PEH-loh) RROH-hoh |
| redhead | **pelirrojo[a]**<br>peh-lee-ROH-hoh[-hah] |
| crew cut | **corte cepillo**<br>KOHR-teh seh-PEE-yoh |
| curly | **rizado**<br>rree-SAH-thoh |
| fine | **fino**<br>FEE-noh |
| greasy | **grasoso**<br>grah-SOH-soh |
| hairy | **velludo[a] ~ peludo[a]**<br>beh-YOO-thoh[-thah] ~<br>peh-LOO-thoh[-thah] |
| length | |
| long | **largo**<br>LAHR-goh |
| short | **corto**<br>KOHR-toh |
| medium | **mediano**<br>meh-DYAH-noh |

## Hairstyle
El estilo de pelo o cabello

military — **militar**
mee-lee-TAHR

ponytail — **la colita de caballo**
koh-LEE-tah deh kah-BAH-yoh

receding — **un poco calvo**
oon POH-koh KAHL-boh

shaved — **afeitado**
ah-feh-TAH-thoh

straight — **lico**
LEE-koh

wavy — **crespo**
KREH-spoh

wig — **con peluca**
kohn peh-LOO-kah

## Face
La cara

broad — **ancha**
AHN-chah

high cheek — **mejilla alta**
meh-HEE-yah AHL-tah
**cachete alto**
kah-CHEH-teh AHL-toh

long — **larga**
LAHR-gah

oval — **ovalada**
oh-bah-LAH-thah

round — **redonda**
rreh-THOHN-dah

square — **cuadrada**
kwah-DRAH-thah

## Complexion
El cutis

| | |
|---|---|
| acne | **el acné**<br>ahk-NEH |
| blackheads | **los barros**<br>BAH-rrohs |
| freckles | **con pecas**<br>kohn PEH-kahs |
| mole | **el lunar**<br>loo-NAHR |
| pimples | **las espinillas**<br>eh-spee-NEE-yahs |
| pockmarks | **con marcas de viruela**<br>kohn MAHR-kahs deh bee-roo-EH-lah |

## Facial Hair
El pelo de cara

| | |
|---|---|
| beard | **la barba**<br>BAHR-bah |
| full beard | **la barba completa ~ la barba llena**<br>BAHR-bah kohm-PLEH-tah ~ BAHR-bah YEH-nah |
| clean shaven | **afeitado**<br>ah-feh-TAH-thoh |
| goatee | **la barba de chivo**<br>BAHR-bah de CHEE-boh |
| mustache | **el bigote**<br>bee-GOH-teh |
| sideburns | **las patillas**<br>pah-TEE-yahs |
| unshaven | **no afeitado**<br>noh ah-feh-TAH-thoh |

## Glasses
Los lentes ~ los anteojos

colored — **con color**
kohn koh-LOHR

mirrored — **los lentes con espejos**
LEHN-tehs kohn eh-SPEH-hohs

shaded — **sombro**
SOHM-broh

tinted — **tinte**
TEEN-teh

prescription — **con prescripción**
kohn preh-skreep-SYOHN

contact lenses — **los lentes de contacto**
LEHN-tehs deh kohn-TAHK-toh

frame — **el aro ~ el marco**
AH-roh ~ MAHR-koh

wire — **de metal**
deh meh-TAHL

plastic — **de plástico**
deh PLAH-stee-koh

sunglasses — **los lentes de sol ~ las gafas de sol**
LEHN-tes deh sohl ~ GAH-fahs deh sohl

## Voice
La voz

accent

speaks with an accent — **habla con acento**
AH-blah kohn ah-SEHN-toh

disguised — **disfrazada**
dees-frah-SAH-thah

lisp

speaks with a lisp — **habla con "zeta"**
AH-blah kohn SEH-tah

monotone — **monótona**
moh-NOH-toh-nah

nasal — **nasal**
nah-SAHL

| | |
|---|---|
| pleasant | **agradable**<br>ah-grah-THAH-bleh |
| raspy | **chillona**<br>chee-YOH-nah |
| stuttering | **tartamudea**<br>tahr-tah-moo-THEH-ah |

## Other Descriptors
Los otros descriptores

Here are some questions that you can ask witnesses to obtain a physical description of the suspect, followed by a list of additional descriptors.

| | |
|---|---|
| Big or little? | **¿Grande o pequeño[a]?**<br>GRAHN-deh oh peh-KEH-nyoh[-nyah] |
| | **¿Grande o chico[a]?**<br>GRAHN-deh oh CHEE-koh[-kah] |
| Clean or dirty? | **¿Limpio[a] o sucio[a]?**<br>LEEM-pyoh[-pyah] oh SOO-syoh[-syah] |
| Fat or thin? | **¿Gordo[a] o flaco[a]?**<br>GOHR-thoh[-thah] oh FLAH-koh[-kah] |
| | **¿Gordo[a] o delgado[a]?**<br>GOHR-thoh[-thah] oh dehl-GAH-thoh[-thah] |
| Handsome or ugly? | **¿Guapo[a] o feo[a]?**<br>GWAH-poh[-pah] oh FEH-oh[-ah] |
| Hurt or unhurt? | **¿Herido[a] o ileso[a]?**<br>eh-REE-thoh[-thah] oh ee-LEH-soh[-sah] |
| Left- or right-handed? | **¿Escribe con la mano izquierda o con la derecha?**<br>eh-SKREE-beh kohn lah MAH-noh ees-KYEHR-thah oh kohn lah deh-REH-chah |

To identify a suspect's gender, ask **¿Hombre o mujer?** ("Man or woman?"). If you ask **¿El sexo?**, you may get the surprising response **¿Mi casa o su casa?** ("My house or yours?").

| | |
|---|---|
| Man or woman? | **¿Hombre o mujer?**<br>OHM-breh oh moo-HEHR |
| Old or young? | **¿Mayor o menor de edad?**<br>mah-YOHR oh meh-NOHR deh eh-THAHTH |
| Rich or poor? | **¿Rico[a] o pobre?**<br>RREE-koh[-kah] oh POH-breh |
| Smelly or pleasant odor? | **¿Huele mal o bien?**<br>WEH-leh mahl oh byehn |
| Strong or weak? | **¿Fuerte o débil?**<br>FWEHR-teh oh DEH-beel |
| Tall or short? | **¿Alto[a] o bajo[a]?**<br>AHL-toh[-tah] oh BAH-hoh[-hah] |
| Tired or rested? | **¿Cansado[a] o descansado[a]?**<br>kahn-SAH-thoh[-thah] oh dehs-kahn-SAH-thoh[-thah] |
| Well or badly dressed? | **¿Bien o mal vestido[a]?**<br>byehn oh mahl beh-STEE-thoh[-thah] |
| Wet or dry? | **¿Mojado[a] o seco[a]?**<br>moh-HAH-thoh[-thah] oh SEH-koh[-kah] |

Here are more useful descriptive words:

| | |
|---|---|
| bald | **calvo[a]**<br>KAHL-boh[-bah]<br>**pelón / pelona**<br>peh-LOHN / peh-LOH-nah |

| | |
|---|---|
| barefoot | **descalzo[a]**<br>dehs-KAHL-soh[-sah] |
| beauty mark | **el lunar**<br>loo-NAHR |
| birthmark | **la marca de nacimiento**<br>MAHR-kah deh nah-see-MYEHN-toh |
| blind | **ciego[a]**<br>SYEH-goh[-gah] |
| breathing | |
| fast breathing | **la respiración rápida**<br>rreh-spee-rah-SYOHN RRAH-pee-thah |
| cross-eyed | **bizco[a]**<br>BEE-skoh[-skah] |
| deaf | **sordo[a]**<br>SOHR-thoh[-thah] |
| disabled | **incapacitado[a]**<br>een-kah-pah-see-TAH-thoh[-thah] |
| gold chain | **la cadena de oro**<br>kah-THEH-nah deh OH-roh |
| gold ring | **el anillo de oro**<br>ah-NEE-yoh deh OH-roh |
| gold tooth | **el diente de oro**<br>DYEHN-teh deh OH-roh |
| hairy | **velludo[a] ~ peludo[a]**<br>beh-YOO-thoh[-thah] ~ peh-LOO-thoh[-thah] |
| jewelry | **las joyas**<br>HOH-yahs |
| lame/limping | **cojo[a]**<br>KOH-hoh[-hah] |
| marks | **las marcas**<br>MAHR-kahs |
| mute | **mudo[a]**<br>MOO-thoh[-thah] |
| pregnant | **embarazada**<br>ehm-bah-rah-SAH-thah |
| scars | **las cicatrices**<br>see-kah-TREE-sehs |

tattoo — **el tatuaje ~ el tatú**
tah-TWAH-heh ~ tah-TOO

wart — **la verruga**
beh-RROO-gah

## DEMEANOR
La conducta

Now ask about a person's demeanor, attitude, personality, and mannerisms.

What's the suspect like? (*male*) — **¿Cómo es el sospechoso?**
KOH-moh ehs ehl soh-speh-CHOH-soh

What's the suspect like? (*female*) — **¿Cómo es la sospechosa?**
KOH-moh ehs lah soh-speh-CHOH-sah

What's the victim like? — **¿Cómo es la víctima?**
KOH-moh ehs lah BEEK-tee-mah

Aggressive or calm? — **¿Agresivo[a] o calmado[a]?**
ah-greh-SEE-boh[-bah] oh kahl-MAH-thoh[-thah]

Angry? — **¿Enojado[a]? ~ ¿Enfadado[a]?**
eh-noh-HAH-thoh[-thah] ~ ehn-fah-THAH-thoh[-thah]

Anxious? — **¿Ansioso[a]?**
ahn-SYOH-soh[-sah]

Confused? — **¿Confundido[a]?**
kohn-foon-DEE-thoh[-thah]

Cheap or generous? — **¿Tacaño[a] o generoso[a]?**
tah-KAH-nyoh[-nyah] oh heh-neh-ROH-soh[-sah]

Crazy or sane? — **¿Loco[a] o sano[a]?**
LOH-koh[-kah] oh SAH-noh[-nah]

Dangerous or safe? — **¿Peligroso[a] o seguro[a]?**
peh-lee-GROH-soh[-sah] oh seh-GOO-roh[-rah]

Most descriptive words (adjectives) that describe males end in **-o**. You change the **-o** to **-a** when you're describing females.

| | |
|---|---|
| He's angry. | **(Él) está enojado.** |
| She's angry. | **(Ella) está enojada.** |

| | |
|---|---|
| Depressed? | **¿Deprimido[a]?**<br>deh-pree-MEE-thoh[-thah] |
| Drugged? | **¿Drogado[a]?**<br>droh-GAH-thoh[-thah] |
| Drunk or sober? | **¿Borracho[a] o sobrio[a]?**<br>boh-RRAH-choh[-chah] oh SOH-bree-oh[-ah] |
| Fast or slow? | **¿Rápido[a] o lento[a]?**<br>RRAH-pee-thoh[-thah] oh LEHN-toh[-tah] |
| | **¿Rápido[a] o despacio[a]?**<br>RRAH-pee-thoh[-thah] oh deh-SPAH-syoh[-syah] |
| Friendly or timid? | **¿Amistoso[a] o tímido[a]?**<br>ah-mee-STOH-soh[-sah] oh TEE-mee-thoh[-thah] |
| Furious or happy? | **¿Furioso[a] o contento[a]?**<br>foo-ree-OH-soh[-sah] oh kohn-TEHN-toh[-tah] |
| Good or bad manners? | **¿De buenos o malos modales?**<br>deh BWEH-nohs oh MAH-lohs moh-THAH-lehs |
| Good or bad mood? | **¿De buen o de mal humor?**<br>deh-BWEHN oh deh MAHL oo-MOHR |
| Uneasy? | **¿Inquieto[a]?**<br>een-KYEH-toh[-tah] |
| Upset? | **¿Molesto[a]?**<br>moh-LEH-stoh[-stah] |

| | |
|---|---|
| Healthy or sick? | **¿De buena salud o enfermo[a]?**<br>deh BWEH-nah sah-LOOTH oh ehn-FEHR-moh[-mah] |
| | **¿Saludable o enfermo[a]?**<br>sah-loo-DAH-bleh oh ehn-FEHR-moh[-mah] |
| Heavy or light? | **¿Pesado[a] o ligero[a]?**<br>peh-SAH-thoh[-thah] oh lee-HEH-roh[-rah] |
| Intelligent or stupid? | **¿Inteligente o estúpido[a]?**<br>een-teh-lee-HEHN-teh oh eh-STOO-pee-thoh[-thah] |
| Irritable or happy? | **¿Irritable o contento[a]?**<br>ee-rree-TAH-bleh oh kohn-TEHN-toh[-tah] |
| Nervous or relaxed? | **¿Nervioso[a] o relajado[a]?**<br>nehr-BYOH-soh[-sah] oh rreh-lah-HAH-thoh[-thah] |
| Nice or nasty? | **¿Simpático[a] o antipático[a]?**<br>seem-PAH-tee-koh[-kah] oh ahn-tee-PAH-tee-koh[-kah] |
| Patient or impatient? | **¿Paciente o impaciente?**<br>pah-SYEHN-teh oh eem-pah-SYEHN-teh |
| Polite or rude? | **¿Cortés o descortés?**<br>kohr-TEHS oh dehs-kohr-TEHS |
| Quiet or noisy? | **¿Calmado[a] o ruidoso[a]?**<br>kahl-MAH-thoh[-thah] oh rroo-ee-DOH-soh[-sah] |
| Relaxed or nervous? | **¿Relajado[a] o nervioso[a]?**<br>rreh-lah-HAH-thoh[-thah] oh nehr-BYOH-soh[-sah] |
| Sad or happy? | **¿Triste o contento[a]?**<br>TREE-steh oh kohn-TEHN-toh[-tah] |

| | |
|---|---|
| Violent or calm? | **¿Violento[a] o tranquilo[a]?** bee-oh-LEHN-toh[-tah] oh trahn-KEE-loh[-lah] |
| Worried or relaxed? | **¿Preocupado[a] o relajado[a]?** preh-oh-koo-PAH-thoh[-thah] oh rreh-lah-HAH-thoh[-thah] |
| Are you / Is he/she nauseated? | **¿Tiene náuseas?** TYEH-neh NAH-oo-seh-ahs |

## Scenario · A LOST CHILD

Un niño perdido

In this scenario, Deputy Luis de Anda obtains a detailed description of a missing child.

| | |
|---|---|
| Good morning, ma'am. I'm Deputy Luis de Anda. Is there anyone missing here? | **Buenos días, señora. Soy Oficial Luis de Anda. ¿Hay alguien desaparecido aquí?** |
| I need information to find your son. | **Necesito información para encontrar a su hijo.** |
| What's his name? How old is he? Does he take medicine, drugs, or alcohol? | **¿Cómo se llama? ¿Cuántos años tiene? ¿Toma medicina, drogas o alcohol?** |
| I want a complete description of your son from head to toe. | **Deseo una descripción de su hijo de la cabeza a los pies.** |
| What's he like—blond, redhead, dark-haired? | **¿Cómo es—rubio, pelirrojo, moreno?** |
| Is he tall, average, short? | **¿Es alto, mediano, bajo?** |
| How much does he weigh (in pounds)? | **¿Cuánto pesa (en libras)?** |
| What color are his eyes? | **¿De qué color son sus ojos?** |
| What is he wearing? What does he have on? | **¿Qué ropa lleva? ¿Qué tiene puesto?** |
| What color are his pants, his T-shirt, his shoes? | **¿De qué color son sus pantalones, su camiseta, sus zapatos?** |

| | |
|---|---|
| Does he have special marks, scars, tattoos? | **¿Tiene marcas específicas, cicatrices, tatuajes?** |
| Does he have money? How much? | **¿Tiene dinero? ¿Cuánto?** |
| Why isn't he here? | **¿Por qué no está aquí?** |
| Place, date, and who saw him last? | **¿Sitio, fecha y quién lo vio último?** |
| Do you have a picture (photo) of him? | **¿Tiene una foto de él?** |
| Here's my card. If you have more information, call the station. | **Aquí tiene mi tarjeta. Si tiene más información, llame a la estación.** |

## ■ POSSESSIONS—STOLEN OBJECTS

### Las posesiones—los objetos robados

My detective students have provided this list for robbery reports. For stolen vehicles, see pp. 101–107.

| | |
|---|---|
| alarm system | **el sistema de alarma** see-STEH-mah deh ah-LAHR-mah |
| antiques | **las antigüedades** ahn-tee-gweh-THAH-thehs |
| articles | **los artículos** ahr-TEE-koo-lohs |
| backpack | **la mochila** moh-CHEE-lah |
| bag | **la bolsa** BOHL-sah |
| bicycle | **la bicicleta** bee-see-KLEH-tah |
| box | **la caja** KAH-hah |
| bracelet (gold) | **la pulsera (de oro)** pool-SEH-rah (deh OH-roh) |
| briefcase | **el maletín** mah-leh-TEEN |
| camera | **la cámara** KAH-mah-rah |

To make a Spanish word ending in a vowel plural, add **-s**. For words ending in a consonant (anything but a vowel), add **-es**. For plural words (things and people), **el** changes to **los** and **la** changes to **las**.

**el zapato → los zapatos**
**la blusa → las blusas**
**el suéter → los suéteres**

| | |
|---|---|
| digital camera | **la cámara digital** KAH-mah-rah dee-hee-TAHL |
| CD | **el disco compacto** DEE-skoh kohm-PAHK-toh |
| | **el CD** see-DEE |
| chain (gold) | **la cadena (de oro)** kah-THEH-nah (deh OH-roh) |
| checkbook | **la chequera** cheh-KEH-rah |
| cigarettes | **los cigarrillos** see-gah-RREE-yohs |
| coin | **la moneda** moh-NEH-thah |
| collection | **la colección** koh-lehk-SYOHN |
| computer | **la computadora** kohm-poo-tah-THOH-rah |
| credit card | **la tarjeta de crédito** tahr-HEH-tah deh KREH-thee-toh |
| diamond | **el diamante** dee-ah-MAHN-teh |
| document | **el documento** doh-koo-MEHN-toh |
| DVD | **el DVD** dee-bee-DEE |
| earrings | **los aretes** ah-REH-tehs |

| | |
|---|---|
| emerald | **la esmeralda**<br>ehs-meh-RAHL-dah |
| equipment | **el equipaje**<br>eh-kee-PAH-heh |
| firearm | **el arma de fuego**<br>AHR-mah deh FWEH-goh |
| furniture | **los muebles**<br>MWEH-blehs |
| gold | **el oro**<br>OH-roh |
| instrument | **el instrumento**<br>een-stroo-MEHN-toh |
| jewelry/jewels | **las joyas**<br>HOH-yahs |
| letters | **las cartas**<br>KAHR-tahs |
| luggage | **el equipaje**<br>eh-kee-PAH-heh |
| mail | **el correo**<br>koh-RREH-oh |
| money | **el dinero**<br>dee-NEH-roh |
| necklace (pearl) | **el collar (de perla)**<br>koh-YAHR (deh PEHR-lah) |
| objects of value | **los objetos de valor**<br>ohb-HEH-tohs deh bah-LOHR |
| painting | **el cuadro**<br>KWAH-droh |
| paycheck | **el cheque de sueldo**<br>CHEH-keh deh SWEHL-doh |
| pendant | **el pendiente**<br>pehn-DYEHN-teh |
| perfume | **el perfume**<br>pehr-FOO-meh |
| photo | **la foto**<br>FOH-toh |
| purse | **la bolsa**<br>BOHL-sah<br>**el bolso**<br>BOHL-soh |

| | |
|---|---|
| radio | **el radio**<br>RRAH-dyoh |
| razor (electric) | **la afeitadora**<br>ah-feh-tah-THOH-rah |
| recorder | **la grabadora**<br>grah-bah-THOH-rah |
| ring | **el anillo**<br>ah-NEE-yoh |
| safe | **la caja fuerte**<br>KAH-hah FWEHR-teh |
| silver | **la plata**<br>PLAH-tah |
| stereo | **el estéreo**<br>eh-STEH-reh-oh |
| suitcase | **la maleta**<br>mah-LEH-tah |
| tape | **la cinta**<br>SEEN-tah |
| tools | **las herramientas**<br>eh-rrah-MYEHN-tahs |
| TV | **el televisor**<br>teh-leh-bee-SOHR |
| umbrella | **el paraguas**<br>pah-RAH-gwahs |
| VCR | **la videograbadora**<br>bee-theh-oh-grah-bah-THOH-rah |
| video camera | **la cámara de video**<br>KAH-mah-rah deh BEE-theh-oh |
| wallet | **la billetera**<br>bee-yeh-TEH-rah |
| | **la cartera**<br>kahr-TEH-rah |
| watch | **el reloj**<br>rreh-LOH |
| weapon | **el arma**<br>AHR-mah |

## BURGLARY INVESTIGATION
### Una investigación sobre un robo

As a detective gathering facts on a burglary, you need to know who entered and how, and full descriptions of what was taken. All verbs in this section are in the past (the preterite). See the investigation scenarios, pp. 251–257.

| | |
|---|---|
| Where did they enter? | **¿Por dónde entraron?** pohr DOHN-deh ehn-TRAH-rohn |
| What time did they enter? | **¿A qué hora entraron?** ah keh OH-rah ehn-TRAH-rohn |
| How many were there? | **¿Cuántos había?** KWAHN-tohs ah-BEE-ah |
| Their clothing? | **¿Su ropa?** soo RROH-pah |
| The thieves ... | **Los ladrones...** lah-DROH-nehs |
| The suspects ... | **Los sospechosos...** soh-speh-CHOH-sohs |
| The intruders ... | **Los intrusos...** een-TROO-sohs |
| broke ... | **rompieron...** rrohm-PYEH-rohn |
| the chain | **la cadena** kah-THEH-nah |
| the deadbolt | **el pestillo** peh-STEE-yoh |
| They forced ... | **Forzaron...** fohr-SAH-rohn |
| the lock | **la cerradura** seh-rrah-THOO-rah |
| the door | **la puerta** PWEHR-tah |
| What did they steal? | **¿Qué robaron?** keh rroh-BAH-rohn |
| What did they take? | **¿Qué llevaron?** keh yeh-BAH-rohn |

| | |
|---|---|
| They stole ... | **Robaron...**<br>rroh-BAH-rohn |
| They took ... | **Llevaron...**<br>yeh-BAH-rohn |
| a camera | **una cámara**<br>KAH-mah-rah |
| the stereo | **el estéreo**<br>eh-STEH-reh-oh |
| How did they enter? | **¿Cómo entraron?**<br>KOH-moh ehn-TRAH-rohn |
| How did they leave? | **¿Cómo salieron?**<br>KOH-moh sah-lee-EH-rohn |
| They entered through ... | **Entraron por...**<br>ehn-TRAH-rohn pohr |
| They left through ... | **Salieron por...**<br>sah-lee-EH-rohn pohr |
| the door | **la puerta**<br>PWEHR-tah |
| the balcony | **el balcón**<br>bahl-KOHN |
| the patio | **el patio**<br>PAH-tyoh |
| the roof | **el techo**<br>TEH-choh |
| the window | **la ventana**<br>behn-TAH-nah |
| Here is your case number. | **Aquí está su número de caso.**<br>ah-KEE eh-STAH soo NOO-meh-roh deh KAH-soh |
| Here is your report number. | **Aquí está su número de reporte.**<br>ah-KEE eh-STAH soo NOO-meh-roh deh rreh-POHR-teh |
| Call this number. | **Llame este número.**<br>YAH-meh EH-steh NOO-meh-roh |
| We'll be in touch with you. | **Vamos a estar en contacto con usted.**<br>BAH-mohs ah eh-STAHR ehn kohn-TAHK-toh kohn oo-STEHTH |

| | |
|---|---|
| We found your vehicle. | **Encontramos su vehículo.** ehn-kohn-TRAH-mohs soo beh-EE-koo-loh |
| It was ... | **Estaba...** eh-STAH-bah |
| broken | **roto** RROH-toh |
| burned | **quemado** keh-MAH-thoh |
| cut | **cortado** kohr-TAH-toh |
| destroyed | **destruido** deh-stroo-EE-thoh |
| found | **encontrado ~ hallado** ehn-kohn-TRAH-thoh ~ ah-YAH-thoh |
| sold | **vendido** behn-DEE-thoh |
| stolen | **robado** rroh-BAH-thoh |
| We found it in ... | **Lo encontramos en...** loh ehn-kohn-TRAH-mohs ehn |
| the street | **la calle** KAH-yeh |
| the garage | **el garaje** gah-RAH-heh |

## ■ ASSAULT AND BATTERY INVESTIGATION

### Una investigación sobre el asalto y la agresión

With the questions below, you can take a report from an assault victim. Most verbs are in the past. Just have the victim substitute one word for another, like "They assaulted/attacked/bit/cut me."

| | |
|---|---|
| What happened? | **¿Qué pasó?** keh pah-SOH |
| Where did it happen? | **¿Dónde pasó?** DOHN-deh pah-SOH |

| | |
|---|---|
| When did it happen? | **¿Cuándo pasó?**<br>KWAHN-doh pah-SOH |
| What did they do to you? | **¿Qué le hicieron?**<br>keh leh ee-SYEH-rohn |
| Did they leave on foot? | **¿Salieron a pie?**<br>sah-lee-EH-rohn ah pyeh |
| Did they leave by car? | **¿Salieron en carro?**<br>sah-lee-EH-rohn ehn KAH-rroh |
| How many were there? | **¿Cuántos había?**<br>KWAHN-tohs ah-BEE-ah |
| How long ago? | **¿Hace cuánto tiempo?**<br>AH-seh KWAHN-toh TYEHM-poh |
| What direction were they going? | **¿En qué dirección iban?**<br>ehn keh dee-rehk-SYOHN EE-bahn |
| Do you need medical help? | **¿Necesita ayuda médica?**<br>neh-seh-SEE-tah ah-YOO-thah MEH-thee-kah |
| Can you get home? | **¿Puede ir a casa?**<br>PWEH-theh eer ah KAH-sah |
| There were (some) ... | **Había...**<br>ah-BEE-ah |
| delinquents | **delincuentes**<br>deh-leen-KWEHN-tehs |
| muggers | **ladrones**<br>lah-DROH-nehs |
| They stole my ... | **Robaron mi(s)...**<br>rroh-BAH-rohn mee(s) |
| They removed my ... | **Quitaron mi(s)...**<br>kee-TAH-rohn mee(s) |
| They took my ... | **Tomaron mi(s)...**<br>toh-MAH-rohn mee(s) |
| money | **dinero**<br>dee-NEH-roh |
| wallet | **cartera**<br>kahr-TEH-rah |
| Where were they? | **¿Dónde estaban?**<br>DOHN-deh eh-STAH-bahn |

| | |
|---|---|
| They were at/in ... | **Estaban en...**<br>eh-STAH-bahn ehn |
| the party | **la fiesta**<br>FYEH-stah |
| the restaurant | **el restaurante**<br>rreh-stah-oo-RAHN-teh |
| What did they do to you then? | **¿Qué le hicieron entonces?**<br>keh leh ee-SYEH-rohn ehn-TOHN-sehs |
| They ... me. | **Me...**<br>meh |
| assaulted | **asaltaron**<br>ah-sahl-TAH-rohn |
| attacked | **atacaron**<br>ah-tah-KAH-rohn |
| bit | **mordieron**<br>mohr-DYEH-rohn |
| cut | **cortaron**<br>kohr-TAH-rohn |
| grabbed | **agarraron**<br>ah-gah-RRAH-rohn |
| hit | **pegaron**<br>peh-GAH-rohn |
| injured | **hirieron**<br>ee-ree-EH-rohn |
| kicked | **patearon**<br>pah-teh-AH-rohn |
| punched | **golpearon**<br>gohl-peh-AH-rohn |
| pushed | **empujaron**<br>ehm-poo-HAH-rohn |
| ran over | **atropellaron**<br>ah-troh-peh-YAH-rohn |
| raped | **violaron**<br>bee-oh-LAH-rohn |
| robbed | **robaron**<br>rroh-BAH-rohn |
| shot at | **dispararon**<br>dee-spah-RAH-rohn |
| slapped | **abofetearon**<br>ah-boh-feh-teh-AH-rohn |

| | |
|---|---|
| stabbed | **apuñalaron**<br>ah-poo-nyah-LAH-rohn |
| threatened | **amenazaron**<br>ah-meh-nah-SAH-rohn |
| They sprayed me with pepper spray. | **Me rociaron con espray de pimienta.**<br>meh rroh-SYAH-rohn kohn eh-SPREH deh pee-MYEHN-tah |
| They knocked me down. | **Me tumbaron.**<br>meh toom-BAH-rohn |
| They pulled my hair. | **Me tiraron el pelo.**<br>meh tee-RAH-rohn ehl PEH-loh |
| | **Me tiraron el cabello.**<br>meh tee-RAH-rohn ehl kah-BEH-yoh |
| They scratched my eyes. | **Me rasguñaron los ojos.**<br>meh rrahs-goo-NYAH-rohn lohs OH-hohs |
| They kneed me in the groin. | **Me dieron con la rodilla en el miembro.**<br>meh DYEH-rohn kohn lah rroh-THEE-yah ehn ehl MYEHM-broh |

# TRANSPORTATION El transporte

We have useful transportation terms: vehicles, parts, identification, traffic signs, and even a traffic stop.

## Vehicles Los vehículos

| | |
|---|---|
| airplane | **el avión**<br>ah-BYOHN |
| ambulance | **la ambulancia**<br>ahm-boo-LAHN-syah |
| armored car | **el carro blindado**<br>KAH-rroh bleen-DAH-thoh |
| bicycle/bike | **la bicicleta ~ la bici**<br>bee-see-KLEH-tah ~ BEE-see |

| | |
|---|---|
| boat (small) | **el barco ~ el bote**<br>BAHR-koh ~ BOH-teh |
| bus | **el autobús ~ el camión**<br>ah-oo-toh-BOOS ~ kah-MYOHN |
| camper | **la camioneta de campamento**<br>kah-myoh-NEH-tah deh kahm-pah-MEHN-toh |
| car | **el carro ~ el auto ~ el automóvil ~ el coche**<br>KAH-rroh ~ AH-oo-toh ~ ah-oo-toh-MOH-beel ~ KOH-cheh |
| convertible | **el convertible**<br>kohn-behr-TEE-bleh |
| delivery truck | **el camión de reparto**<br>kah-MYOHN deh rreh-PAHR-toh |
| fire truck | **el camión de bomberos**<br>kah-MYOHN deh bohm-BEH-rohs |
| helicopter | **el helicóptero**<br>eh-lee-KOHP-teh-roh |
| jeep | **el jip**<br>yeep |
| motorcycle | **la motocicleta ~ la moto**<br>moh-toh-see-KLEH-tah ~ MOH-toh |
| pickup (truck) | **el pickup**<br>PEEK-oop |
| police patrol car | **la patrulla ~ el carro de patrulla**<br>pah-TROO-yah ~ KAH-rroh deh pah-TROO-yah |
| recreation vehicle | **el vehículo de recreo ~ el RV**<br>beh-EE-koo-loh deh rreh-KREH-oh ~ EH-reh beh |
| school bus | **el autobús escolar ~ el camión escolar**<br>ah-oo-toh-BOOS eh-skoh-LAHR ~ kah-MYOHN eh-skoh-LAHR |

| | |
|---|---|
| sports car | **el carro deportivo**<br>KAH-rroh deh-pohr-TEE-boh |
| station wagon | **el station wagon**<br>eh-stah-SYOHN WAH-gohn |
| tank truck | **el camión cisterna ~ el petrolero**<br>kah-MYOHN see-STEHR-nah ~ peh-troh-LEH-roh |
| taxi | **el taxi**<br>TAHK-see |
| tow truck | **la grúa ~ el remolque**<br>GROO-ah ~ rreh-MOHL-keh |
| tractor | **el tractor**<br>trahk-TOHR |
| tractor trailer | **el semi-remolque**<br>SEH-mee-rreh-MOHL-keh |
| train | **el tren**<br>trehn |
| tricycle/trike | **el triciclo**<br>tree-SEE-kloh |
| truck | **la camioneta ~ la troca ~ el troque**<br>kah-myoh-NEH-tah ~ TROH-kah ~ TROH-keh |
| van | **la furgoneta ~ el ven ~ el van**<br>foor-goh-NEH-tah ~ behn ~ bahn |

## Car Theft, Vehicle Parts, and DMV Terms

El robo de carros, las partes del vehículo y los términos de DMV

| | |
|---|---|
| Did they steal your vehicle? | **¿Le robaron el vehículo?**<br>leh rroh-BAH-rohn ehl beh-EE-koo-loh |
| Who is the owner of the car? | **¿Quién es el dueño del carro?**<br>kyehn ehs ehl DWEH-nyoh dehl KAH-rroh |

| | |
|---|---|
| Where was it stolen from? | **¿De dónde estaba robado?** deh DOHN-deh eh-STAH-bah rroh-BAH-thoh |
| Type of vehicle, registration, license number, state, VIN? | **¿Tipo de vehículo, registro, número de licencia, estado, número de la identificación?** |
| Year, make, model, body type, style, color of paint, license number? | **¿Año, marca, modelo, tipo de carrocería, estilo, color de pintura, número de licencia?** |
| Last driver of vehicle, date and time reported stolen? | **¿Último conductor/chofer, fecha y hora reportado robado?** |
| Proof of insurance | **Prueba de seguro ~ Prueba de aseguranza** |
| Proof of ownership | **Prueba de propiedad** |
| Proof of registration | **Prueba de registro** |

Here is a complete list of car parts.

| | |
|---|---|
| accelerator | **el acelerador** ahk-seh-leh-rah-THOHR |
| air conditioning | **el aire (acondicionado)** AY-reh (ah-kohn-dee-syoh-NAH-thoh) |
| alarm | **la alarma** ah-LAHR-mah |
| antenna | **la antena** ahn-TEH-nah |
| axle | **el eje** EH-heh |
| back seat | **el asiento de atrás** ah-SYEHN-toh deh ah-TRAHS |
| battery | **la batería** bah-teh-REE-ah |
| brakes | **los frenos** FREH-nohs |
| bumper | **el parachoques** pah-rah-CHOH-kehs |
| carburetor | **el carburador** kahr-boo-rah-THOHR |

| | |
|---|---|
| dashboard | **el tablero**<br>tah-BLEH-roh |
| doors | **las puertas**<br>PWEHR-tahs |
| two doors | **dos puertas**<br>dohs PWEHR-tahs |
| four doors | **cuatro puertas**<br>KWAH-troh PWEHR-tahs |
| engine | **el motor**<br>moh-TOHR |
| exhaust | **el aspirador**<br>ah-spee-rah-THOHR |
| exhaust pipe | **el tubo de escape**<br>TOO-boh deh eh-SKAH-peh |
| exterior | **el exterior**<br>ehks-tee-ree-OHR |
| fan | **el ventilador**<br>behn-tee-lah-THOHR |
| fan belt | **la correa del ventilador**<br>koh-RREH-ah dehl behn-tee-lah-THOHR |
| fender | **el guardafango**<br>gwahr-thah-FAHN-goh |
| front seat | **el asiento de enfrente**<br>ah-SYEHN-toh deh ehn-FREHN-teh |
| fuel pump | **la bomba de gasolina**<br>BOHM-bah deh gah-soh-LEE-nah |
| fuse | **el fusible**<br>foo-SEE-bleh |
| gas | **la gasolina**<br>gah-soh-LEE-nah |

**La bomba de gasolina** ("fuel pump") and **la bomba de agua** ("water pump") have nothing to do with a bomb, **la bomba**! See "False Friends" on pp. 277–278.

| | |
|---|---|
| gas cap | **el tapón del tanque**<br>tah-POHN dehl TAHN-keh |
| gas tank | **el tanque de gasolina**<br>TAHN-keh deh<br>gah-soh-LEE-nah |
| gear | **el engranaje**<br>ehn-grah-NAH-heh |
| gearshift | **el cambio de velocidades**<br>KAHM-byoh deh<br>beh-loh-see-THAH-thehs |
| glove compartment | **la guantera ~ la cajuelita**<br>gwahn-TEH-rah ~<br>kah-hweh-LEE-tah |
| handle | **el tirador**<br>tee-rah-THOHR |
| headlights | **las luces ~ las delanteras ~ los faros delanteros**<br>LOO-sehs ~ deh-lahn-TEH-rahs<br>~ FAH-rohs deh-lahn-TEH-rohs |
| heater | **el calentador**<br>kah-lehn-tah-THOHR |
| high beams | **las luces altas ~ los faros altos**<br>LOO-sehs AHL-tahs ~<br>FAH-rohs AHL-tohs |
| hood | **la cubierta ~ el capó**<br>koo-BYEHR-tah ~ kah-POH |
| horn | **la bocina**<br>boh-SEE-nah |
| hubcap | **el tapacubos**<br>tah-pah-KOO-bohs |
| infant seat | **el asiento infantil ~ el asiento para el bebé**<br>ah-SYEHN-toh een-fahn-TEEL ~<br>ah-SYEHN-toh PAH-rah ehl<br>beh-BEH |
| interior | **el interior**<br>een-teh-ree-OHR |
| jack | **el gato**<br>GAH-toh |
| keys | **las llaves**<br>YAH-behs |

| | |
|---|---|
| license plate | **la placa (de matrícula)** PLAH-kah (deh mah-TREE-koo-lah) |
| lock | **la cerradura** seh-rrah-THOO-rah |
| low beams | **las luces bajas** LOO-sehs BAH-hahs |
| mirror | **el espejo** eh-SPEH-hoh |
| rear view mirror | **el espejo de retrovisión** eh-SPEH-hoh deh rreh-troh-bee-SYOHN |
| side mirror | **el espejo de los lados** eh-SPEH-hoh deh lohs LAH-thohs |
| right mirror | **el espejo derecho** eh-SPEH-hoh deh-REH-choh |
| left mirror | **el espejo izquierdo** eh-SPEH-hoh ees-KYEHR-thoh |
| muffler | **el amortiguador ~ el mofle** ah-mohr-tee-gwah-THOHR ~ MOH-fleh |
| pedal | **el pedal** peh-THAHL |
| rack | **el portamaletas** pohr-tah-mah-LEH-tahs |
| radiator | **el radiador** rrah-dyah-THOHR |
| radio | **el radio** RRAH-dyoh |
| roof | **el techo** TEH-choh |
| safety/seat belt | **el cinturón ~ el cinto de seguridad** seen-too-ROHN ~ SEEN-toh deh seh-goo-ree-THAHTH |
| seat | **el asiento** ah-SYEHN-toh |
| back seat | **el asiento de atrás** ah-SYEHN-toh deh ah-TRAHS |

| | |
|---|---|
| front seat | **el asiento delantero**<br>ah-SYEHN-toh deh-lahn-TEH-roh |
| infant seat | **el asiento infantil ~ el asiento para el bebé**<br>ah-SYEHN-toh een-fahn-TEEL ~ ah-SYEHN-toh PAH-rah ehl beh-BEH |
| shocks | **el amortiguador**<br>ah-mohr-tee-gwah-THOHR |
| smog control devices | **los aparatos para controlar el smog**<br>ah-pah-RAH-tohs PAH-rah kohn-troh-LAHR ehl smohg |
| speedometer | **el indicador de velocidad**<br>een-dee-kah-THOHR deh beh-loh-see-THAHTH |
| steering wheel | **el volante**<br>boh-LAHN-teh |
| stick shift | **el cambio manual**<br>KAHM-byoh mah-NWAHL |
| stop lights | **las luces de parada**<br>LOO-sehs deh pah-RAH-thah |
| taillights | **las luces traseras ~ los faros traseros**<br>LOO-sehs trah-SEH-rahs ~ FAH-rohs trah-SEH-rohs |
| tire | **la llanta**<br>YAHN-tah |
| spare tire | **la llanta de repuesto**<br>YAHN-tah deh rreh-PWEH-stoh |
| transmission | **la transmisión**<br>trahns-mee-SYOHN |
| trunk | **la cajuela ~ el maletero**<br>kah-HWEH-lah ~ mah-leh-TEH-roh |
| turn signal lights | **las luces direccionales**<br>LOO-sehs dee-rehk-syoh-NAH-lehs |
| type | **el tipo**<br>TEE-poh |

upholstery — **la tapicería**
tah-pee-seh-REE-ah

VIN (vehicle identification number) — **el número de identificación (del vehículo)**
NOO-meh-roh deh ee-dehn-tee-fee-kah-SYOHN (dehl beh-EE-koo-loh)

water pump — **la bomba de agua**
BOHM-bah deh AH-gwah

wheel — **la rueda**
rroo-EH-thah

window — **la ventana**
behn-TAH-nah

rear window — **la ventana trasera**
behn-TAH-nah trah-SEH-rah

windshield — **el parabrisas**
pah-rah-BREE-sahs

windshield wiper — **el limpiaparabrisas**
leem-pyah-pah-rah-BREE-sahs

wire — **el alambre**
ah-LAHM-breh

year — **el año**
AH-nyoh

## AUTO ACCIDENT INVESTIGATION
### Una investigación de un accidente de auto

This section deals with the rules of the road, investigating an auto accident, traffic signs, road hazards, plus driving locations. This reads easier than a DMV manual!

(Is) anybody hurt? — **¿Alguien (está) herido?**
AHL-gyehn eh-STAH eh-REE-thoh

Passengers? — **¿Pasajeros?**
pah-sah-HEH-rohs

Where are you / is he/she hurt? — **¿Dónde está herido[a]?**
DOHN-deh eh-STAH eh-REE-thoh[-thah]

How fast (were you driving)? | **¿Qué velocidad (manejaba)?** keh beh-loh-see-THAHTH (mah-neh-HAH-bah)

How did the accident happen? | **¿Cómo pasó el accidente?** KOH-moh pah-SOH ehl ahk-see-THEHN-teh

What caused the accident? | **¿Qué causó el accidente?** keh kah-oo-SOH ehl ahk-see-THEHN-teh

(How were) the road conditions? | **¿En que estado estaba el camino?** ehn keh eh-STAH-thoh eh-STAH-bah ehl kah-MEE-noh

Dry or wet? | **¿Seco o mojado?** SEH-koh oh moh-HAH-thoh

Slippery? | **¿Resbaloso?** rrehs-bah-LOH-soh

Flooded? | **¿Inundado?** een-oon-DAH-thoh

In bad shape? | **¿En mal estado?** ehn mahl eh-STAH-thoh

Icy? | **¿Con hielo?** kohn YEH-loh

In what direction (were you going)? | **¿En cuál dirección (iba)?** ehn kwahl dee-rehk-SYOHN (EE-bah)

Have you been drinking (alcohol)? | **¿Ha estado tomando (alcohol)?** ah eh-STAH-thoh toh-MAHN-doh (ahl-koh-OHL)

How much? | **¿Cuánto?** KWAHN-toh

Who crashed into whom? | **¿Quién chocó a quién?** kyehn choh-KOH ah kyehn

| | |
|---|---|
| Did you stop before (entering) the intersection? | **¿Paró antes de (entrar en) la intersección?** pah-ROH AHN-tehs deh (ehn-TRAHR ehn) lah een-tehr-sehk-SYOHN |
| (*to a male*) (Were you the) driver or passenger? | **¿(Era) el conductor o el pasajero?** (EH-rah) ehl kohn-dook-TOHR oh ehl pah-sah-HEH-roh |
| (*to a female*) (Were you the) driver or passenger? | **¿(Era) la conductora o la pasajera?** (EH-rah) lah kohn-dook-TOH-rah oh lah pah-sah-HEH-rah |
| Was it a hit and run? | **¿Chocó y huyó?** choh-KOH ee oo-YOH |
| How many vehicles? | **¿Cuántos carros?** KWAHN-tohs KAH-rrohs |
| Who hit you? | **¿Quién chocó contra usted?** kyehn choh-KOH kohn-trah oo-STEHTH |
| Who lost control? | **¿Quién perdió el control?** kyehn pehr-DYOH ehl kohn-TROHL |
| How many passengers? | **¿Cuántos pasajeros?** KWAHN-tohs pah-sah-HEH-rohs |
| (Were you wearing a) seat belt? | **¿(Tenía puesto[a] el) cinturón ~ cinto (de seguridad)?** (teh-NEE-ah PWEH-stoh[-stah] ehl) seen-too-ROHN ~ SEEN-toh (deh seh-goo-ree-THAHTH) |
| How was your car damaged? | **¿Cómo fue dañado su carro?** KOH-moh fweh dah-NYAH-thoh soo KAH-rroh |
| How much damage? | **¿Cuánto daño?** KWAHN-toh DAH-nyoh |

## Road and Traffic Terms
Las palabras del camino y del tráfico

| | |
|---|---|
| alley | **el callejón**<br>kah-yeh-HOHN |
| blind alley | **el callejón sin salida**<br>kah-yeh-HOHN seen sah-LEE-thah |
| arrow | **la flecha**<br>FLEH-chah |
| avenue | **la avenida**<br>ah-beh-NEE-thah |
| barricade | **la barricada**<br>bah-rree-KAH-thah |
| bike lane | **el carril para bicicletas**<br>kah-RREEL PAH-rah bee-see-KLEH-tahs |
| block | **la cuadra ~ el bloque**<br>KWAH-drah ~ BLOH-keh |
| boulevard | **el bulevar**<br>boo-leh-BAHR |
| bridge | **el puente**<br>PWEHN-teh |
| narrow bridge | **el puente estrecho**<br>PWEHN-teh eh-STREH-choh |
| bump (in the road) | **el hoyo**<br>OH-yoh |
| canal | **el canal**<br>kah-NAHL |
| car pool lane | **el carril con dos o más personas por carro**<br>kah-RREEL kohn dohs oh mahs pehr-SOH-nahs pohr KAH-rroh |
| center divider | **la división del centro**<br>dee-vee-SYOHN dehl SEHN-troh |
| collision | **el choque**<br>CHOH-keh |
| corner (street) | **la esquina**<br>eh-SKEE-nah |

**El choque** ("crash") has nothing to do with "to choke," **sofocar** or **asfixiar**. See "False Friends" on pp. 277–278.

| | |
|---|---|
| crash | **el choque**<br>CHOH-keh |
| crossing | **el cruce ~ el crucero**<br>KROO-seh ~ kroo-SEH-roh |
| crosswalk | **el cruce de peatones**<br>KROO-seh deh peh-ah-TOH-nehs |
| curb | **el borde ~ el bordillo**<br>BOHR-theh ~ bohr-THEE-yoh |
| curve | **la curva**<br>KOOR-bah |
| dangerous curve | **la curva peligrosa**<br>KOOR-bah peh-lee-GROH-sah |
| detour | **la desviación ~ el desvío**<br>dehs-bee-ah-SYOHN ~ dehs-BEE-oh |
| ditch | **la zanja**<br>SAHN-hah |
| entry | **la entrada**<br>ehn-TRAH-thah |
| no entry | **prohibido entrar**<br>proh-ee-BEE-thoh ehn-TRAHR |
| exit | **la salida**<br>sah-LEE-thah |
| fence | **la cerca ~ el cerco**<br>SEHR-kah ~ SEHR-koh |
| freeway begins | **la autopista comienza**<br>ah-oo-toh-PEE-stah koh-MYEHN-sah |
| garbage can | **el bote de basura**<br>BOH-teh deh bah-SOO-rah |
| gasoline | **la gasolina**<br>gah-soh-LEE-nah |

| | |
|---|---|
| HAZMAT (hazardous materials) | **los materiales peligrosos**<br>mah-teh-ree-AH-lehs peh-lee-GROH-sohs |
| highway | **la carretera**<br>kah-rreh-TEH-rah |
| public highway | **la carretera pública**<br>kah-rreh-TEH-rah POO-blee-kah |
| hill | **la colina**<br>koh-LEE-nah |
| hydrant | **la llave de incendios ~ la boca de incendios**<br>yah-beh deh een-SEHN-dyohs ~ BOH-kah deh een-SEHN-dyohs |
| intersection | **la intersección**<br>een-tehr-sehk-SYOHN |
| island | **la isla**<br>EES-lah |
| lane | **el carril**<br>kah-RREEL |
| car pool lane | **el carril con dos o más personas por carro**<br>kah-RREEL kohn dohs oh mahs pehr-SOH-nahs pohr KAH-rroh |
| passing lane | **el carril para pasar ~ el carril para rebasar**<br>kah-RREEL PAH-rah pah-SAHR ~ kah-RREEL PAH-rah rreh-bah-SAHR |
| wrong lane | **el carril equivocado**<br>kah-REEL eh-kee-boh-KAH-thoh |
| leak | **la gotera**<br>goh-TEH-rah |
| gas leak | **la gotera de gasolina**<br>goh-TEH-rah deh gah-soh-LEE-nah |
| oil leak | **la gotera de aceite**<br>goh-TEH-rah deh ah-SEH-teh |
| license | **la licencia**<br>lee-SEHN-syah |

| | |
|---|---|
| revoked license | **la licencia cancelada**<br>lee-SEHN-syah<br>kahn-seh-LAH-thah |
| light | **la luz ~ el faro**<br>loos ~ FAH-roh |
| brake light | **la luz de freno**<br>loos deh FREH-noh |
| change of light | **el cambio de luz**<br>KAHM-byoh deh loos |
| fog light | **la luz de neblina**<br>loos deh neh-BLEE-nah |
| green light | **la luz verde**<br>loos BEHR-theh |
| license plate light | **la luz para la placa**<br>loos PAH-rah lah PLAH-kah |
| lights not working | **las luces no funcionando**<br>LOO-sehs noh<br>foon-syoh-NAHN-doh |
| red light | **la luz roja**<br>loos RROH-hah |
| to run a red light | **pasar la luz roja**<br>pah-SAHR lah loos RROH-hah |
| street light | **luz de la calle**<br>loos deh lah KAH-yeh |
| traffic light | **la luz de tránsito ~<br>el semáforo**<br>loos deh TRAHN-see-toh ~<br>seh-MAH-foh-roh |
| yellow light | **la luz amarilla**<br>loos ah-mah-REE-yah |
| line | **la línea**<br>LEE-neh-ah |
| broken line | **la línea quebrada**<br>LEE-neh-ah keh-BRAH-thah |
| double line | **la línea doble**<br>LEE-neh-ah DOH-bleh |
| solid line | **la línea sólida**<br>LEE-neh-ah SOH-lee-thah |
| white line | **la línea blanca**<br>LEE-neh-ah BLAHN-kah |

| | |
|---|---|
| mud | **el lodo ~ el barro**<br>LOH-thoh ~ BAH-rroh |
| oil | **el aceite**<br>ah-SEH-teh |
| one-way street | **la calle de dirección única**<br>KAH-yeh deh dee-rehk-SYOHN OO-nee-kah |
| overpass | **el pasaje sobre el camino**<br>pah-SAH-heh SOH-breh ehl kah-MEE-noh |
| parking | **el estacionamiento**<br>eh-stah-syoh-nah-MYEHN-toh |
| parking brakes | **los frenos de estacionamiento**<br>FREH-nohs deh eh-stah-syoh-nah-MYEHN-toh |
| parking lights | **las luces de estacionamiento**<br>LOO-sehs deh eh-stah-syoh-nah-MYEHN-toh |
| parking lot | **el lote de estacionamiento**<br>LOH-teh deh eh-stah-syoh-nah-MYEHN-toh |
| parking meter | **el parquímetro**<br>pahr-KEE-meh-troh |
| parking space | **el espacio de estacionamiento**<br>eh-SPAH-syoh deh eh-stah-syoh-nah-MYEHN-toh |
| handicapped parking | **el estacionamiento para minusválidos**<br>eh-stah-syoh-nah-MYEHN-toh PAH-rah mee-noos-BAH-lee-thohs |
| reserved parking | **el estacionamiento reservado**<br>eh-stah-syoh-nah-MYEHN-toh rreh-sehr-BAH-thoh |
| no parking | **no estacionarse**<br>noh eh-stah-syoh-NAHR-seh |
| pavement | **el pavimento**<br>pah-bee-MYEHN-toh |

|  |  |
|---|---|
| wet pavement | **el pavimento mojado** pah-bee-MYEHN-toh moh-HAH-thoh |
| pedestrian | **el peatón** peh-ah-TOHN |
| plates | **las placas** PLAH-kahs |
| expired plates | **las placas expiradas** PLAH-kahs ehks-pee-RAH-thahs |
| pothole | **el bache** BAH-cheh |
| puddle | **el charco** CHAHR-koh |
| railroad | **el ferrocarril** feh-rroh-kah-RREEL |
| railroad crossing | **el crucero de ferrocarril ~ el cruce de ferrocarril** kroo-SEH-roh deh feh-rroh-kah-RREEL ~ KROO-seh deh feh-rroh-kah-RREEL |
| not stopping for a train | **no parar para un tren** noh pah-RAHR PAH-rah oon trehn |
| ramp | **la rampa** RRAHM-pah |
| off (exit) ramp | **la rampa de salida** RRAHM-pah deh sah-LEE-thah |
| on (entrance) ramp | **la rampa de entrada** RRAHM-pah deh ehn-TRAH-thah |
| reflector | **el reflector** rreh-flehk-TOHR |
| road | **el camino** kah-MEE-noh |
| road blocked | **el camino bloqueado** kah-MEE-noh bloh-keh-AH-thoh |
| road closed | **el camino cerrado** kah-MEE-noh seh-RRAH-thoh |

| | |
|---|---|
| divided road | **el camino dividido**<br>kah-MEE-noh dee-bee-THEE-thoh |
| narrow road | **el camino estrecho ~ el camino angosto**<br>kah-MEE-noh eh-STREH-choh ~ kah-MEE-noh ahn-GOH-stoh |
| rocks | **las piedras**<br>PYEH-drahs |
| route | **la ruta**<br>RROO-tah |
| sand | **la arena**<br>ah-REH-nah |
| school | **la escuela**<br>eh-SKWEH-lah |
| school: slow | **despacio, escuela**<br>deh-SPAH-syoh eh-SKWEH-lah |
| school bus | **el autobús escolar ~ el camión escolar**<br>ah-oo-toh-BOOS eh-skoh-LAHR ~ kah-MYOHN eh-skoh-LAHR |
| school zone | **la zona escolar**<br>SOH-nah eh-skoh-LAHR |
| shoulder | **el borde**<br>BOHR-theh |
| sidewalk | **la acera ~ la banqueta**<br>ah-SEH-rah ~ bahn-KEH-tah |
| sign | **la señal**<br>seh-NYAHL |
| street sign | **la señal de calle**<br>seh-NYAHL deh KAH-yeh |
| traffic sign | **la señal de tráfico**<br>seh-NYAHL deh TRAH-fee-koh |
| siren | **la sirena**<br>see-REH-nah |
| slow | **lento ~ despacio**<br>LEHN-toh ~ deh-SPAH-syoh |
| smoke | **el humo**<br>OO-moh |

| | |
|---|---|
| speed limit | **la velocidad máxima ~ el límite de velocidad**<br>beh-loh-see-THAHTH MAHK-see-mah ~ LEE-mee-teh deh beh-loh-see-THAHTH |
| spill | **el derramiento**<br>deh-rrah-MYEHN-toh |
| stop | **la parada**<br>pah-RAH-thah |
| bus stop | **la parada de autobús**<br>pah-RAH-thah deh ah-oo-toh-BOOS |
| taxi stop | **la parada de taxi**<br>pah-RAH-thah deh TAHK-see |
| street | **la calle**<br>KAH-yeh |
| one-way street | **la calle de única dirección**<br>KAH-yeh deh OO-nee-kah dee-rehk-SYOHN |
| two-way street | **la calle de doble dirección**<br>KAH-yeh deh DOH-bleh dee-rehk-SYOHN |
| telephone booth | **la cabina de teléfono**<br>kah-BEE-nah deh teh-LEH-foh-noh |
| telephone pole | **el poste de teléfono**<br>POH-steh deh teh-LEH-foh-noh |
| traffic | **el tráfico ~ el tránsito**<br>TRAH-fee-koh ~ TRAHN-see-toh |
| traffic circle | **el círculo de tráfico ~ la glorieta**<br>SEER-koo-loh deh TRAH-fee-koh ~ gloh-ree-EH-tah |
| slow traffic | **tráfico lento**<br>TRAH-fee-koh LEHN-toh |
| two-way traffic | **tráfico de doble circulación**<br>TRAH-fee-koh deh DOH-bleh seer-koo-lah-SYOHN |

|  |  |
|---|---|
| trash can | **el cubo de basura ~ el bote de basura**<br>KOO-boh deh bah-SOO-rah ~ BOH-teh deh bah-SOO-rah |
| tunnel | **el túnel**<br>TOO-nehl |
| turn | **la vuelta**<br>BWEHL-tah |
| illegal turn | **la vuelta ilegal**<br>BWEHL-tah ee-leh-GAHL |
| no left turn | **no vuelta a la izquierda**<br>noh BWEHL-tah ah lah ees-KYEHR-thah |
| no right turn | **no vuelta a la derecha**<br>noh BWEHL-tah ah lah deh-REH-chah |
| no turns | **no dé vuelta**<br>noh deh BWEHL-tah |
| no U-turn | **no dé vuelta en "U"**<br>noh deh BWEHL-tah ehn oo |
| visibility | **la visibilidad**<br>bee-see-bee-lee-THAHTH |
| obstructed visibility | **la visibilidad obstruida**<br>bee-see-bee-lee-THAHTH ohb-stroo-EE-thah |
| way | |
| one way | **una vía ~ un solo camino**<br>OO-nah BEE-ah ~ oon SOH-loh kah-MEE-noh |
| wrong way | **la dirección contra el tráfico**<br>dee-rehk-SYOHN KOHN-trah ehl TRAH-fee-koh |
| yield | **ceda el paso**<br>SEH-thah ehl PAH-soh |
| zone | **la zona**<br>SOH-nah |
| green zone | **la zona verde**<br>SOH-nah BEHR-theh |
| red zone | **la zona roja**<br>SOH-nah RROH-hah |
| yellow zone | **la zona amarilla**<br>SOH-nah ah-mah-REE-yah |

## TRAFFIC VIOLATIONS

Las violaciones de tráfico

Here is a list of traffic violations, as well as useful phrases in a vehicle stop.

| | |
|---|---|
| I'm arresting you for ... | **Lo / La arresto por...** loh/lah ah-RREH-stoh pohr |
| I'm citing you for ... | **Lo / La cito por...** loh/lah SEE-toh pohr |
| I'm warning you for ... | **Le doy un aviso por...** leh doy oon ah-BEE-soh pohr |
| The ticket is for ... | **El tíquete es por...** ehl TEE-keh-teh ehs pohr |

### License, Registration, and Insurance Violations

Las violaciones de licencia, registro y seguro

| | |
|---|---|
| driving without a license | **manejar sin licencia** mah-neh-HAHR seen lee-SEHN-syah |
| having a revoked license | **tener una licencia cancelada** teh-NEHR OO-nah lee-SEHN-syah kahn-seh-LAH-thah |
| having an expired license | **tener la licencia expirada** teh-NEHR lah lee-SEHN-syah ehks-pee-RAH-thah |
| having an expired plate | **tener la placa expirada** teh-NEHR lah PLAH-kah ehks-pee-RAH-thah |
| having an expired car registration | **tener el registro expirado** teh-NEHR ehl rreh-HEE-stroh ehks-pee-RAH-thoh |

### Parking Violations

Las violaciones de estacionamiento

| | |
|---|---|
| blocking the driveway | **tapar la entrada** tah-PAHR lah ehn-TRAH-thah |
| obstructing traffic | **obstruir el tráfico** ohb-stroo-EER ehl TRAH-fee-koh |

| | |
|---|---|
| parking in handicapped spaces | **estacionar en sitios para minusválidos**<br>eh-stah-syoh-NAHR ehn SEE-tyohs PAH-rah mee-noos-BAH-lee-thohs |
| no parking | **estacionamiento prohibido**<br>eh-stah-syoh-nah-MYEHN-toh proh-ee-BEE-thoh |

## Moving Violations

Las violaciones en marcha

| | |
|---|---|
| driving against the traffic | **manejar contra el tráfico**<br>mah-neh-HAHR KOHN-trah ehl TRAH-fee-koh |
| driving too slow | **manejar demasiado despacio**<br>mah-neh-HAHR deh-mah-SYAH-thoh deh-SPAH-syoh |
| | **manejar demasiado lento**<br>mah-neh-HAHR deh-mah-SYAH-thoh LEHN-toh |
| backing out unsafely | **retroceder de una manera peligrosa**<br>rreh-troh-seh-THEHR deh OO-nah mah-NEH-rah peh-lee-GROH-sah |
| obstructing traffic | **obstruir el tráfico**<br>ohb-stroo-EER ehl TRAH-fee-koh |
| crossing the double line | **cruzar la línea doble**<br>kroo-SAHR lah LEE-neh-ah DOH-bleh |
| driving the wrong way | **manejar en el sentido contrario**<br>mah-neh-HAHR ehn ehl sehn-TEE-thoh kohn-TRAH-ree-oh |
| following too closely | **seguir demasiado cerca**<br>seh-GEER deh-mah-SYAH-thoh SEHR-kah |

| | |
|---|---|
| making an unsafe lane change | **hacer un cambio de carril peligroso**<br>ah-SEHR oon KAHM-byoh deh kah-RREEL peh-lee-GROH-soh |
| passing a school bus | **doblar un camión escolar**<br>doh-BLAHR oon kah-MYOHN eh-skoh-LAHR |
| | **doblar un autobús escolar**<br>doh-BLAHR oon ah-oo-toh-BOOS eh-skoh-LAHR |
| passing illegally | **doblar ilegalmente**<br>doh-BLAHR ee-leh-gahl-MEHN-teh |
| | **pasar ilegalmente**<br>pah-SAHR ee-leh-gahl-MEHN-teh |
| reckless driving | **manejar con descuido**<br>mah-neh-HAHR kohn dehs-KWEE-thoh |
| driving on the sidewalk | **manejar sobre la banqueta**<br>mah-neh-HAHR SOH-breh lah bahn-KEH-tah |
| | **manejar sobre la acera**<br>mah-neh-HAHR SOH-breh lah ah-SEH-rah |
| not signaling | **no hacer las señales**<br>noh ah-SEHR lahs seh-NYAH-lehs |
| starting out when it's unsafe | **arrancar cuando es peligroso**<br>ah-rrahn-KAHR KWAHN-doh ehs peh-lee-GROH-soh |
| not stopping for … | **no parar para…**<br>noh pah-RAHR PAH-rah |
| an ambulance | **una ambulancia**<br>OO-nah ahm-boo-LAHN-syah |
| emergency vehicles | **los vehículos de emergencia**<br>los beh-EE-koo-lohs deh eh-mehr-HEHN-syah |

not stopping for ... — **no parar para...**
noh pah-RAHR PAH-rah

a school bus — **un autobús escolar ~ un camión escolar**
oon ah-oo-toh-BOOS eh-skoh-LAHR ~ oon kah-MYOHN eh-skoh-LAHR

a train — **un tren**
oon trehn

stopping suddenly without signaling — **parar de repente sin señalar**
pah-RAHR deh rreh-PEHN-teh seen seh-nyah-LAHR

towing another vehicle — **remolcar otro carro**
rreh-mohl-KAHR OH-troh KAH-rroh

making an illegal turn — **dar una vuelta ilegal**
dahr OO-nah BWEHL-tah ee-leh-GAHL

making a U-turn — **dar una vuelta en "U"**
dahr OO-nah BWEHL-tah ehn oo

driving in the wrong direction — **manejar en la dirección contraria**
mah-neh-HAHR ehn lah dee-rehk-SYOHN kohn-TRAH-ree-ah

driving in the wrong lane — **manejar en el carril incorrecto**
mah-neh-HAHR ehn ehl kah-RREEL een-koh-RREHK-toh

not yielding the right of way — **no ceder el derecho de vía**
noh seh-THEHR ehl deh-REH-choh deh BEE-ah

## Safety Violations

Las violaciones contra la seguridad

driving without an adult — **manejar sin adulto**
mah-neh-HAHR seen ah-THOOL-toh

| | |
|---|---|
| not having a bike helmet | **no tener un casco en bici** noh teh-NEHR oon KAH-skoh ehn BEE-see |
| not having a motorcycle helmet | **no tener un casco en moto** noh teh-NEHR oon KAH-skoh ehn MOH-toh |
| not wearing a seat belt | **no tener puesto[a] el cinturón** noh teh-NEHR PWEH-stoh[-stah] ehl seen-too-ROHN |
| being a passenger in the bed of a pickup | **ser pasajero[a] en la cama de un pickup** sehr pah-sah-HEH-roh[-rah] ehn lah KAH-mah deh oon PEEK-oop |
| having too many passengers | **tener demasiados pasajeros** teh-NEHR deh-mah-SYAH-thohs pah-sah-HEH-rohs |
| not signaling | **no hacer las señales** noh ah-SEHR lahs seh-NYAH-lehs |
| towing another vehicle unsafely | **remolcar otro carro de una manera insegura** rreh-mohl-KAHR OH-troh KAH-rroh deh OO-nah mah-NEH-rah een-seh-GOO-rah |
| having obstructed visibility | **tener la visibilidad obstruida** teh-NEHR lah bee-see-bee-lee-THAHTH ohb-stroo-EE-thah |
| tinted windows | **ventanas con tinte** behn-TAH-nahs kohn TEEN-teh |

## Speeding Violations
Las violaciones con exceso de velocidad

| | |
|---|---|
| driving too fast | **manejar demasiado rápido** mah-neh-HAHR deh-mah-SYAH-thoh RRAH-pee-thoh |

| | |
|---|---|
| driving at (100) mph | **manejar a (cien) millas por hora**<br>mah-neh-HAHR ah (syehn) MEE-yahs pohr OH-rah |
| exceeding the speed limit | **pasar la velocidad máxima**<br>pah-SAHR lah beh-loh-see-THAHTH MAHK-see-mah |
| speeding | **manejar muy rápido**<br>mah-neh-HAHR MOO-ee RRAH-pee-thoh |
| | **manejar con exceso de velocidad**<br>mah-neh-HAHR kohn ehk-SEH-soh deh beh-loh-see-THAHTH |
| exhibition of speed (burning rubber) | **la exhibición de velocidad (quemando llanta)**<br>ehks-ee-bee-SYOHN deh beh-loh-see-THAHTH (keh-MAHN-doh YAHN-tah) |
| racing and spectators | **hacer carreras y espectadores**<br>ah-SEHR kah-RREH-rahs ee eh-spehk-tah-THOH-rehs |
| impeding traffic | **impedir el tráfico**<br>eem-peh-THEER ehl TRAH-fee-koh |

## Traffic Sign and Signal Violations
Las violaciones de señales de tráfico

| | |
|---|---|
| not stopping at the intersection | **no parar en la intersección**<br>noh pah-RAHR ehn lah een-tehr-sehk-SYOHN |
| not stopping at a pedestrian crossing | **no parar en el cruce de peatones**<br>noh pah-RAHR ehn ehl KROO-seh deh peh-ah-TOH-nehs |
| running a red light | **pasar una luz roja**<br>pah-SAHR OO-nah loos RROH-hah |

| | |
|---|---|
| running a red arrow | **pasar una flecha roja**<br>pah-SAHR OO-nah FLEH-chah RROH-hah |
| not stopping completely behind the limit line | **no parar completamente detrás de la línea de límite**<br>noh pah-RAHR kohm-pleh-tah-MEHN-teh deh-TRAHS deh lah LEE-neh-ah deh LEE-mee-teh |
| not stopping for ... | **no parar para...**<br>noh pah-RAHR PAH-rah |
| a red light | **una luz roja**<br>OO-nah loos RROH-hah |
| a stop sign | **una señal de alto**<br>OO-nah seh-NYAHL deh AHL-toh |

## Mechanical Violations
Las violaciones mecánicas

| | |
|---|---|
| brakes not working | **no funcionar los frenos**<br>noh foon-syoh-NAHR lohs FREH-nohs |
| having too heavy a load | **tener la carga demasiado grande**<br>teh-NEHR lah KAHR-gah deh-mah-SYAH-thoh GRAHN-deh |
| muffler too loud | **el amortiguador demasiado alto**<br>ah-mohr-tee-gwah-THOHR deh-mah-SYAH-thoh AHL-toh |
| (letting out) too much smoke | **(echando) demasiado humo**<br>(eh-CHAHN-doh) deh-mah-SYAH-thoh OO-moh |
| taillights not working | **no funcionando las luces traseras**<br>noh foon-SYOH-nahn-doh lahs LOO-sehs trah-SEH-rahs |
| license plate missing | **faltar la placa de licencia**<br>fahl-TAHR lah PLAH-kah deh lee-SEHN-syah |

| | |
|---|---|
| tire too small | **la llanta demasiado chica ~ pequeña**<br>yahn-tah deh-mah-SYAH-thoh CHEE-kah ~ peh-KEH-nyah |
| having worn tires | **tener las llantas gastadas**<br>teh-NEHR lahs YAHN-tahs gah-STAH-thahs |
| driving an unsafe vehicle | **manejar un vehículo no seguro**<br>mah-neh-HAHR oon beh-EE-koo-loh noh seh-GOO-roh |
| having obstructed visibility | **tener la visibilidad obstruida**<br>teh-NEHR lah bee-see-bee-lee-THAHTH ohb-stroo-EE-thah |

## End of Citation

El fin de tíquete

| | |
|---|---|
| You have to go to the police station. | **Tiene que ir a la estación de policía.**<br>TYEH-neh keh eer ah lah eh-stah-SYOHN deh poh-lee-SEE-ah |
| You have to go to court. | **Tiene que ir a la corte.**<br>TYEH-neh keh eer ah lah KOHR-teh |
| | **Tiene que ir al tribunal.**<br>TYEH-neh keh eer ahl tree-boo-NAHL |
| Sign here, please. | **Firme aquí, por favor.**<br>FEER-meh ah-KEE pohr fah-BOHR |
| Your signature does not mean you are guilty. | **Su firma no es una admisión de culpa.**<br>soo FEER-mah noh ehs OO-nah ahd-mee-SYOHN deh KOOL-pah |

| | |
|---|---|
| We're going to store your car. | **Vamos a guardar su carro.** BAH-mohs ah gwahr-THAHR soo KAH-rroh |
| The tow truck is taking your car to the tow yard. | **La grúa lleva su carro al corralón.** lah GROO-ah YEH-bah soo KAH-rroh ahl koh-rrah-LOHN |
| Drive carefully. | **Maneje con cuidado.** mah-NEH-heh kohn kwee-THAH-thoh |
| Be careful now. | **Tenga cuidado ahora.** TEHN-gah kwee-THAH-thoh ah-OH-rah |

## LEGAL TERMS
### Los términos legales

Here are words and phrases for criminal charges and the courtroom.

| | |
|---|---|
| accomplice | **el / la cómplice** KOHM-plee-seh |
| accusation | **la denuncia** deh-NOON-syah |
| acquittal | **la absolución** ahb-soh-loo-SYOHN |
| affidavit | **la declaración jurada** deh-klah-rah-SYOHN hoo-RAH-thah |
| alibi | **la coartada** koh-ahr-TAH-thah |
| allegation | **la alegación ~ la acusación** ah-leh-gah-SYOHN ~ ah-koo-sah-SYOHN |
| arraignment | **la denuncia** deh-NOON-syah |
| arrest | **el arresto ~ la detención** ah-RREH-stoh ~ deh-tehn-SYOHN |
| attorney | **el abogado / la abogada** ah-boh-GAH-thoh / ah-boh-GAH-thah |

**La citación** is the legal term for "citation." The street term is **tíquete** or **tiquete** ("ticket").

| | |
|---|---|
| autopsy | **la autopsia**<br>ah-oo-TOHP-syah |
| bail | **la fianza**<br>fee-AHN-sah |
| bailiff | **el / la alguacil**<br>ahl-gwah-SEEL |
| bigamy | **la bigamia**<br>bee-GAH-mee-ah |
| blackmail | **el chantaje**<br>chahn-TAH-heh |
| bondsman | **el póliza**<br>POH-lee-sah |
| charge | **el cargo**<br>KAHR-goh |
| citation | **la citación ~ el tíquete**<br>see-tah-SYOHN ~ TEE-keh-teh |
| claim | **la demanda**<br>deh-MAHN-dah |
| complaint | **la queja**<br>KEH-hah |
| confession | **la confesión**<br>kohn-feh-SYOHN |
| corruption | **la corrupción**<br>koh-rroop-SYOHN |
| counterfeiting | **la falsificación**<br>fahl-see-fee-kah-SYOHN |
| court | **la corte ~ el tribunal**<br>KOHR-teh ~ tree-boo-NAHL |
| court order | **la orden de la corte**<br>OHR-thehn deh lah KOHR-teh |
| crime | **el crimen ~ el delito**<br>KREE-mehn ~ deh-LEE-toh |
| cross-examination | **la interrogación**<br>een-teh-rroh-gah-SYOHN |

| | |
|---|---|
| custody warrant | **la orden de custodia**<br>OHR-thehn deh koo-STOH-dyah |
| damages | **los daños**<br>DAH-nyohs |
| defendant | **el acusado / la acusada**<br>ah-koo-SAH-thoh / ah-koo-SAH-thah |
| defense attorney/lawyer | **el abogado defensor / la abogada defensora**<br>ah-boh-GAH-thoh deh-fehn-SOHR / ah-boh-GAH-thah deh-fehn-SOH-rah |
| deposition | **la declaración oral**<br>deh-klah-rah-SYOHN oh-RAHL |
| district attorney | **el / la fiscal**<br>fee-SKAHL |
| evidence | **la evidencia**<br>eh-bee-THEHN-syah |
| extortion | **la extorsión**<br>ehks-tohr-SYOHN |
| felony | **el delito grave ~ la felonía**<br>deh-LEE-toh GRAH-beh ~ feh-loh-NEE-ah |
| fine | **la multa**<br>MOOL-tah |
| forgery | **la falsificación**<br>fahl-see-fee-kah-SYOHN |
| fraud | **el fraude**<br>FRAH-oo-deh |
| freedom on bail | **la libertad bajo fianza**<br>lee-behr-TAHTH BAH-hoh fee-AHN-sah |
| grand theft | **el hurto mayor**<br>OOR-toh mah-YOHR |
| guilt | **la culpa**<br>KOOL-pah |
| guilty | **culpable**<br>kool-PAH-bleh |
| not guilty | **no culpable**<br>noh kool-PAH-bleh |

|  |  |
|---|---|
| harassment | **el acosamiento**<br>ah-koh-sah-MYEHN-toh |
| sexual harassment | **el acosamiento sexual**<br>ah-koh-sah-MYEHN-toh sehk-SWAHL |
| hearing | **la audiencia**<br>ah-oo-DYEHN-syah |
| homicide | **el homicidio**<br>oh-mee-SEE-dyoh |
| incarceration | **el encarcelamiento**<br>ehn-kahr-seh-lah-MYEHN-toh |
| infraction | **la infracción**<br>een-frahk-SYOHN |
| innocent | **inocente**<br>ee-noh-SEHN-teh |
| interrogation | **el interrogatorio**<br>een-teh-rroh-gah-TOH-ree-oh |
| investigation | **la investigación**<br>een-beh-stee-gah-SYOHN |
| judge | **el juez**<br>hwehs |
| juror/jury | **el jurado**<br>hoo-RAH-thoh |
| justice | **la justicia**<br>hoo-STEE-syah |
| juvenile court | **la corte de menores**<br>KOHR-teh deh meh-NOH-rehs |
| juvenile delinquency | **la delincuencia juvenil**<br>deh-leen-KWEHN-syah hoo-beh-NEEL |
| law | **la ley**<br>LEH-ee |
| law enforcement | **la aplicación de la ley**<br>ah-plee-kah-SYOHN deh lah LEH-ee |
| lawyer | **el abogado / la abogada**<br>ah-boh-GAH-thoh/ ah-boh-GAH-thah |
| legal aid | **la asistencia legal**<br>ah-see-STEHN-syah leh-GAHL |

| | |
|---|---|
| lie detector | **el detector de mentiras**<br>deh-tehk-TOHR deh mehn-TEE-rahs |
| manslaughter | **el homicidio sin premeditación**<br>oh-mee-SEE-dyoh seen preh-meh-thee-tah-SYOHN |
| misdemeanor | **el delito menor**<br>deh-LEE-toh meh-NOHR |
| murder | **el homicidio**<br>oh-mee-SEE-dyoh |
| oath | **el juramento**<br>hoo-rah-MEHN-toh |
| under oath | **bajo juramento**<br>BAH-hoh hoo-rah-MEHN-toh |
| order/warrant | **la orden**<br>OHR-thehn |
| parole | **el parole ~ la libertad condicional**<br>pah-ROH-leh ~ lee-behr-TAHTH kohn-dee-syoh-NAHL |
| petty theft | **el hurto menor**<br>OOR-toh meh-NOHR |
| plaintiff | **el / la demandante**<br>deh-mahn-DAHN-teh |
| plea | **la declaración**<br>deh-klah-rah-SYOHN |
| probation | **la probación ~ la libertad condicional**<br>pro-bah-SYOHN ~ lee-behr-TAHTH kohn-dee-syoh-NAHL |
| proof | **la prueba**<br>proo-EH-bah |
| punishment | **la pena**<br>PEH-nah |
| record | **el archivo**<br>ahr-CHEE-boh |
| police record | **el archivo de policía**<br>ahr-CHEE-boh deh poh-lee-SEE-ah |

| | |
|---|---|
| prior record/priors | **el archivo de antecedentes anteriores**<br>ahr-CHEE-boh deh ahn-teh-seh-THEHN-tehs ahn-teh-ree-OH-rehs |
| released from jail | **puesto[a] en libertad de la cárcel**<br>PWEH-stoh[-stah] ehn lee-behr-TAHTH deh lah KAHR-sehl |
| resistance to arrest | **la resistencia a la autoridad**<br>rreh-see-STEHN-syah ah lah ah-oo-toh-ree-THAHTH |
| restraining order | **la orden de retiro y restricción**<br>OHR-thehn deh rreh-TEE-roh ee rreh-streek-SYOHN |
| rights | **los derechos**<br>deh-REH-chohs |
| robbery | **el robo ~ el hurto**<br>RROH-boh ~ OOR-toh |
| sentence | **la sentencia ~ la pena**<br>sehn-TEHN-syah ~ PEH-nah |
| suit | **la demanda**<br>deh-MAHN-dah |
| testimony | **el testimonio**<br>teh-stee-MOH-nyoh |
| ticket | **la citación ~ el tíquete**<br>see-tah-SYOHN ~ TEE-keh-teh |
| trial | **el juicio**<br>HWEE-syoh |
| vandalism | **el vandalismo**<br>bahn-dah-LEEZ-moh |
| verdict | **el veredicto**<br>beh-reh-THEEK-toh |
| violence | **la violencia**<br>bee-oh-LEHN-syah |
| warrant/order | **la orden**<br>OHR-thehn |
| arrest warrant | **la orden de arresto**<br>OHR-thehn deh ah-RREH-stoh |

| | |
|---|---|
| custody warrant | **la orden de custodia**<br>OHR-thehn deh koo-STOH-dyah |
| judge's warrant | **la orden del juez**<br>OHR-thehn dehl hwehs |
| search warrant | **la orden de registro**<br>OHR-thehn deh rreh-HEE-stroh |
| | **la orden de esculque**<br>OHR-thehn deh eh-SKOOL-keh |
| welfare fraud | **el fraude del bienestar**<br>FRAH-oo-deh dehl byehn-eh-STAHR |
| witness | **el / la testigo**<br>teh-STEE-goh |
| eyewitness | **el / la testigo ocular**<br>teh-STEE-goh oh-koo-LAHR |

There is no feminine ending for **testigo** ("witness"): **El testigo** is a male witness, and **la testigo** is a female witness.

## WEAPONS
## Las armas

Here are useful expressions dealing with firearms and assorted weapons.

| | |
|---|---|
| Drop the weapon. | **Suelte el arma.**<br>SWEHL-teh ehl AHR-mah |
| Drop the weapons. | **Suelte las armas.**<br>SWEHL-teh lahs AHR-mahs |
| Drop the gun. | **Suelte la pistola.**<br>SWEHL-teh lah pee-STOH-lah |
| Whose is it? | **¿De quién es?**<br>deh kyehn ehs |
| What type of weapon? | **¿Qué tipo de arma?**<br>keh TEE-poh deh AHR-mah |

"A weapon" is **un arma**. "The weapon" is **el arma**. "The weapons," **las armas**.

| | |
|---|---|
| What type of knife? | **¿Qué tipo de navaja?**<br>keh TEE-poh deh nah-BAH-hah |
| Is it your weapon? | **¿Es su arma?**<br>ehs soo AHR-mah |
| What caliber? | **¿Cuál calibre?**<br>kwahl kah-LEE-breh |
| (*to a male*) What did they shoot you with? | **¿Con qué lo tiraron?**<br>kohn KEH loh tee-RAH-rohn |
| | **¿Con qué lo dispararon?**<br>kohn KEH loh dee-spah-RAH-rohn |
| (*to a female*) What did they shoot you with? | **¿Con qué la tiraron?**<br>kohn KEH lah tee-RAH-rohn |
| | **¿Con qué la dispararon?**<br>kohn KEH lah dee-spah-RAH-rohn |
| They shot me with a handgun. | **Me fusilaron con una pistola.**<br>meh foo-see-LAH-rohn kohn OO-nah pee-STOH-lah |
| | **Me tiraron con una pistola.**<br>meh tee-RAH-rohn kohn OO-nah pee-STOH-lah |
| (*to a male*) Are you the registered owner of the weapon? | **Es usted el dueño registrado del arma?**<br>ehs oo-STEHTH ehl DWEH-nyoh rreh-hee-STRAH-thoh dehl AHR-mah |
| (*to a female*) Are you the registered owner of the weapon? | **Es usted la dueña registrada del arma?**<br>ehs oo-STEHTH lah DWEH-nyah rreh-hee-STRAH-thah dehl AHR-mah |

| | |
|---|---|
| Did you register the gun with the police? | **¿Registró la pistola con el departamento de policía?** rreh-hee-STROH lah pee-STOH-lah kohn ehl deh-pahr-tah-MEHN-toh deh poh-lee-SEE-ah |
| Did you register the gun with the state? | **¿Registró la pistola con el estado?** rreh-hee-STROH lah pee-STOH-lah kohn ehl eh-STAH-thoh |
| Is the gun loaded? | **¿Está cargada la pistola?** eh-STAH kahr-GAH-thah lah pee-STOH-lah |
| Is the gun registered? | **¿Está registrada la pistola?** eh-STAH rreh-hee-STRAH-thah lah pee-STOH-lah |
| a concealed firearm | **un arma de fuego escondida** oon AHR-mah deh FWEH-goh eh-skohn-DEE-thah |

## Firearms
### Las armas de fuego

| | |
|---|---|
| bullet | **la bala** BAH-lah |
| caliber | **el calibre** kah-LEE-breh |
| carbine | **la carabina** kah-rah-BEE-nah |
| cartridge | **el cartucho** kahr-TOO-choh |
| gun/pistol | **la pistola** pee-STOH-lah |
| holster | **la funda de pistola** FOON-dah deh pee-STOH-lah |
| machine gun | **la ametralladora** ah-meh-trah-yah-THOH-rah |
| revolver | **el revólver** rreh-BOHL-behr |

| | |
|---|---|
| rifle | **el rifle ~ el fusil**<br>RREE-fleh ~ foo-SEEL |
| round | **el tiro**<br>TEE-roh |
| semiautomatic gun | **la pistola semiautomática**<br>pee-STOH-lah seh-mee-ah-oo-toh-MAH-tee-kah |
| shooting | **un tiroteo**<br>tee-roh-TEH-oh |
| shot | **un disparo ~ un tiro**<br>dee-SPAH-roh ~ TEE-roh |
| shotgun | **la escopeta**<br>eh-skoh-PEH-tah |
| double-barreled shotgun | **la escopeta de dos cañones**<br>eh-skoh-PEH-tah deh dohs kah-NYOH-nehs |
| toy gun | **la pistola de juguete**<br>pee-STOH-lah deh hoo-GEH-teh |

## Cutting and Stabbing Weapons
## Las armas que cortan y apuñalan

| | |
|---|---|
| (*to a male*) What did they stab you with? | **¿Con qué lo apuñalaron?**<br>kohn keh loh ah-poo-nyah-LAH-rohn |
| (*to a female*) What did they stab you with? | **¿Con qué la apuñalaron?**<br>kohn keh lah ah-poo-nyah-LAH-rohn |
| They stabbed me with a knife. | **Me apuñalaron con un cuchillo.**<br>meh ah-poo-nyah-LAH-rohn kohn oon koo-CHEE-yoh |
| stabbing | **la apuñalada**<br>ah-poo-nyah-LAH-thah |
| (*to a male*) What did they cut you with? | **¿Con qué lo cortaron?**<br>kohn keh loh kohr-TAH-rohn |
| (*to a female*) What did they cut you with? | **¿Con qué la cortaron?**<br>kohn keh lah kohr-TAH-rohn |

| | |
|---|---|
| They cut me with a knife. | **Me cortaron con un cuchillo.**<br>meh kohr-TAH-rohn kohn oon koo-CHEE-yoh |
| ax | **el hacha**<br>AH-chah |
| bow and arrow | **el arco y la flecha**<br>AHR-koh ee lah FLEH-chah |
| butcher's knife | **el cuchillo de carnicero**<br>koo-CHEE-yoh deh kahr-nee-SEH-roh |
| can opener | **el abrelatas**<br>ah-breh-LAH-tahs |
| dagger | **el puñal**<br>poo-NYAHL |
| drill | **el taladro**<br>tah-LAH-droh |
| fork | **el tenedor**<br>teh-neh-THOHR |
| hatchet | **el hacha**<br>AH-chah |
| ice pick | **el picahielos**<br>pee-kah-YEH-lohs |
| knife | **el cuchillo**<br>koo-CHEE-yoh |
| folding knife/ switchblade | **la navaja**<br>nah-BAH-hah |
| kitchen knife | **el cuchillo**<br>koo-CHEE-yoh |
| machete | **el machete**<br>mah-CHEH-teh |
| pitchfork | **la horca**<br>OHR-kah |
| pliers | **los alicates**<br>ah-lee-KAH-tehs |
| razor | **la navaja**<br>nah-BAH-hah |
| shaving razor | **la navaja de afeitar**<br>nah-BAH-hah deh ah-feh-TAHR |
| razor blade | **la hoja de afeitar**<br>OH-hah deh ah-feh-TAHR |

| | |
|---|---|
| saw (hand) | **el serrucho**<br>seh-RROO-choh |
| scissors | **las tijeras**<br>tee-HEH-rahs |
| screwdriver | **el destornillador ~**<br>**el atornillador ~**<br>**el desarmador**<br>dehs-tohr-nee-yah-THOHR ~<br>ah-tohr-nee-yah-THOHR ~<br>dehs-ahr-mah-THOHR |
| switchblade | **la navaja**<br>nah-BAH-hah |
| sword | **la espada**<br>eh-SPAH-thah |

## Explosives and Igniting Weapons
Los explosivos y las armas que encienden

| | |
|---|---|
| bomb | **la bomba**<br>BOHM-bah |
| time bomb | **la bomba de tiempo**<br>BOHM-bah deh-TYEHM-poh |
| dynamite | **la dinamita**<br>dee-nah-MEE-tah |
| explosion | **la explosión**<br>ehks-ploh-SYOHN |
| grenade | **la granada**<br>grah-NAH-thah |
| hand grenade | **la granada de mano**<br>grah-NAH-thah deh<br>MAH-noh |
| highway flare | **la señal luminosa**<br>seh-NYAHL loo-mee-NOH-sah |
| torch | **la antorcha**<br>ahn-TOHR-chah |

## Weapons of Opportunity
Las otras armas

baseball bat — **el bate de béisbol**
BAH-teh deh BEHS-bohl

baton — **la porra**
POH-rrah

belt — **el cinturón ~ el cinto**
seen-too-ROHN ~ SEEN-toh

blackjack — **la macana**
mah-KAH-nah

bottle — **la botella**
boh-TEH-yah

brass knuckles — **las manoplas**
mah-NOH-plahs

brick — **el ladrillo**
lah-DREE-yoh

broomstick — **el palo de escoba**
PAH-loh deh eh-SKOH-bah

car jack — **el gato de carro**
GAH-toh deh KAH-rroh

chain — **la cadena**
kah-THEH-nah

chair — **la silla**
SEE-yah

club — **el garrote**
gah-RROH-teh

cord — **la cuerda**
KWEHR-thah

crowbar — **la palanca**
pah-LAHN-kah

file — **la lima**
LEE-mah

flashlight — **la linterna**
leen-TEHR-nah

frying pan — **la sartén**
sahr-TEHN

hammer — **el martillo**
mahr-TEE-yoh

hose — **la manguera**
mahn-GEH-rah

| | |
|---|---|
| lug wrench | **la palanca ~ la barra de hierro**<br>pah-LAHN-kah ~ BAH-rrah deh YEH-rroh |
| nightstick | **el bastón**<br>bah-STOHN |
| pepper spray | **el espray de pimienta**<br>eh-SPREH deh pee-MYEHN-tah |
| pipe (metal) | **el tubo**<br>TOO-boh |
| rock | **la piedra**<br>PYEH-drah |
| rope | **la cuerda ~ la soga**<br>KWEHR-thah ~ SOH-gah |
| rubber hose | **la manguera**<br>mahn-GEH-rah |
| shovel | **la pala**<br>PAH-lah |
| stick | **el palo**<br>PAH-loh |
| stone | **la piedra**<br>PYEH-drah |
| stun gun | **la pistola de toque ~ el stun gun**<br>pee-STOH-lah deh TOH-keh ~ stahn gahn |
| tire iron | **la llave de la llanta**<br>YAH-beh deh lah YAHN-tah |
| whip | **el látigo**<br>LAH-tee-goh |
| wire | **el alambre**<br>ah-LAHM-breh |
| wrench | **la llave inglesa**<br>YAY-beh een-GLEH-sah |

## ALCOHOL AND DRUGS
### El alcohol y las drogas

The following expressions are useful in alcohol, DUI, and drug busts.

| | |
|---|---|
| You're under arrest for driving under the influence of alcohol. | **Está arrestado[a] por manejar bajo la influencia de alcohol.**<br>eh-STAH ah-rreh-STAH-thoh[-thah] pohr mah-neh-HAHR BAH-hoh lah een-floo-EHN-syah deh ahl-koh-OHL |
| You can't ... | **No se puede...**<br>noh seh PWEH-theh |
| drink and drive in public. | **manejar y tomar en público.**<br>mah-neh-HAHR ee toh-MAHR ehn POO-blee-koh |
| have an open container in public. | **tener un envase abierto en público.**<br>teh-NEHR oon ehn-BAH-seh ah-BYEHR-toh ehn POO-blee-koh |
| Can anybody drive your car? | **¿Alguien puede manejar su carro?**<br>AHL-gyehn PWEH-theh mah-neh-HAHR soo KAH-rroh |
| Can you get home? | **¿Puede llegar a casa?**<br>PWEH-theh yeh-GAHR ah KAH-sah |
| Are you taking drugs? | **¿Toma drogas?**<br>TOH-mah DROH-gahs |
| Are you selling drugs? | **¿Vende drogas?**<br>BEHN-deh DROH-gahs |
| Are you pushing drugs? | **¿Anda empujando drogas?**<br>AHN-dah ehm-poo-HAHN-doh DROH-gahs |
| What are you selling? | **¿Qué vende?**<br>keh BEHN-deh |

What are you buying? | **¿Qué compra?** keh KOHM-prah

Where is your ...? | **¿Dónde está su...?** DOHN-deh eh-STAH soo

spoon | **cucharita** koo-chah-REE-tah

stash (heroin) | **clavo (heroína)** KLAH-boh (eh-roh-EE-nah)

straw | **paja** PAH-hah

syringe | **jeringa** heh-REEN-gah

Who is your contact? | **¿Quién es su conexión?** kyehn ehs soo koh-nehk-SYOHN

acid | **el ácido ~ el sello** AH-see-thoh ~ SEH-yoh

alcohol | **el alcohol** ahl-koh-OHL

amphetamines | **las anfetaminas** ahn-feh-tah-MEE-nahs

angel dust | **el polvo de ángel** POHL-boh deh AHN-hehl

bag | **la bolsa** BOHL-sah

balloon | **el globo** GLOH-boh

beer | **la cerveza** sehr-BEH-sah

brandy | **el brandy** BRAHN-dee

brick | **el ladrillo** lah-DREE-yoh

can | **el bote ~ la lata** BOH-teh ~ LAH-tah

champagne | **la champaña** chahm-PAH-nyah

cigarette | **el cigarrillo ~ el pitillo** see-gah-RREE-yoh ~ pee-TEE-yoh

| | |
|---|---|
| clip | **las pinzas**<br>PEEN-sahs |
| cocaine/coke | **la cocaína ~ la coca**<br>koh-kah-EE-nah ~ KOH-cah |
| cocktail | **el cóctel**<br>KOHK-tehl |
| connection | **la conexión**<br>koh-nehk-SYOHN |
| crack | **el crak ~ el crack**<br>krahk |
| crank | **el crank**<br>krahnk |
| depressants | **los sedantes**<br>seh-THAHN-tehs |
| dime bag | **el diez ~ el daime**<br>dyehs ~ DAY-meh |
| disinfectants | **los desinfectantes**<br>dehs-een-fehk-TAHN-tehs |
| downers | **los abajos**<br>ah-BAH-hohs |
| drink | **la bebida**<br>beh-BEE-thah |
| alcoholic drink | **la bebida alcohólica**<br>beh-BEE-thah<br>ahl-koh-OH-lee-kah |
| drug abuse | **el abuso de drogas**<br>ah-BOO-soh deh DROH-gahs |
| drug addict | **el droguero / la droguera**<br>droh-GEH-roh / droh-GEH-rah |
| | **el drogadicto / la drogadicta**<br>droh-gah-THEEK-toh /<br>droh-gah-THEEK-tah |
| drug dealer | **el / la narcotraficante**<br>nahr-koh-trah-fee-KAHN-teh |
| drug traffic | **el narcotráfico ~**<br>**el tráfico de drogas**<br>nahr-koh-TRAH-fee-koh ~<br>TRAH-fee-koh deh DROH-gahs |

| | |
|---|---|
| drunk | **borracho[a]**<br>boh-RRAH-choh[-chah]<br>**ebrio[a]**<br>EH-bree-oh[-ah] |
| fix | **el filerazo**<br>fee-leh-RAH-soh |
| gasoline | **la gasolina**<br>gah-soh-LEE-nah |
| gin | **la ginebra**<br>hee-NEH-brah |
| glass | **el vaso**<br>BAH-soh |
| glue | **la cola ~ el pegamiento**<br>KOH-lah ~ peh-gah-MYEHN-toh |
| grass | **la hierba**<br>YEHR-bah |
| habit | **el hábito**<br>AH-bee-toh |
| hashish | **el hashish**<br>ah-SHEESH |
| heroin | **la heroína**<br>eh-roh-EE-nah |
| illegal possession | **la posesión ilegal**<br>poh-seh-SYOHN ee-leh-GAHL |
| informant | **el / la informante**<br>een-fohr-MAHN-teh |
| inhalants | **los inhaladores**<br>een-ah-lah-THOH-rehs |
| injection | **la inyección**<br>een-yehk-SYOHN |
| intoxicated | **intoxicado[a]**<br>een-tohk-see-KAH-thoh[-thah] |
| joint | **el leño ~ el caballo**<br>LEH-nyoh ~ kah-BAH-yoh |
| kilogram | **el kilo**<br>KEE-loh |
| lid | **el bote**<br>BOH-teh |
| lighter | **el encendedor**<br>ehn-sehn-deh-THOHR |

| | |
|---|---|
| liquor | **el licor**<br>lee-KOHR |
| LSD/acid | **el LSD ~ el ácido**<br>EH-leh EH-seh deh ~ AH-see-thoh |
| marijuana | **la marihuana**<br>mah-ree-WAH-nah |
| mescaline | **la mescalina**<br>meh-skah-LEE-nah |
| methedrine/speed | **la metadrina**<br>meh-tah-DREE-nah |
| mirror | **el espejo**<br>eh-SPEH-hoh |
| morphine | **la morfina**<br>mohr-FEE-nah |
| narcotics | **los narcóticos**<br>nahr-KOH-tee-kohs |
| needle | **la aguja**<br>ah-GOO-hah |
| dirty needle | **la aguja sucia**<br>ah-GOO-hah SOO-syah |
| nickel bag | **el cinco ~ el nicle**<br>SEEN-koh ~ NEEK-leh |
| opium | **el opio**<br>OH-pyoh |
| ounce | **la onza**<br>OHN-sah |
| overdose | **la sobredosis**<br>soh-breh-THOH-sees |
| paint | **la pintura**<br>peen-TOO-rah |
| pills | **las pastillas**<br>pah-STEE-yahs |
| pipe | **la pipa**<br>PEE-pah |
| pot/weed | **la marihuana**<br>mah-ree-WAH-nah |
| pound | **la libra**<br>LEE-brah |
| powder | **el polvo**<br>POHL-boh |

| | |
|---|---|
| quarter | **el cuarto**<br>KWAHR-toh |
| rainbows | **los írises**<br>EE-ree-sehs |
| razor | **la navaja**<br>nah-BAH-hah |
| red devils | **los diablos rojos**<br>dee-AH-blohs RROH-hohs |
| roach | **la cucaracha**<br>koo-kah-RAH-chah |
| rum | **el ron**<br>rrohn |
| shot | **el vasito**<br>bah-SEE-toh |
| shot glass | **el tequilero**<br>teh-kee-LEH-roh |
| six-pack | **el paquete de seis ~ el six pack**<br>pah-KEH-teh deh sehs ~ seeks pahk |
| sleeping pills | **las pastillas para dormir**<br>pah-STEE-yahs PAH-rah dohr-MEER |
| speed | **la pep**<br>pehp |
| spoon/teaspoon | **la cucharita**<br>koo-chah-REE-tah |
| stash (heroin) | **el clavo (heroína)**<br>KLAH-boh (eh-roh-EE-nah) |
| stimulants | **los estimulantes**<br>eh-stee-moo-LAHN-tehs |
| straw | **la paja**<br>PAH-hah |
| sugar cube | **el cubo de azúcar**<br>KOO-boh deh ah-SOO-kahr |
| syringe | **la jeringa**<br>heh-REEN-gah |
| tablet | **la tableta**<br>tah-BLEH-tah |

teaspoon — **la cucharadita**
koo-chah-rah-THEE-tah

tequila — **el tequila**
teh-KEE-lah

tranquilizer — **el tranquilizante**
trahn-kee-lee-SAHN-teh

uppers — **los estimulantes**
eh-stee-moo-LAHN-tehs

vodka — **el vodka**
BOHD-kah

weed/pot — **la marihuana**
mah-ree-WAH-nah

whiskey — **el whisky**
WEE-skee

whites — **las blancas**
BLAHN-kahs

wine — **el vino**
BEE-noh

wine glass — **la copa**
KOH-pah

yellow jackets — **las amarillas**
ah-mah-REE-yahs

## JAIL
### La cárcel

Here are some expressions to help you with inmate booking and release.

You have the right to make a phone call. — **Tiene el derecho a hacer una llamada telefónica.**
TYEH-neh ehl deh-REH-choh ah ah-SEHR OO-nah yah-MAH-thah teh-leh-FOH-nee-kah

Empty your pockets. — **Vacíe los bolsillos.**
bah-SEE-eh lohs bohl-SEE-yohs

**Vacíe las bolsas.**
bah-SEE-eh lahs BOHL-sahs

|  |  |
|---|---|
| Put everything on the counter. | **Ponga todo sobre el mostrador.**<br>POHN-gah TOH-thoh SOH-breh ehl moh-strah-THOHR |
| We're going to take your picture. | **Le vamos a sacar la foto.**<br>leh BAH-mohs ah sah-KAHR lah FOH-toh |
| We're going to take your fingerprints. | **Le vamos a tomar las huellas digitales.**<br>leh BAH-mohs ah toh-MAHR lahs WEH-yahs dee-hee-TAH-lehs |
| booking center | **el centro de fichar**<br>SEHN-troh deh fee-CHAHR |
| cell | **la celda**<br>SEHL-dah |
| fingerprints | **las huellas digitales**<br>WEH-yahs dee-hee-TAH-lehs |
| guard | **el / la guardia**<br>GWAHR-dyah |
| handcuffs | **las esposas**<br>eh-SPOH-sahs |
| inmate | **el preso / la presa**<br>PREH-soh / PREH-sah |
| prison | **la prisión**<br>pree-SYOHN |
| prisoner | **el prisionero / la prisionera**<br>pree-syoh-NEH-roh / pree-syoh-NEH-rah |
| release | **soltar en libertad**<br>sohl-TAHR ehn lee-behr-TAHTH<br>**poner en libertad**<br>poh-NEHR ehn lee-behr-TAHTH |
| strip search | **el registro sin ropa**<br>rreh-HEE-stroh seen RROH-pah<br>**el esculque sin ropa**<br>eh-SKOOL-keh seen RROH-pah |

## Application for Bail and Own Recognizance (O.R.) Release
La aplicación para la fianza y la palabra de honor de estar en la corte

How long (have you been living) at your home address?
**¿Cuánto tiempo (vive) en su casa?**
KWAHN-toh TYEHM-poh (BEE-beh) ehn soo KAH-sah

In the county?
**¿En el condado?**
ehn ehl kohn-DAH-thoh

Are you renting or buying your house?
**¿Renta o compra su casa?**
RREHN-tah oh KOHM-prah soo KAH-sah
**¿Alquila o compra su casa?**
ahl-KEE-lah oh KOHM-prah soo KAH-sah

(Do you have) a personal reference who is not living with you?
**¿(Tiene) una referencia personal no en la casa con usted?**
(TYEH-neh) OO-nah rreh-feh-REHN-syah pehr-soh-NAHL noh ehn lah KAH-sah kohn oo-STEHTH

(Do you have) any other pending cases?
**¿(Tiene) otros casos pendientes?**
(TYEH-neh) OH-trohs KAH-sohs pehn-DYEHN-tehs

How were you released?
**¿Cómo fue soltado[a]?**
KOH-moh fweh sohl-TAH-thoh[-thah]

Have you failed to appear in court?
**¿Ha faltado en una promesa de estar en la corte en la fecha prevista?**
ah fahl-TAH-thoh ehn OO-nah proh-MEH-sah deh eh-STAHR ehn lah KOHR-teh ehn lah FEH-chah preh-BEE-stah

(Give me) all your prior arrests, including out of state.

**(Déme) todos los arrestos previos, incluyendo fuera del estado.**
(DEH-meh) TOH-thohs lohs ah-RREH-stohs PREH-byohs een-kloo-YEHN-doh FWEH-rah dehl eh-STAH-thoh

## Medical Questions
Las preguntas médicas

Are you now under a doctor's care for any medical or psychiatric reasons?

**¿Está viendo un doctor por razones médicas o psiquiátricas?**
eh-STAH BYEHN-doh oon dohk-TOHR pohr rrah-SOH-nehs MEH-thee-kahs oh see-kee-AH-tree-kahs

Do you now have or have you ever had ...?

**¿Tiene ahora o ha tenido...?**
TYEH-neh ah-OH-rah oh ah teh-NEE-thoh

convulsions

**las convulsiones**
kohn-bool-SYOH-nehs

diabetes

**la diabetes**
dee-ah-BEH-tehs

emphysema

**el enfisema**
ehn-fee-SEH-mah

heart problems

**los problemas del corazón**
proh-BLEH-mahs dehl koh-rah-SOHN

seizures

**las convulsiones**
kohn-bool-SYOH-nehs

Do you have an alcohol or drug habit that causes withdrawal problems?

**¿Tiene problemas con alcohol o drogas causando problemas de retracción?**
TYEH-neh proh-BLEH-mahs kohn ahl-koh-OHL oh DROH-gahs kah-oo-SAHN-doh proh-BLEH-mahs deh rreh-trahk-SYOHN

Type and amount used daily?

**¿Cuál y cuánto diario?**
KWAHL ee KWAHN-toh dee-AH-ree-oh

Have you thought of suicide?

**¿Ha pensado en el suicidio?**
ah pehn-SAH-thoh ehn ehl soo-ee-SEE-dyoh

Do you feel that way now?

**¿Está pensando en esto ahorita?**
eh-STAH pehn-SAHN-doh ehn EH-stoh ah-oh-REE-tah

Are you allergic to any food or medicine?

**¿Está alérgico[a] a una comida o a alguna medicina?**
eh-STAH ah-LEHR-hee-koh[-kah] ah OO-nah koh-MEE-thah oh ah ahl-GOO-nah meh-thee-SEE-nah

If yes, what is it?

**Si responde que sí, ¿qué es?**
see rreh-SPOHN-deh keh see keh ehs

Do you have any other medical problems?

**¿Tiene otros problemas médicos?**
TYEH-neh OH-trohs proh-BLEH-mahs MEH-thee-kohs

Do you have medical insurance?

**¿Tiene seguro médico?**
TYEH-neh seh-GOO-roh MEH-thee-koh

**¿Tiene aseguranza médica?**
TYEH-neh ah-seh-goo-RAHN-sah MEH-thee-kah

Insurance carrier?

**¿Nombre del seguro?**
NOHM-breh dehl seh-GOO-roh

## Searching
### Registrando / esculcando

Take off your shoes and socks and put them behind you.

**Quítese los zapatos y los calcetines y póngalos atrás de usted.**
KEE-teh-seh lohs sah-PAH-tohs ee lohs kahl-seh-TEE-nehs ee POHN-gah-lohs ah-TRAHS deh oo-STEHTH

| | |
|---|---|
| Open your mouth and lift up your tongue. | **Abra la boca y levante la lengua.**<br>AH-brah lah BOH-kah ee leh-BAHN-teh lah LEHN-gwah |
| Open your cheeks. | **Abra las mejillas.**<br>AH-brah lahs meh-HEE-yahs |
| | **Abra los cachetes.**<br>AH-brah lohs kah-CHEH-tehs |
| Pull down your lower lip and pull up your upper lip. | **Baje el labio inferior y levante el labio superior.**<br>BAH-heh ehl LAH-byoh een-feh-ree-OHR ee leh-BAHN-teh ehl LAH-byoh soo-peh-ree-OHR |
| Bend over and run your fingers through your hair. | **Agáchese y sacuda el pelo.**<br>ah-GAH-cheh-seh ee sah-KOO-thah ehl PEH-loh |
| | **Agáchese y sacuda el cabello.**<br>ah-GAH-cheh-seh ee sah-KOO-thah ehl kah-BEH-yoh |
| Take off your shirt, pants, and underwear. | **Quítese la camisa, los pantalones y los chones.**<br>KEE-teh-seh lah kah-MEE-sah lohs pahn-tah-LOH-nehs ee lohs CHOH-nehs |
| | **Quítese la camisa, los pantalones y la ropa interior.**<br>KEE-teh-seh lah kah-MEE-sah lohs pahn-tah-LOH-nehs ee lah RROH-pah een-teh-ree-OHR |
| Put your hands behind (you). | **Ponga las manos atrás.**<br>POHN-gah lahs MAH-nohs ah-TRAHS |
| Spread your feet. | **Abra los pies.**<br>AH-brah lohs pyehs |
| Give me your belt. | **Déme su cinturón.**<br>DEH-meh soo seen-too-ROHN |
| | **Déme su cinto.**<br>DEH-meh soo SEEN-toh |

| | |
|---|---|
| Take off your shoes. | **Quítese los zapatos.**<br>KEE-teh-seh lohs sah-PAH-tohs |
| Take off your socks. | **Quítese los calcetines.**<br>KEE-teh-seh lohs kahl-seh-TEE-nehs |
| Take off your clothes. | **Quítese la ropa.**<br>KEE-teh-seh lah RROH-pah |
| Lift your left foot. | **Levante el pie izquierdo.**<br>leh-BAHN-teh ehl pyeh ees-KYEHR-thoh |
| Lift your right foot. | **Levante el pie derecho.**<br>leh-BAHN-teh ehl pyeh deh-REH-choh |
| Lift your tongue. | **Levante la lengua.**<br>leh-BAHN-teh lah LEHN-gwah |
| Raise your hands. | **Levante las manos.**<br>leh-BAHN-teh lahs MAH-nohs |
| Lift your testicles. | **Levante los testículos.**<br>leh-BAHN-teh lohs teh-STEE-koo-lohs<br>**Levante los huevos.**<br>leh-BAHN-teh lohs WEH-bohs |
| Bend over and open your butt cheeks and cough twice. | **Agáchese y abra las mejillas de las nalgas y tosa dos veces.**<br>ah-GAH-cheh-seh ee AH-brah lahs meh-HEE-yahs deh lahs NAHL-gahs ee TOH-sah dohs BEH-sehs<br>**Agáchese y abra los cachetes de las nalgas y tosa dos veces.**<br>ah-GAH-cheh-seh ee AH-brah lohs kah-CHEH-tehs deh lahs NAHL-gahs ee TOH-sah dohs BEH-sehs |

## Releasing
Poniendo en libertad/soltando

(*to a male*) We're going to release you on bail.

**Lo vamos a soltar en libertad bajo fianza.**
loh BAH-mohs ah sohl-TAHR ehn lee-behr-TAHTH BAH-hoh FYAHN-sah

**Lo vamos a poner en libertad bajo fianza.**
loh BAH-mohs ah poh-NEHR ehn lee-behr-TAHTH BAH-hoh FYAHN-sah

(*to a female*) We're going to release you on bail.

**La vamos a soltar en libertad bajo fianza.**
lah BAH-mohs ah sohl-TAHR ehn lee-behr-TAHTH BAH-hoh FYAHN-sah

**La vamos a poner en libertad bajo fianza.**
lah BAH-mohs ah poh-NEHR ehn lee-behr-TAHTH BAH-hoh FYAHN-sah

Sign here.

**Firme aquí.**
FEER-meh ah-KEE

Here is ...

**Aquí está...**
ah-KEE eh-STAH

your date to be in court.

**la fecha de la corte.**
FEH-chah deh lah KOHR-teh

**la fecha del tribunal.**
FEH-chah dehl tree-boo-NAHL

your booking slip.

**la palabra de honor de estar en la corte.**
pah-LAH-brah deh oh-NOHR deh eh-STAHR ehn lah KOHR-teh

the name of your probation officer.

**el nombre del oficial de probación.**
NOHM-breh dehl oh-fee-SYAHL deh proh-bah-SYOHN

Here is your personal property.

**Aquí están sus pertenencias personales.**
ah-KEE eh-STAHN soos pehr-teh-NEHN-syahs pehr-soh-NAH-lehs

## FISH AND GAME, ANIMALS, AND CAMPING
### Los peces, la caza, los animales y el campamento

Here are fish and game, camping, domestic and wild animals, and animal control terms.

I am a fish and game warden.

**Soy agente de la pesca y la caza.**
soy ah-HEHN-teh deh lah PEH-skah ee lah KAH-sah

You are in violation of the fish and game code.

**Está en violación del código de la pesca y la caza.**
eh-STAH ehn bee-oh-lah-SYOHN dehl KOH-thee-goh deh lah PEH-skah ee lah KAH-sah

It attacked me.

**Me atacó.**
meh ah-tah-KOH

It injured me.

**Me hirió.**
meh ee-ree-OH

It bit me.

**Me mordió.**
meh mohr-DYOH

It stung me.

**Me picó.**
meh pee-KOH

What are you hunting?

**¿Qué está cazando?**
keh eh-STAH kah-SAHN-doh

What are you fishing?

**¿Qué está pescando?**
keh eh-STAH peh-SKAHN-doh

May I see your hunting license?

**¿Puedo ver su licencia de cazar?**
PWEH-thoh BEHR soo lee-SEHN-syah deh kah-SAHR

| | |
|---|---|
| May I see your fishing license? | **¿Puedo ver su licencia de pescar?**<br>PWEH-thoh BEHR soo lee-SEHN-syah deh peh-SKAHR |
| This animal is illegal. | **Este animal es ilegal.**<br>EH-steh ah-nee-MAHL ehs ee-leh-GAHL |
| This fish is illegal. | **Este pez es ilegal.**<br>EH-steh pehs ehs ee-leh-GAHL |
| Do you have permission from the landowner? | **¿Tiene permiso del dueño de la propiedad?**<br>TYEH-neh pehr-MEE-soh dehl DWEH-nyoh deh lah proh-pyeh-THAHTH |
| Did you see the "no hunting/no trespassing" sign? | **¿Vio el aviso que dice: Prohibido cazar o pasar?**<br>byoh ehl ah-BEE-soh keh DEE-seh proh-ee-BEE-thoh kah-SAHR oh pah-SAHR |
| Did you see the "no fishing/no trespassing" sign? | **¿Vio el aviso que dice: Prohibido pescar o pasar?**<br>byoh ehl ah-BEE-soh keh DEE-seh proh-ee-BEE-thoh peh-SKAHR oh pah-SAHR |
| It's against the law to hunt here. | **Es contra la ley cazar aquí.**<br>ehs KOHN-trah lah LEH-ee kah-SAHR ah-KEE |
| It's against the law to fish here. | **Es contra la ley pescar aquí.**<br>ehs KOHN-trah lah LEH-ee peh-SKAHR ah-KEE |
| Is this your fishing rod? | **¿Es su caña de pesca?**<br>ehs soo KAH-nyah deh PEH-skah |
| Is this your fishing equipment? | **¿Es su equipo de pesca?**<br>ehs soo eh-KEE-poh deh PEH-skah |

| | |
|---|---|
| I'm an animal control officer. | **Soy oficial para el control de animales.**<br>soy oh-fee-SYAHL PAH-rah ehl kohn-TROHL deh ah-nee-MAH-lehs |
| | **Soy agente para el control de animales.**<br>soy ah-HEHN-teh PAH-rah ehl kohn-TROHL deh ah-nee-MAH-lehs |
| What pets do you have at home? | **¿Cuáles animales domésticos tiene en casa?**<br>KWAH-lehs ah-nee-MAHL-ehs doh-MEH-stee-kohs TYEH-neh ehn KAH-sah |
| | **¿Cuáles mascotas tiene en casa?**<br>KWAH-lehs mah-SKOH-tahs TYEH-neh ehn KAH-sah |
| Where do they sleep? | **¿Dónde duermen?**<br>DOHN-deh DWEHR-mehn |
| Where do they eat? | **¿Dónde comen?**<br>DOHN-deh KOH-mehn |
| Do you have chickens and roosters? | **¿Tiene gallinas y gallos?**<br>TYEH-neh gah-YEE-nahs ee GAH-yohs |
| Your animal is causing lots of problems in the neighborhood. | **Su animal causa muchos problemas en el vecindario.**<br>soo ah-nee-MAHL KAH-oo-sah MOO-chohs proh-BLEH-mahs ehn ehl beh-seen-DAH-ree-oh |
| It's destroying public property. | **Destruye la propiedad pública.**<br>deh-STROO-yeh lah proh-pyeh-THAHTH POO-blee-kah |

| | |
|---|---|
| Put the animal in ... | **Ponga el animal en...** POHN-gah ehl ah-nee-MAHL ehn |
| a cage | **una jaula** OO-nah HAH-oo-lah |
| a pen | **un corral** oon koh-RAHL |
| a doghouse | **una perrera** OO-nah peh-RREH-rah |
| Do you have a license for your animal? | **¿Tiene una licencia para su animal?** TYEH-neh OO-nah lee-SEHN-syah PAH-rah soo ah-nee-MAHL |
| Do you have a vaccination certificate for your animal? | **¿Tiene una vacuna para su animal?** TYEH-neh OO-nah bah-KOO-nah PAH-rah soo ah-nee-MAHL |
| Has your dog bitten anyone? | **¿Ha mordido a alguien su perro?** ah mohr-THEE-thoh ah AHL-gyehn soo PEH-rroh |
| Has your cat bitten anyone? | **¿Ha mordido a alguien su gato?** ah mohr-THEE-thoh ah AHL-gyehn soo GAH-toh |
| (*to a male*) What bit you? | **¿Qué lo mordió?** keh loh mohr-DYOH |
| (*to a female*) What bit you? | **¿Qué la mordió?** keh lah mohr-DYOH |
| A dog bit me. | **Un perro me mordió.** oon PEH-rroh meh mohr-DYOH |
| A cat bit me. | **Un gato me mordió.** oon GAH-toh meh mohr-DYOH |
| A rat bit me. | **Una rata me mordió.** OO-nah RRAH-tah meh mohr-DYOH |

| | |
|---|---|
| A person bit me. | **Una persona me mordió.**<br>OO-nah pehr-SOH-nah meh mohr-DYOH |
| I think your animal is sick. | **Pienso que su animal está enfermo.**<br>PYEHN-soh keh soo ah-nee-MAHL eh-STAH ehn-FEHR-moh |
| I think your animal is injured. | **Pienso que su animal está lastimado ~ herido.**<br>PYEHN-soh keh soo ah-nee-MAHL eh-STAH lah-stee-MAH-thoh ~ eh-REE-thoh |
| I think it has rabies. | **Pienso que tiene rabia.**<br>PYEHN-soh keh TYEH-neh RRAH-byah |
| It's neutered/castrated. | **Está castrado.**<br>eh-STAH kah-STRAH-thoh |
| It's not neutered/castrated. | **No está castrado.**<br>noh eh-STAH kah-STRAH-thoh |
| It's spayed. | **Está arreglada.**<br>eh-STAH ah-rreh-GLAH-thah<br>**Han sacado los ovarios.**<br>ahn sah-KAH-thoh lohs oh-BAH-ree-ohs |
| I'm taking your dog to the dog pound. | **Llevo a su perro a la perrera.**<br>YEH-boh ah soo PEH-rroh ah lah peh-RREH-rah<br>**Llevo a su perro al corralón.**<br>YEH-boh ah soo PEH-rroh ahl koh-rrah-LOHN |
| We are going to dispose of your animal. | **Vamos a disponer de su animal.**<br>BAH-mohs ah dee-spoh-NEHR deh soo ah-nee-MAHL |
| It's trapped. | **Está atrapado.**<br>eh-STAH ah-trah-PAH-thoh |

(*to a male*) What cruelty. I'm arresting you for abusing your pet.

**Qué crueldad. Lo arresto por abusar a su animal doméstico.**
keh kroo-ehl-DAHTH loh ah-RREH-stoh pohr ah-boo-SAHR ah soo ah-nee-MAHL doh-MEH-stee-koh

**Qué crueldad. Lo arresto por abusar a su mascota.**
keh kroo-ehl-DAHTH loh ah-RREH-stoh pohr ah-boo-SAHR ah soo mah-SKOH-tah

(*to a female*) What cruelty. I'm arresting you for abusing your pet.

**Qué crueldad. La arresto por abusar a su animal doméstico.**
keh kroo-ehl-DAHTH lah ah-RREH-stoh pohr ah-boo-SAHR ah soo ah-nee-MAHL doh-MEH-stee-koh

**Qué crueldad. La arresto por abusar a su mascota.**
keh kroo-ehl-DAHTH lah ah-RREH-stoh pohr ah-boo-SAHR ah soo mah-SKOH-tah

animal — **el animal**
ah-nee-MAHL

abused animal — **el animal abusado**
ah-nee-MAHL ah-boo-SAH-thoh

animal control — **el control de animales**
kohn-TROHL deh ah-nee-MAH-lehs

animal shelter — **el refugio de animales**
rreh-FOO-hee-oh deh ah-nee-MAH-lehs

tame animal — **el animal doméstico**
ah-nee-MAHL doh-MEH-stee-koh

wild animal — **el animal salvaje**
ah-nee-MAHL sahl-BAH-heh

**el animal silvestre**
ah-nee-MAHL seel-BEH-streh

| | |
|---|---|
| backpack | **la mochila**<br>moh-CHEE-lah |
| bear | **el oso**<br>OH-soh |
| beaver | **el castor**<br>kah-STOHR |
| bird | **el pájaro**<br>PAH-hah-roh |
| bobcat | **el lince**<br>LEEN-seh |
| | **el gato montés**<br>GAH-toh mohn-TEHS |
| bonfire | **la hoguera**<br>oh-GEH-rah |
| | **la lumbrada**<br>loom-BRAH-thah |
| buck | **el venado**<br>beh-NAH-thoh |
| bull | **el toro**<br>TOH-roh |
| burner | **el hornillo**<br>ohr-NEE-yoh |
| butane gas | **el gas butano**<br>gahs boo-TAH-noh |
| cage | **la jaula**<br>HAH-oo-lah |
| in a cage | **en una jaula**<br>ehn OO-nah HAH-oo-lah |
| campfire | **el fuego de campamento**<br>FWEH-goh deh kahm-pah-MEHN-toh |
| canary | **el canario**<br>kah-NAH-ree-oh |
| carp | **la carpa**<br>KAHR-pah |
| cat | **el gato**<br>GAH-toh |
| catfish | **el bagre**<br>BAH-greh |
| chicken | **el pollo**<br>POH-yoh |

| | |
|---|---|
| cords | **las cuerdas**<br>KWEHR-thahs |
| cow | **la vaca**<br>BAH-kah |
| coyote | **el coyote**<br>koh-YOH-teh |
| crab | **el cangrejo**<br>kahn-GREH-hoh |
| deer | **el ciervo**<br>SYEHR-boh |
| doe | **la cierva**<br>SYEHR-bah |
| dog | **el perro**<br>PEH-rroh |
| doghouse/dog pound | **la perrera**<br>peh-RREH-rah |
| donkey | **el burro**<br>BOO-rroh |
| drinking water | **el agua potable**<br>AH-gwah poh-TAH-bleh |
| duck | **el pato**<br>PAH-toh |
| eagle | **el águila**<br>AH-gee-lah |
| firewood | **la leña**<br>LEH-nyah |
| fish | |
| live fish | **el pez**<br>pehs |
| fish on a plate | **el pescado**<br>peh-SKAH-thoh |
| tropical fish | **los peces tropicales**<br>PEH-sehs troh-pee-KAH-lehs |
| fishing | **la pesca**<br>PEH-skah |
| fishing rod | **la caña de pesca**<br>KAH-nyah deh PEH-skah |
| fishing without a license | **la pesca sin licencia de pescar**<br>PEH-skah seen lee-SEHN-syah deh peh-SKAHR |

| | |
|---|---|
| harpoon/spear | **el arpón de pesca**<br>ahr-POHN deh PEH-skah |
| illegal fishing | **la pesca ilegal**<br>PEH-skah ee-leh-GAHL |
| fox | **el zorro**<br>SOH-rroh |
| frog | **la rana**<br>RRAH-nah |
| goat | **la cabra**<br>KAH-brah |
| goose | **el ganso**<br>GAHN-soh |
| hawk | **el halcón**<br>ahl-KOHN |
| hen | **la gallina**<br>gah-YEE-nah |
| hike | **la caminata**<br>kah-mee-NAH-tah |
| mountain hike | **la caminata en las montañas**<br>kah-mee-NAH-tah ehn lahs mohn-TAH-nyahs |
| horse | **el caballo**<br>kah-BAH-yoh |
| hunting | **la caza**<br>KAH-sah |
| hunting without a hunting license | **la caza sin licencia de cazar**<br>KAH-sah seen lee-SEHN-syah deh kah-SAHR |
| kitten | **el gatito**<br>gah-TEE-toh |
| lion | **el león**<br>leh-OHN |
| litter (*trash*) | **la basura**<br>bah-SOO-rah |
| lizard | **el lagarto**<br>lah-GAHR-toh |
| monkey | **el mono**<br>MOH-noh |
| mountain lion | **el puma**<br>POO-mah |
| mouse | **el ratón**<br>rrah-TOHN |

| | |
|---|---|
| parakeet | **el perico**<br>peh-REE-koh |
| parrot | **el loro**<br>LOH-roh |
| pet | **el animal doméstico**<br>ah-nee-MAHL doh-MEH-stee-koh |
| | **la mascota**<br>mah-SKOH-tah |
| pig | **el cerdo ~ el puerco**<br>SEHR-thoh ~ PWEHR-koh |
| wild pig | **el jabalí**<br>hah-bah-LEE |
| pigeon | **el pichón**<br>pee-CHOHN |
| poles | **las estacas**<br>eh-STAH-kahs |
| puppy | **el perrito**<br>peh-RREE-toh |
| quail | **la codorniz**<br>koh-thohr-NEES |
| rabbit | **el conejo**<br>koh-NEH-hoh |
| rabies | **la rabia**<br>RRAH-byah |
| rat | **la rata**<br>RRAH-tah |
| rattlesnake | **la serpiente de cascabel**<br>sehr-PYEHN-teh deh kah-skah-BEHL |
| rooster | **el gallo**<br>GAH-yoh |
| shark | **el tiburón**<br>tee-boo-ROHN |
| shots (*immunizations*) | **las vacunas**<br>bah-KOO-nahs |
| skunk | **el zorrillo**<br>soh-RREE-yoh |
| sleeping bag | **el saco para dormir**<br>SAH-koh PAH-rah dohr-MEER |

| | |
|---|---|
| snake | **la culebra**<br>koo-LEH-brah |
| | **la serpiente**<br>sehr-PYEHN-teh |
| poisonous snake | **la víbora**<br>BEE-boh-rah |
| spider | **la araña**<br>ah-RAH-nyah |
| black widow spider | **la araña viuda negra**<br>ah-RAH-nyah bee-OO-thah NEH-grah |
| squirrel | **la ardilla**<br>ahr-THEE-yah |
| tarantula | **la tarántula**<br>tah-RAHN-too-lah |
| tent | **la tienda de campamento**<br>TYEHN-dah deh kahm-pah-MEHN-toh |
| trail | **el sendero**<br>sehn-DEH-roh |
| trailer | **la caravana**<br>kah-rah-BAH-nah |
| | **el trailer**<br>TRAY-lehr |
| trap | **la trampa**<br>TRAHM-pah |
| trout | **la trucha**<br>TROO-chah |
| turkey | **el pavo ~ el guajolote**<br>PAH-boh ~ gwah-hoh-LOH-teh |
| turtle | **la tortuga**<br>tohr-TOO-gah |
| vaccination | **la vacuna**<br>bah-KOO-nah |
| It's vaccinated. | **Está vacunado.**<br>eh-STAH bah-koo-NAH-thoh |
| veterinarian | **el veterinario**<br>beh-teh-ree-NAH-ree-oh |
| wolf | **el lobo**<br>LOH-boh |

# DISPATCH
El despacho

Dispatch/communications is a vital link between citizens and the department! As you improve your language skills, you can prepare ahead for police, fire, and medical 9-1-1 calls. We include crimes and misdemeanors.

## Dispatcher Call Types
Los tipos de llamadas para
el despachador/la despachadora

| | |
|---|---|
| Do you want help from the police, the fire department, or an ambulance? | **¿Quiere ayuda de la policía, los bomberos o una ambulancia?**<br>KYEH-reh ah-YOO-thah deh lah poh-lee-SEE-ah lohs bohm-BEH-rohs oh OO-nah ahm-boo-LAHN-syah |
| Please speak in short, clear sentences. | **Por favor, hable con frases cortas y claras.**<br>pohr fah-BOHR AH-bleh kohn FRAH-sehs KOHR-tahs ee KLAH-rahs |
| (*to a male*) Wait a minute. I'm transferring you to someone who speaks Spanish. | **Espere un momento, lo estoy transfiriendo a alguien que habla español.**<br>eh-SPEH-reh oon moh-MEHN-toh loh eh-STOY trahns-fee-ree-EHN-doh ah AHL-gyehn keh AH-blah eh-spah-NYOHL |
| (*to a female*) Wait a minute. I'm transferring you to someone who speaks Spanish. | **Espere un momento, la estoy transfiriendo a alguien que habla español.**<br>eh-SPEH-reh oon moh-MEHN-toh lah eh-STOY trahns-fee-ree-EHN-doh ah AHL-gyehn keh AH-blah eh-spah-NYOHL |

| | |
|---|---|
| I'm sending an ambulance. | **Mando una ambulancia.**<br>MAHN-doh OO-nah ahm-boo-LAHN-syah |
| I'm sending a fire truck. | **Mando un camión de bomberos.**<br>MAHN-doh oon kah-MYOHN deh bohm-BEH-rohs |
| I'm sending a patrol car. | **Mando una patrulla.**<br>MAHN-doh OO-nah pah-TROO-yah |
| | **Mando un carro de patrulla.**<br>MAHN-doh oon KAH-rroh deh pah-TROO-yah |
| abandoned vehicle | **el vehículo abandonado**<br>beh-EE-koo-loh ah-bahn-doh-NAH-thoh |
| abuse | **el abuso**<br>ah-BOO-soh |
| animal abuse | **el abuso de animales**<br>ah-BOO-soh deh ah-nee-MAH-lehs |
| child abuse | **el abuso de niños**<br>ah-BOO-soh deh NEE-nyohs |
| | **el abuso de menores**<br>ah-BOO-soh deh meh-NOH-rehs |
| domestic abuse | **el abuso doméstico**<br>ah-BOO-soh doh-MEH-stee-koh |
| spousal abuse | **el abuso conyugal**<br>ah-BOO-soh kohn-yoo-GAHL |
| accident | **el accidente**<br>ahk-see-THEHN-teh |
| vehicle accident | **el accidente de vehículo**<br>ahk-see-THEHN-teh deh beh-EE-koo-loh |
| alarm | **la alarma**<br>ah-LAHR-mah |

animal

- animal abuse — **el abuso de animales** ah-BOO-soh deh ah-nee-MAH-lehs
- wild animal — **el animal salvaje** ah-nee-MAHL sahl-BAH-heh

allergic reaction — **la reacción alérgica** rreh-ahk-SYOHN ah-LEHR-hee-kah

arson — **el incendio premeditado** een-SEHN-dyoh preh-meh-thee-TAH-thoh

assassination — **el asesinato** ah-seh-see-NAH-toh

assault and battery — **el asalto y la agresión** ah-SAHL-toh ee lah ah-greh-SYOHN

assault with a weapon — **el asalto con arma** ah-SAHL-toh kohn AHR-mah

auto theft — **el robo de un carro** RROH-boh deh oon KAH-rroh

bike stolen — **la bicicleta robada** bee-see-KLEH-tah rroh-BAH-thah

birth (*delivery*) — **el parto de un bebé** PAHR-toh deh oon beh-BEH

bite — **la mordedura** mohr-theh-THOO-rah

body (dead) — **el cadáver** kah-THAH-behr

**la persona muerta** pehr-SOH-nah MWEHR-tah

bomb — **la bomba** BOHM-bah

- bomb found — **la bomba hallada** BOHM-bah ah-YAH-thah
- bomb threat — **la amenaza de bomba** ah-meh-NAH-sah deh BOHM-bah

| | |
|---|---|
| breathe | **respirar**<br>rreh-spee-RAHR |
| difficulty breathing | **la dificultad respirando**<br>dee-fee-kool-TAHTH<br>rreh-spee-RAHN-doh |
| bribery | **el soborno**<br>soh-BOHR-noh |
| burglary | **el robo ~ el hurto**<br>RROH-boh ~ OOR-toh |
| burn | **la quemadura**<br>keh-mah-THOO-rah |
| car | **el carro**<br>KAH-rroh |
| car stolen/carjacking | **el carro robado**<br>KAH-rroh rroh-BAH-thoh |
| cars dragging | **la carrera de carros**<br>kah-RREH-rah deh KAH-rrohs |
| child/minor | **el niño ~ el menor**<br>NEE-nyoh ~ meh-NOHR |
| child abuse | **el abuso de niños**<br>ah-BOO-soh deh NEE-nyohs |
| | **el abuso de menores**<br>ah-BOO-soh deh<br>meh-NOH-rehs |
| child found | **el niño hallado**<br>NEE-nyoh ah-YAH-thoh |
| child missing | **el niño perdido**<br>NEE-nyoh pehr-THEE-thoh |
| child neglect | **el descuido de niños**<br>dehs-KWEE-thoh deh<br>NEE-nyohs |
| | **el descuido de menores**<br>dehs-KWEE-thoh deh<br>meh-NOH-rehs |
| choking person | **la persona sofocando ~ la persona asfixiando**<br>pehr-SOH-nah<br>soh-foh-KAHN-doh ~<br>pehr-SOH-nah<br>ahs-feek-SYAHN-doh |

| | |
|---|---|
| crazy person | **la persona loca**<br>pehr-SOH-nah LOH-kah |
| cruelty to animals | **la crueldad a animales**<br>kroo-ehl-DAHTH ah ah-nee-MAH-lehs |
| dead person | **el cadáver**<br>kah-THAH-behr |
| | **la persona muerta**<br>pehr-SOH-nah MWEHR-tah |
| delinquency | **la delincuencia**<br>deh-leen-KWEHN-syah |
| diabetes | **la diabetes**<br>dee-ah-BEH-tehs |
| disorderly conduct | **el desorden público**<br>dehs-OHR-thehn POO-blee-koh |
| dog | **el perro**<br>PEH-rroh |
| lost dog | **el perro perdido**<br>PEH-rroh pehr-THEE-thoh |
| domestic abuse | **el abuso doméstico**<br>ah-BOO-soh doh-MEH-stee-koh |
| domestic violence | **la violencia doméstica**<br>bee-oh-LEHN-syah doh-MEH-stee-kah |
| drive-by shooting | **el tiroteo de un carro en marcha**<br>tee-roh-TEH-oh deh oon KAH-rroh ehn MAHR-chah |
| drown | **ahogarse**<br>ah-oh-GAHR-seh |
| He's/She's drowning (in the pool). | **Se está ahogando (en la piscina).**<br>seh eh-STAH ah-oh-GAHN-doh (ehn lah pee-SEE-nah) |
| drunk (person) in public | **(la persona) borracha en público**<br>(pehr-SOH-nah) boh-RRAH-chah ehn POO-blee-koh |

| | |
|---|---|
| elevator | **el ascensor ~ el elevador**<br>ah-sehn-SOHR ~<br>eh-leh-bah-THOHR |
| stopped elevator | **el ascensor parado ~ el elevador parado**<br>ah-sehn-SOHR pah-RAH-thoh ~ eh-leh-bah-THOHR pah-RAH-thoh |
| explosion | **la explosión**<br>ehks-ploh-SYOHN |
| fall | **la caída**<br>kah-EE-thah |
| family dispute | **el argumento entre familiares**<br>ahr-goo-MEHN-toh EHN-treh fah-mee-lee-AH-rehs |
| fight | **la pelea**<br>peh-LEH-ah |
| find | **hallar**<br>ah-YAHR |
| found child | **el niño hallado**<br>NEE-nyoh ah-YAH-thoh |
| found person | **la persona hallada**<br>pehr-SOH-nah ah-YAH-thah |
| fire in … | **el fuego en…**<br>FWEH-goh ehn |
| grass | **la hierba**<br>YEHR-bah |
| rubbish/trash | **la basura**<br>bah-SOO-rah |
| structure/building | **el edificio**<br>eh-dee-FEE-syoh |
| vehicle | **el vehículo**<br>beh-EE-koo-loh |
| flood | **la inundación**<br>een-oon-dah-SYOHN |
| gambling | **el juego**<br>HWEH-goh |
| gas leak | **la fuga de gas**<br>FOO-gah deh gahs |

| | |
|---|---|
| graffiti | **el graffiti ~ el grafiti**<br>grah-FEE-tee |
| gunshot victim | **la víctima herida de bala**<br>BEEK-tee-mah eh-REE-thah deh BAH-lah |
| HAZMAT | **los materiales peligrosos**<br>mah-teh-ree-AH-lehs peh-lee-GROH-sohs |
| heart attack | **el ataque al corazón**<br>ah-TAH-keh ahl koh-rah-SOHN |
| hijacking | **el secuestro**<br>seh-KWEH-stroh |
| holdup | **el atraco ~ el asalto**<br>ah-TRAH-koh ~ ah-SAHL-toh |
| home invasion | **la invasión del hogar**<br>een-bah-SYOHN dehl oh-GAHR |
| hostage | **el rehén**<br>rreh-EHN |
| illegal entry | **la entrada sin permiso**<br>ehn-TRAH-thah seen pehr-MEE-soh |
| indecent exposure (public) | **la persona sin ropa en público**<br>pehr-SOH-nah seen RROH-pah ehn POO-blee-koh |
| injury | **la herida**<br>eh-REE-thah |
| back injury | **la herida de espalda**<br>eh-REE-thah deh eh-SPAHL-dah |
| neck injury | **la herida de cuello**<br>eh-REE-thah deh KWEH-yoh |
| keys | **las llaves**<br>YAH-behs |
| lost keys | **las llaves perdidas**<br>YAH-behs pehr-THEE-thahs |
| kidnapping | **el secuestro**<br>seh-KWEH-stroh |
| larceny | **el hurto**<br>OOR-toh |
| lights out | **las luces apagadas**<br>LOO-sehs ah-pah-GAH-thahs |

| | |
|---|---|
| locked door | **la puerta cerrada con llave** PWEHR-tah seh-RRAH-thah kohn YAH-beh |
| lost property | **los objetos personales perdidos** ohb-HEH-tohs pehr-soh-NAH-lehs pehr-THEE-thohs |
| loud party | **la fiesta con mucho ruido** FYEH-stah kohn MOO-choh roo-EE-thoh |
| mentally ill person | **la persona loca** pehr-SOH-nah LOH-kah |
| missing child | **el niño perdido** NEE-nyoh pehr-THEE-thoh |
| missing person | **la persona perdida** pehr-SOH-nah pehr-THEE-thah |
| murder | **el homicidio ~ el asesinato** oh-mee-SEE-dyoh ~ ah-seh-see-NAH-toh |
| music disturbance | **la música molestando** MOO-see-kah moh-leh-STAHN-doh |
| narcotics violation | **la violación de narcóticos** bee-oh-lah-SYOHN deh nahr-KOH-tee-kohs |
| obscene phone call | **la llamada obscena** yah-MAH-thah ohb-SEH-nah |
| overdose (drug) | **la sobredosis (de drogas)** soh-breh-THOH-sees (deh DROH-gahs) |
| package | **el paquete** pah-KEH-teh |
| mysterious package | **el paquete misterioso** pah-KEH-teh mee-steh-ree-OH-soh |
| pain | |
| abdominal pain | **el dolor de estómago** doh-LOHR deh eh-STOH-mah-goh |
| chest pain | **el dolor de pecho** doh-LOHR deh PEH-choh |

|  |  |
|---|---|
| person | |
| person found | **la persona hallada**<br>pehr-SOH-nah ah-YAH-thah |
| person missing | **la persona perdida**<br>pehr-SOH-nah pehr-THEE-thah |
| poison | **el veneno**<br>beh-NEH-noh |
| poisoning | **el envenenamiento**<br>ehn-beh-neh-nah-MYEHN-toh |
| rape | **la violación**<br>bee-oh-lah-SYOHN |
| restraining order violation | **la violación de una orden de restricción**<br>bee-oh-lah-SYOHN deh OO-nah OHR-thehn deh rreh-streek-SYOHN |
| riot | **el motín ~ el alboroto**<br>moh-TEEN ~ ahl-boh-ROH-toh |
| robbery | **el robo ~ el hurto**<br>RROH-boh ~ OOR-toh |
| seizure(s)/convulsions | **las convulsiones**<br>kohn-bool-SYOH-nehs |
| sexual assault | **el asalto sexual**<br>ah-SAHL-toh sehk-SWAHL |
| shock | **el choque**<br>CHOH-keh |
| electrical shock | **el choque eléctrico**<br>CHOH-keh eh-LEHK-tree-koh |
| nervous shock | **el choque de nervios**<br>CHOH-keh deh NEHR-byohs |
| shooters (people firing weapons) | **las personas disparando armas**<br>pehr-SOH-nahs dee-spah-RAHN-doh AHR-mahs |
| shots fired | **los disparos ~ el tiroteo**<br>dee-SPAH-rohs ~ tee-roh-TEH-oh |
| smoke | **el humo**<br>OO-moh |

|  |  |
|---|---|
| spousal abuse | **el abuso conyugal**<br>ah-BOO-soh kohn-yoo-GAHL |
| stabbed person | **la persona puñalada**<br>pehr-SOH-nah<br>poo-nyah-LAH-thah |
| sting | **la picadura**<br>pee-kah-THOO-rah |
| street light out | **la luz de la calle apagada**<br>loos deh lah KAH-yeh<br>ah-pah-GAH-thah |
| stroke | **la embolia ~**<br>**el ataque del cerebro**<br>ehm-BOH-lee-ah ~<br>ah-TAH-keh dehl seh-REH-broh |
| suffocation | **la sofocación**<br>soh-foh-kah-SYOHN |
| suicide | **el suicidio**<br>soo-ee-SEE-dyoh |
| suicidal subject | **la persona pensando**<br>**en suicidarse**<br>pehr-SOH-nah pehn-SAHN-doh<br>ehn soo-ee-see-THAHR-seh |
| suspicious package | **el paquete sospechoso**<br>pah-KEH-teh<br>soh-speh-CHOH-soh |
| suspicious subject | **la persona sospechosa**<br>pehr-SOH-nah<br>soh-speh-CHOH-sah |
| terrorist threat | **la amenaza de terrorismo**<br>ah-meh-NAH-sah deh<br>teh-rroh-REEZ-moh |
| theft | **el robo ~ el hurto**<br>RROH-boh ~ OOR-toh |
| threatening phone call | **la llamada amenazando**<br>yah-MAH-thah<br>ah-meh-nah-SAHN-doh |
| traffic collision | **el choque de tráfico**<br>CHOH-keh deh TRAH-fee-koh |
| train | **el tren**<br>trehn |
| trauma | **el trauma**<br>TRAH-oo-mah |

| | |
|---|---|
| trespassing | **la entrada sin permiso**<br>ehn-TRAH-thah seen pehr-MEE-soh |
| unconscious person | **la persona perdiendo el conocimiento**<br>pehr-SOH-nah pehr-DYEHN-doh ehl koh-noh-see-MYEHN-toh |
| vagrancy | **la vagancia**<br>bah-GAHN-syah |
| vandalism | **el vandalismo**<br>bahn-dah-LEEZ-moh |

## Scenario · DISPATCHER CALL

Una llamada para el despachador

Time is of the essence when identifying, categorizing, and responding to fire, medical, or police calls. Keep it short and simple. Brevity saves lives. Follow-up questions are omitted. Medical questions may involve liability issues.

| | |
|---|---|
| What are you reporting? | **¿Qué está reportando?** |
| Where is it happening? | **¿Dónde está pasando?** |
| When did it happen? | **¿Cuándo pasó?** |
| Where are you now? | **¿Dónde está ahorita?** |
| (What's your) phone number? | **¿(Cuál es su) número de teléfono?** |
| (What's your) complete name? | **¿(Cuál es su) nombre completo?** |
| (Any) weapons? | **¿(Hay) armas?** |
| Suspect description. (*male*) | **La descripción del sospechoso.** |
| Suspect description. (*female*) | **La descripción de la sospechosa.** |
| Vehicle description. | **La descripción del vehículo.** |
| What direction were they heading? | **¿En qué dirección iban?** |

| | |
|---|---|
| (*to a male*) Don't worry. We're going to help you. | **No se preocupe. Vamos a ayudarlo.** |
| (*to a female*) Don't worry. We're going to help you. | **No se preocupe. Vamos a ayudarla.** |
| They're coming right away. | **Vienen en seguida.** |
| They're on their way. | **Están en camino.** |
| Don't hang up, please. | **No cuelgue, por favor.** |
| Stay with me. | **Quédese conmigo.** |

## MEDICAL CARE AND EMERGENCY TOOLS

### Cuidado médico y las herramientas de emergencia

Here are useful expressions in medical emergencies before the paramedics arrive.

| | |
|---|---|
| Do you have a medical problem? | **¿Tiene un problema médico?**<br>TYEH-neh oon proh-BLEH-mah MEH-thee-koh |
| Where does it hurt? | **¿Dónde le duele?**<br>DOHN-deh leh DWEH-leh |
| Do you have pain? | **¿Tiene dolor?**<br>TYEH-neh doh-LOHR |
| Do you need a doctor? | **¿Necesita un doctor?**<br>neh-seh-SEE-tah oon dohk-TOHR |
| Do you need an ambulance? | **¿Necesita una ambulancia?**<br>neh-seh-SEE-tah OO-nah ahm-boo-LAHN-syah |
| Are you taking medicine? | **¿Toma medicina?**<br>TOH-mah meh-thee-SEE-nah |
| ache | **el dolor**<br>doh-LOHR |
| backache | **el dolor de espalda**<br>doh-LOHR deh eh-SPAHL-dah |
| headache | **el dolor de cabeza**<br>doh-LOHR deh kah-BEH-sah |

| | |
|---|---|
| anxiety attack | **el ataque de ansiedad** ah-TAH-keh deh ahn-syeh-THAHTH |
| assault | **un asalto** ah-SAHL-toh |
| attack | **el ataque** ah-TAH-keh |
| anxiety attack | **el ataque de ansiedad** ah-TAH-keh deh ahn-syeh-THAHTH |
| heart attack | **el ataque al corazón ~ el ataque cardíaco** ah-TAH-keh ahl koh-rah-SOHN ~ ah-TAH-keh kahr-THEE-ah-koh |
| nervous attack | **el ataque de nervios** ah-TAH-keh deh NEHR-byohs |
| Band-Aid | **la curita** koo-REE-tah |
| bandage | **el vendaje ~ la venda** behn-DAH-heh ~ BEHN-dah |
| bite | **la mordedura** mohr-theh-THOO-rah |
| animal bite | **la mordedura de animales** mohr-theh-THOO-rah deh ah-nee-MAH-lehs |
| blanket | **la cobija ~ la manta** koh-BEE-hah ~ MAHN-tah |
| bone | **el hueso** HWEH-soh |
| broken bone | **el hueso roto ~ el hueso quebrado** HWEH-soh RROH-toh ~ HWEH-soh keh-BRAH-thoh |
| breathing problems | **los problemas de respiración** proh-BLEH-mahs deh rreh-spee-rah-SYOHN |
| bruise | **el moretón** moh-reh-TOHN |
| burn | **la quemadura** keh-mah-THOO-rah |

| | |
|---|---|
| burned | **quemado[a]**<br>keh-MAH-thoh[-thah] |
| chest pain | **el dolor de pecho**<br>doh-LOHR deh PEH-choh |
| choking | **sofocante ~ asfixiante**<br>soh-foh-KAHN-teh ~<br>ahs-feek-SYAHN-teh |
| convulsions/seizure(s) | **las convulsiones**<br>kohn-bool-SYOH-nehs |
| CPR | **la resucitación cardiopulmonar**<br>rreh-soo-see-tah-SYOHN<br>kahr-dyoh-pool-moh-NAHR |
| cut | **la cortada**<br>kohr-TAH-thah |
| cut | **cortado[a]**<br>kohr-tah-THOH[-thah] |
| knife gash | **la cuchillada**<br>koo-chee-YAH-thah |
| dislocation | **la dislocación**<br>dees-loh-kah-SYOHN |
| dizziness | **el mareo**<br>mah-REH-oh |
| dizzy | **mareado[a]**<br>mah-reh-AH-thoh[-thah] |
| drown | **ahogarse**<br>ah-oh-GAHR-seh |
| He's/She's drowning. | **Se está ahogando.**<br>seh eh-STAH ah-oh-GAHN-doh |
| He/She drowned. | **Se ahogó.**<br>seh ah-oh-GOH |
| epilepsy | **la epilepsia**<br>eh-pee-LEHP-syah |
| epileptic | **epiléptico[a]**<br>eh-pee-LEHP-tee-koh[-kah] |
| exhaustion | **el agotamiento**<br>ah-goh-tah-MYEHN-toh |
| fainting | **el desmayo**<br>dehs-MAH-yoh |
| fall | **la caída**<br>kah-EE-thah |

| | |
|---|---|
| first aid kit | **el botiquín (de primeros auxilios)**<br>boh-tee-KEEN<br>(deh pree-MEH-rohs<br>ah-ook-SEE-lee-ohs) |
| fracture | **la fractura**<br>frahk-TOO-rah |
| fractured | **fracturado[a]**<br>frahk-too-RAH-thoh[-thah] |
| gash (knife) | **la cuchillada**<br>koo-chee-YAH-thah |
| gloves | **los guantes**<br>GWAHN-tehs |
| gunshot wound | **la herida de bala**<br>eh-REE-thah deh BAH-lah |
| heart attack | **el ataque al corazón**<br>ah-TAH-keh ahl koh-rah-SOHN<br>**el ataque cardíaco**<br>ah-TAH-keh kahr-THEE-ah-koh |
| heart disease | **la enfermedad del corazón**<br>ehn-fehr-meh-THAHTH<br>dehl koh-rah-SOHN |
| hyperventilation | **la hiperventilación**<br>ee-pehr-behn-tee-lah-SYOHN<br>**el ataque de ansiedad**<br>ah-TAH-keh deh<br>ahn-syeh-THAHTH |
| infection | **la infección**<br>een-fehk-SYOHN |
| injury | **la herida**<br>eh-REE-thah |
| insulin | **la insulina**<br>een-soo-LEE-nah |
| laceration | **la laceración**<br>lah-seh-rah-SYOHN |
| medical problems | **los problemas médicos**<br>proh-BLEH-mahs<br>MEH-thee-kohs |
| medication | **el medicamento**<br>meh-thee-kah-MEHN-toh |

**El choque** ("shock") has nothing to do with "to choke," **sofocar** or **asfixiar**. See "False Friends" on pp. 277–278.

| | |
|---|---|
| medicine | **la medicina**<br>meh-thee-SEE-nah |
| nervous attack | **el ataque de nervios**<br>ah-TAH-que deh NEHR-byohs |
| overdose | **la sobredosis**<br>soh-breh-THOH-sees |
| pain | **el dolor**<br>doh-LOHR |
| poison | **el veneno**<br>beh-NEH-noh |
| poisoned | **envenenado[a]**<br>ehn-beh-neh-NAH-thoh[-thah] |
| poisoning | **el envenenamiento**<br>ehn-beh-neh-nah-MYEHN-toh |
| puncture | **la perforación**<br>pehr-foh-rah-SYOHN |
| rope | **la cuerda**<br>KWEHR-thah |
| run over | **atropellado[a]**<br>ah-troh-peh-YAH-thoh[-thah] |
| scrape/scratch | **el rasguño**<br>rrahs-GOO-nyoh |
| seizure(s)/convulsions | **las convulsiones**<br>kohn-bool-SYOH-nehs |
| shock (trauma) | **el choque**<br>CHOH-keh |
| shooting | **el tiroteo**<br>tee-roh-TEH-oh |
| shot | **balaceado[a]**<br>bah-lah-seh-AH-thoh[-thah] |
| sprain | **la torcedura**<br>tohr-seh-THOO-rah |
| sprained/twisted | **torcido[a]**<br>tohr-SEE-thoh[-thah] |

| | |
|---|---|
| sting | **la picadura**<br>pee-kah-THOO-rah |
| bee stings | **las picaduras de abejas**<br>pee-kah-THOO-rahs deh ah-BEH-hahs |
| strangulation | **la estrangulación**<br>eh-strahn-goo-lah-SYOHN |
| stress | **el estrés**<br>eh-STREHS |
| stroke | **la embolia ~ el ataque del cerebro**<br>ehm-BOH-lee-ah ~ ah-TAH-keh dehl seh-REH-broh |
| sunburn | **la quemadura del sol**<br>keh-mah-THOO-rah dehl sohl |
| sunstroke | **la insolación ~ demasiado sol**<br>een-soh-lah-SYOHN ~ deh-mah-SYAH-thoh sohl |
| swelling | **la hinchazón**<br>een-chah-SOHN |
| swollen | **hinchado[a]**<br>een-CHAH-thoh[-thah] |
| tape | **la cinta**<br>SEEN-tah |
| toolbox | **la caja de herramientas**<br>KAH-hah deh eh-rrah-MYEHN-tahs |
| tourniquet | **el torniquete**<br>tohr-nee-KEH-teh |
| trauma | **el trauma**<br>TRAH-oo-mah |
| unconsciousness | **la inconsciencia**<br>een-kohn-SYEHN-syah |
| venereal disease | **la enfermedad venérea**<br>ehn-fehr-meh-THAHTH beh-NEH-reh-ah |
| wound | **la herida**<br>eh-REE-thah |

# Law Enforcement Commands and Key Questions and Statements

## COMMANDS
Los mandatos

As a police officer, you give commands telling people what to do and what not to do. Over the years, we have developed a unique way of presenting commands logically. High-level commands are divided into three groups: quickie, E, and A commands.

Quickie commands are very short: a word or two. E and A commands are formed from action words (verbs). You will find many of these commands in scenarios in Chapter 4.

## Quickie Commands
Los mandatos rápidos

Quickie commands are short and to the point. They are "power" words expressing complete actions, like **¡Atrás!** ("(Get) back!").

against — **contra**
KOHN-trah

Against the wall. — **Contra la pared.**
KOHN-trah lah pah-REHTH

ankles — **tobillos**
toh-BEE-yohs

Ankles together. — **Tobillos juntos.**
toh-BEE-yohs HOON-tohs

If an English expression has two or more equivalent forms in Spanish, they are separated by a "~".

Enough. **Basta. ~ Bastante.**

| | |
|---|---|
| arm(s) | **brazo(s)**<br>BRAH-soh(s) |
| Arms extended. | **Brazos extendidos.**<br>BRAH-sohs ehks-tehn-DEE-thohs |
| Arm extended to forehead. | **Brazo extendido a la frente.**<br>BRAH-soh ehks-tehn-DEE-thoh ah lah FREHN-teh |
| Arms out. | **Brazos afuera.**<br>BRAH-sohs ah-FWEH-rah |
| Attention, please. | **Atención, por favor.**<br>ah-tehn-SYOHN pohr fah-BOHR |
| Back. | **Atrás.**<br>ah-TRAHS |
| Everybody back. | **Todos atrás.**<br>TOH-thohs ah-TRAHS |
| Careful. | **Cuidado.**<br>kwee-THAH-thoh |
| Down. | **Abajo.**<br>ah-BAH-hoh |
| Enough. | **Basta. ~ Bastante.**<br>BAH-stah ~ bah-STAHN-teh |
| eye(s) | **ojo(s)**<br>OH-hoh(s) |
| Eyes closed. | **Ojos cerrados.**<br>OH-hohs seh-RRAH-thohs |
| Look out! | **Ojo.**<br>OH-hoh |
| face | **cara**<br>KAH-rah |
| Face the wall. | **Cara a la pared.**<br>KAH-rah ah lah pah-RETH |

Some commands use words that end in **-o** for males and **-a** for females. For two or more persons (plural), add **-s**.

| | |
|---|---|
| (*to one male*) Freeze. | **Quieto.** |
| (*to more than one male*) Freeze. | **Quietos.** |
| (*to one female*) Freeze. | **Quieta.** |
| (*to more than one female*) Freeze. | **Quietas.** |

| | |
|---|---|
| Fast. | **Rápido. ~ Pronto.**<br>RRAH-pee-thoh ~ PROHN-toh |
| finger | **el dedo**<br>DEH-thoh |
| Index finger up. | **Dedo índice para arriba.**<br>DEH-thoh EEN-dee-seh PAH-rah ah-RREE-bah |
| foot | **el pie**<br>pyeh |
| Feet together. | **Pies juntos.**<br>pyehs HOON-tohs |
| On your feet. | **De pie.**<br>deh pyeh |
| floor | **piso ~ suelo**<br>PEE-soh ~ SWEH-loh |
| On the floor. | **Al piso. ~ Al suelo.**<br>ahl PEE-soh ~ ahl SWEH-loh |
| | **En el piso. ~ En el suelo.**<br>ehn ehl PEE-soh ~ ehn ehl SWEH-loh |
| On the floor, face down. | **En el suelo, boca abajo.**<br>ehn ehl SWEH-loh BOH-kah ah-BAH-hoh |
| On the floor, face up. | **En el suelo, boca arriba.**<br>ehn ehl SWEH-loh BOH-kah ah-RREE-bah |
| Forward. | **Adelante.**<br>ah-deh-LAHN-teh |
| Freeze. | **Quieto. / Quieta.**<br>KYEH-toh / KYEH-tah |

| | |
|---|---|
| Get going. (*to one person*) | **Ándele.**<br>AHN-deh-leh |
| Get going. (*to more than one person*) | **Ándenle.**<br>AHN-dehn-leh |
| Get going, guys! | **Ándenle, muchachos.**<br>AHN-dehn-leh moo-CHAH-chohs |
| ground | **piso ~ suelo**<br>PEE-soh ~ SWEH-loh |
| On the ground. | **Al piso. ~ Al suelo.**<br>ahl PEE-soh ~ ahl SWEH-loh |
| | **En el piso. ~ En el suelo.**<br>ehn ehl PEE-soh ~ ehn ehl SWEH-loh |
| On the ground, face down. | **En el suelo, boca abajo.**<br>ehn ehl SWEH-loh BOH-kah ah-BAH-hoh |
| On the ground, face up. | **En el suelo, boca arriba.**<br>ehn ehl SWEH-loh BOH-kah ah-RREE-bah |
| hand(s) | **mano(s)**<br>MAH-noh(s) |
| Hands at your sides. | **Manos al lado del cuerpo.**<br>MAH-nohs ahl LAH-thoh dehl KWEHR-poh |
| Hands behind you. | **Manos detrás de usted.**<br>MAH-nohs deh-TRAHS deh oo-STEHTH |
| Hand(s) down. | **Mano(s) abajo.**<br>MAH-noh(s) ah-BAH-hoh |
| Hands in sight. | **Manos a la vista.**<br>MAH-nohs ah lah BEE-stah |
| Hands on the ground. | **Manos en el suelo.**<br>MAH-nohs ehn ehl SWEH-loh |
| Hands on the steering wheel. | **Manos en el volante.**<br>MAH-nohs ehn ehl boh-LAHN-teh |
| Hands on the wall. | **Manos en la pared.**<br>MAH-nohs ehn lah pah-REHTH |
| Hands on top of the car. | **Manos encima del carro.**<br>MAH-nohs ehn-SEE-mah dehl KAH-rroh |

| | |
|---|---|
| Hands out of your pockets. | **Manos afuera de los bolsillos.** MAH-nohs ah-FWEH-rah deh lohs bohl-SEE-yohs |
| Hands together. | **Manos juntas.** MAH-nohs HOON-tahs |
| Hands up. | **Manos arriba.** MAH-nohs ah-RREE-bah |
| Hands with your palms up. | **Manos con las palmas arriba.** MAH-nohs kohn lahs PAHL-mahs ah-RREE-bah |
| head | **cabeza** kah-BEH-sah |
| Head (tilted) back. | **Cabeza para atrás.** kah-BEH-sah PAH-rah ah-TRAHS |
| heel | **tacón** tah-KOHN |
| Heel of right foot to toe of left foot. | **Tacón del pie derecho enfrente del pie izquierdo.** tah-KOHN dehl pyeh deh-REH-choh ehn-FREHN-teh dehl pyeh ees-KYEHR-thoh |
| Immediately. | **De inmediato. ~ Inmediatamente.** deh een-meh-DYAH-toh ~ een-meh-dyah-tah-MEHN-teh |
| Inside. | **Adentro.** ah-DEHN-troh |
| knees | **rodillas** rroh-THEE-yahs |
| On your knees. | **De rodillas.** deh rroh-THEE-yahs |
| left | **la izquierda** ees-KYEHR-thah |
| To the left. | **A la izquierda.** ah lah ees-KYEHR-thah |
| left foot | **el pie izquierdo** pyeh ees-KYEHR-thoh |
| left knee | **la rodilla izquierda** rroh-THEE-yah ees-KYEHR-thah |
| Look out! | **Ojo.** OH-hoh |

|  |  |
|---|---|
| Outside. | **Fuera. ~ Afuera.**<br>FWEH-rah ~ ah-FWEH-rah |
| Everybody out(side). | **Todos fuera. ~ Todos afuera.**<br>TOH-thohs FWEH-rah ~<br>TOH-thohs ah-FWEH-rah |
| palms | **las palmas**<br>PAHL-mahs |
| Palms in sight. | **Palmas a la vista.**<br>PAHL-mahs ah lah BEE-stah |
| Palms together. | **Palmas juntas.**<br>PAHL-mahs HOON-tahs |
| Palms up. | **Palmas arriba.**<br>PAHL-mahs ah-RREE-bah |
| Quick. | **Rápido. ~ Pronto.**<br>RRAH-pee-thoh ~ PROHN-toh |
| right | **la derecha**<br>deh-REH-chah |
| To the right. | **A la derecha.**<br>ah lah deh-REH-chah |
| right foot | **el pie derecho**<br>pyeh deh-REH-choh |
| right knee | **la rodilla derecha**<br>rroh-THEE-yah deh-REH-chah |
| Right now. | **Ahora mismo. ~ Ahorita. ~ Ya.**<br>ah-OH-rah MEEZ-moh ~<br>ah-oh-REE-tah ~ yah |
| Silence. | **Silencio.**<br>see-LEHN-syoh |
| Slow./Slowly. | **Despacio. ~ Lentamente.**<br>deh-SPAH-syoh ~<br>lehn-tah-MEHN-teh |
| Stop. | **Alto.**<br>AHL-toh |
| Stop ahead. | **Alto adelante.**<br>AHL-toh ah-theh-LAHN-teh |
| Stop—police. | **Alto—policía.**<br>AHL-toh poh-lee-SEE-ah |
| straight | **derecho ~ recto**<br>deh-REH-choh ~ RREHK-toh |

| | |
|---|---|
| Straight ahead. | **Derecho ~ Recto.**<br>deh-REH-choh ~ RREHK-toh |
| Straight line, hands at sides. | **Línea derecha, manos al lado.**<br>LEE-neh-ah deh-REH-chah MAH-nohs ahl LAH-thoh<br>**Línea recta, manos al lado.**<br>LEE-neh-ah REHK-tah MAH-nohs ahl LAH-thoh |

## E Commands
### Los mandatos con E

To form E commands, remove the **-ar** ending from the dictionary form (infinitive): **habl*ar*** ("to speak") → **habl-**. Then add **-e**: **habl-** + **-e** → **Hable** ("Speak"). When addressing two or more persons, add **-en**: **Hablen** ("(You all) speak"). To say "don't," add **no**: **No hable** ("Don't speak").

| | |
|---|---|
| Abandon. | **Abandone.**<br>ah-bahn-DOH-neh |
| Everyone abandon the premises immediately. | **Abandonen el lugar todos de inmediato.** |
| alert | |
| Be alert. | **Esté alerta.**<br>eh-STEH ah-LEHR-tah |
| Answer. | **Conteste.**<br>kohn-TEH-steh |
| Answer the question. | **Conteste la pregunta.** |
| Answer yes or no. | **Conteste sí o no.** |

☞ *See also* Answer/**Responda** *on p. 204.*

| | |
|---|---|
| arrest | |
| You're under arrest. | **Dése preso[a].**<br>DEH-seh PREH-soh[-sah] |
| Back up. | **Regrese.**<br>rreh-GREH-seh |
| Back up slowly. | **Regrese despacio.** |
| Be alert. | **Esté alerta.**<br>eh-STEH ah-LEHR-tah |

| | |
|---|---|
| Be ready. | **Esté listo[a].** eh-STEH LEE-stoh[-stah] |
| Bend. | **Doble.** DOH-bleh |
| Bend your knees. | **Doble las rodillas.** |
| Bend over. | **Agáchese.** ah-GAH-cheh-seh |
| Bend over near the floor. | **Agáchese cerca del piso. ~ Agáchese cerca del suelo.** |
| Break it up. | **Dispérsese.** dee-SPEHR-seh-seh |
| Break it up, all of you. | **Dispérsense todos.** |
| Breathe. | **Respire.** rreh-SPEE-reh |
| Breathe deeply. | **Respire profundo.** |
| Breathe normally. | **Respire normalmente.** |
| Call. | **Llame.** YAH-meh |
| Call 9-1-1. | **Llame al nueve-uno-uno.** |
| Call an ambulance. | **Llame una ambulancia.** |
| Call off. | **Llame.** |
| Call off the dog. | **Llame al perro.** |
| Calm down./Keep calm. | **Cálmese.** KAHL-meh-seh |
| Check. (inspect) | **Revise.** rreh-BEE-seh |
| Check it out. | **Revíselo.** |
| Check the license. | **Revise la licencia.** |
| Check. (test) | **Compruebe. ~ Pruebe.** kohm-proo-EH-beh ~ proo-EH-beh |
| Check the tires. | **Compruebe las llantas. ~ Pruebe las llantas.** |
| Check. (verify) | **Verifique.** beh-ree-FEE-keh |
| Check the license. | **Verifique la licencia.** |

| | |
|---|---|
| Clean. | **Limpie.**<br>LEEM-pyeh |
| Clean the license plate. | **Limpie la placa.** |
| Clean your hands. | **Límpiese las manos.** |
| Close. | **Cierre.**<br>SYEH-rreh |
| Close the door with your foot. | **Cierre la puerta con un pie.** |
| Close your eyes. | **Cierre los ojos.** |
| Close your mouth. | **Cierre la boca.** |
| Count. | **Cuente.**<br>KWEHN-teh |
| Count backwards from 10 to 1. | **Cuente para atrás de diez hasta uno.** |
| Cover. | **Tape.**<br>TAH-peh |
| Cover your mouth and nose. | **Tápese la boca y la nariz.** |
| Cover yourself. | **Tápese.** |
| Cover yourself with a blanket. | **Tápese con una manta.**<br>**Tápese con una cobija.** |

☞ *See also* Cover/**Cubra** *on p. 205.*

| | |
|---|---|
| Cross. | **Cruce.**<br>KROO-seh |
| Cross your ankles. | **Cruce los tobillos.** |
| Cross your feet. | **Cruce los pies.** |
| Dial 9-1-1. | **Marque nueve-uno-uno.**<br>MAHR-keh NWEH-beh OO-noh OO-noh |

☞ *See* Call/**Llame** *on p. 190 and also* Press/**Oprima** *on p. 208.*

| | |
|---|---|
| Disperse. | **Dispérsese.**<br>dee-SPEHR-seh-seh |
| Disperse, all of you. | **Dispérsense todos.** |

| | |
|---|---|
| Drink. | **Tome.**<br>TOH-meh |
| Don't drink and drive. | **No tome y maneje.**<br>noh TOH-meh ee mah-NEH-heh |

☞ *See also* Drink/**Beba** *on p. 205.*

| | |
|---|---|
| Drive. | **Maneje.**<br>mah-NEH-heh |
| Drive carefully. | **Maneje con cuidado.** |
| Drive slowly. | **Maneje despacio.** |
| If you drink, don't drive. | **Si toma, no maneje.** |
| Drop. | **Suelte. ~ Deje caer.**<br>SWEHL-teh ~ DEH-heh kah-EHR |
| Drop it. | **Suéltelo. ~ Déjelo caer.** |
| Drop the weapon. | **Suelte el arma.**<br>**Deje caer el arma.** |
| Empty your pockets. | **Vacíe los bolsillos.**<br>bah-SEE-eh lohs bohl-SEE-yohs |
| Enter. | **Entre.**<br>EHN-treh |
| Enter the car. | **Entre en el carro.** |
| Do not enter. | **No entrar. ~ Prohibido entrar.** |
| No entry. | **No entrar. ~ Prohibido entrar.** |
| Escape. | **Escápese.**<br>eh-SKAH-peh-seh |
| Escape from the fire. | **Escápese del fuego.** |
| Evacuate. | **Evacue.**<br>eh-BAH-kweh |
| Evacuate the building, everybody. | **Evacuen el edificio, todos.** |
| Get back. | **Échese para atrás. ~ Retírese.**<br>EH-cheh-seh PAH-rah ah-TRAHS ~ reh-TEE-reh-seh |

☞ *See also* Get back/**Póngase** *on p. 206.*

| | |
|---|---|
| Get down. | **Arrástrese. ~ Tírese.**<br>ah-RRAHS-treh-seh ~<br>TEE-reh-seh |
| Get down on the floor. | **Arrástrese al piso. ~ Tírese al piso.** |
| Get down./Get out. | **Baje. ~ Bájese.**<br>BAH-heh ~ BAH-heh-seh |
| Get down from the roof. | **Bájese del techo.** |
| Get down from there. | **Bájese de allí.** |
| Get out of the car. | **Baje del carro. ~ Bájese del carro.** |
| Get in. | **Entre.**<br>EHN-treh |
| Get on your knees. | **Hínquese.**<br>EEN-keh-seh |
| Get out. (leave) | **Quite. ~ Quítese.**<br>KEE-teh ~ KEE-teh-seh |
| Get the car off the road. | **Quite el carro del camino.** |
| Get out of the street. | **Quítese de la calle.** |

☞ *See also* Get out/**Salga** *on p. 206.*

| | |
|---|---|
| Get up. | **Levántese.**<br>leh-BAHN-teh-seh |
| Get up slowly with your hands up. | **Levántese despacio con las manos arriba.** |
| Give. | **Dé.**<br>deh |
| Give me the information. | **Déme la información.** |
| Give me the weapon. | **Déme el arma.** |
| Give up. | **Dése.** |
| You're under arrest. (Give yourself up as prisoner.) | **Dése preso[a].** |
| Give back. | **Regrese.**<br>rreh-GREH-seh |
| Give me back my money. | **Regrese mi dinero.** |

☞ *See also* Give back/**Devuelva** *on p. 206.*

| | |
|---|---|
| Go away. | **Márchese.**<br>MAHR-cheh-seh |
| Everybody go away. | **Márchense todos.** |

☞ *See also* Go away/**Váyase** *on p. 207.*

| | |
|---|---|
| Go back. | **Regrese.**<br>rreh-GREH-seh |
| Go back to your house. | **Regrese a su casa.** |

☞ *See also* Go back/**Vuelva** *on p. 207.*

| | |
|---|---|
| Grab. | **Agarre.**<br>ah-GAH-rreh |
| Grab the man. | **Agarre al hombre.** |
| Hold on to me. | **Agárreme.** |
| Hang. | **Cuelgue.**<br>KWEHL-geh |
| Don't hang up. | **No cuelgue.** |
| Hang up the phone. | **Cuelgue.** |
| Hang a sheet from the window. | **Cuelgue una sábana de la ventana.** |

☞ *See* Pick up the phone/**Descuelgue** *on p. 196.*

| | |
|---|---|
| Help. | **Ayude.**<br>ah-YOO-theh |
| Help me. | **Ayúdeme.** |
| Hurry up. | **Apúrese.**<br>ah-POO-reh-seh |
| Inspect. | **Revise.**<br>rreh-BEE-seh |
| Inspect the license. | **Revise la licencia.** |
| Interlace your fingers. | **Entrelace los dedos.**<br>ehn-treh-LAH-seh lohs DEH-thohs |
| Join. | **Junte.**<br>HOON-teh |
| Jump. | **Brinque. ~ Salte.**<br>BREEN-keh ~ SAHL-teh |
| Don't jump. | **No brinque. ~ No salte.** |

| | |
|---|---|
| Jump to save yourselves. | **Brinquen para salvarse. ~ Salten para salvarse.** |
| Keep. | **Guarde. ~ Conserve.**<br>GWAHR-theh ~ kohn-SEHR-beh |
| Keep quiet. | **Guarde silencio.** |
| Keep to the right. | **Conserve su derecha.** |

☞ *See also* Keep/**Mantenga** *on p. 207.*

| | |
|---|---|
| Kneel down. | **Hínquese. ~ Arrodíllese.**<br>EEN-keh-seh ~ ah-rroh-THEE-yeh-seh |
| Kneel down and don't move. | **Hínquese y no se mueva. ~ Arrodíllese y no se mueva.** |
| Lean. | **Inclínese.**<br>een-KLEE-neh-seh |
| Lean forward and grab your ankles. | **Inclínese y agarre los tobillos.** |
| Let. (allow) | **Deje.**<br>DEH-heh |
| (*to a male*) Let me help you. | **Déjeme ayudarlo.** |
| (*to a female*) Let me help you. | **Déjeme ayudarla.** |
| Let me see the soles of your feet. | **Déjeme ver la planta de los pies.** |
| Let me see your ID. | **Déjeme ver su identificación.** |
| Let me see your license. | **Déjeme ver su licencia.** |

☞ *See also* Let/**Permita** *on p. 208.*

| | |
|---|---|
| Lie back. | **Acuéstese.**<br>ah-KWEH-steh-seh |
| Lie down. | **Acuéstese.**<br>ah-KWEH-steh-seh |
| Lie down on the floor/ground, face up. | **Acuéstese en el suelo, boca arriba.** |
| Lie down on your back, face up. | **Acuéstese en el suelo, boca arriba.** |

| | |
|---|---|
| Lift. | **Levante. ~ Alce.**<br>leh-BAHN-teh ~ AHL-seh |
| Lift one leg six inches off the ground. | **Alce una pierna enfrente seis pulgadas del suelo.** |
| Lift your shirt. | **Levante la camisa.** |
| Listen. | **Escuche.**<br>eh-SKOO-cheh |
| Listen to me. | **Escúcheme.** |
| Look (at). | **Mire.**<br>MEE-reh |
| Look at my nose. | **Mire mi nariz.** |
| Look at me. | **Míreme.** |
| Look (for). | **Busque.**<br>BOO-skeh |
| Look for evidence. | **Busque evidencia.** |
| Don't look for anything. | **No busque nada.** |
| Pass. | **Rebase. ~ Pase.**<br>rreh-BAH-seh ~ PAH-seh |
| Pass with care. | **Rebase con cuidado. ~ Pase con cuidado.** |
| Don't pass. | **No rebase. ~ No pase.** |
| No passing. | **No rebase. ~ No pase.** |
| Pick up. | **Descuelgue.**<br>dehs-KWEHL-geh |
| Pick up the phone. | **Descuelgue.** |
| Pick up the phone and try again. | **Descuelgue y trate otra vez.** |

☞ *See* Hang up the phone/**Cuelgue** *on p. 194.*

| | |
|---|---|
| Place. | **Coloque.**<br>koh-LOH-keh |
| Place it here. | **Colóquelo aquí.** |
| Place your weapon on the ground slowly. | **Coloque su arma en el suelo despacio.** |

| | |
|---|---|
| Pull. | **Tire. ~ Jale.**<br>TEE-reh ~ HAH-leh |
| Pull the alarm. | **Tire la alarma. ~ Jale la alarma.** |
| Pull over. | **Arrime.**<br>ah-RREE-meh |
| Pull the car over to the curb. | **Arrime el carro a la acera.** |
| Pull to the right. | **Arrímese a la derecha.** |

☞ *See also* Pull over/**Hágase** *on p. 209.*

| | |
|---|---|
| Pull up ____. | **Agarre ____.**<br>ah-GAHR-reh |
| Pull up the collar of your shirt. | **Agarre el cuello de su camisa.** |
| Push. | **Empuje.**<br>ehm-POO-heh |
| Don't push. | **No empuje.** |
| Push down. | **Pise.**<br>PEE-seh |
| Push down on the brakes. | **Pise los frenos.** |
| Put. (place) | **Coloque.**<br>koh-LOH-keh |
| Put it here. | **Colóquelo aquí.** |
| Put your weapon on the ground slowly. | **Coloque su arma en el suelo despacio.** |
| Put ____ down. | **Baje ____. ~ Bájese ____.**<br>BAH-heh ~ BAH-heh-seh |
| Put your hand down each time. | **Baje la mano cada vez.** |

☞ *See also* Put/**Ponga** *on p. 209.*

| | |
|---|---|
| Put ____ out. (a burning object) | **Apague ____.**<br>ah-PAH-geh |
| Put out the cigarette. | **Apague el cigarro. ~ Apague el cigarrillo.** |
| Put out the fire. | **Apague el incendio.** |

| | |
|---|---|
| Put together. | **Junte.**<br>HOON-teh |
| Put your feet together. | **Junte los pies.** |
| Put your knees together. | **Junte las rodillas.** |
| Put your legs together. | **Junte las piernas.** |
| Raise. | **Levante. ~ Alce.**<br>leh-BAHN-teh ~ AHL-seh |
| Raise one leg six inches off the ground. | **Alce una pierna enfrente seis pulgadas del suelo.** |
| Raise your hands. | **Levante las manos.** |
| Raise your shirt. | **Levante la camisa.** |
| ready | |
| Be ready. | **Esté listo[a].**<br>eh-STEH LEE-stoh[-stah] |
| Relax. | **Esté tranquilo[a].**<br>eh-STEH trahn-KEE-loh[-lah] |
| | **Relájese.**<br>rreh-LAH-heh-seh |
| Relax and take a deep breath. | **(Esté) tranquilo[a] y respire profundo. ~ Relájese y respire profundo.** |
| Release. | **Suelte. ~ Deje caer.**<br>SWEHL-teh ~ DEH-heh kah-EHR |
| Release it. | **Suéltelo. ~ Déjelo caer.** |
| Release the weapon. | **Suelte el arma. ~ Deje caer el arma.** |
| Remain. | **Quédese.**<br>KEH-theh-seh |
| Remain behind the barricades. | **Quédese detrás de las barricadas.** |
| Remain in the car. | **Quédese en el carro.** |
| Remain in the street. | **Quédese en la calle.** |
| Remove. | **Quite. ~ Quítese.**<br>KEE-teh ~ KEE-teh-seh |
| Remove all the money from your wallet. | **Quite todo el dinero de su cartera.** |

| | |
|---|---|
| Remove the keys from the car. | **Quite las llaves del carro.** |
| Remove your cap. | **Quítese la gorra.** |
| Remove your shoes. | **Quítese los zapatos.** |
| Get the car off the road. | **Quite el carro del camino.** |
| Repair. | **Repare.**<br>rreh-PAH-reh |
| Repair your muffler. | **Repare el mufle.** |
| Get repaired. | **Haga reparar.** |
| Get your car repaired. | **Haga reparar su carro.** |
| Report. | **Reporte.**<br>rreh-POHR-teh |
| Call 9-1-1 and report the crime. | **Llame al nueve-uno-uno y reporte el crimen.** |
| Rest. | **Descanse.**<br>dehs-KAHN-seh |
| Rest a while. | **Descanse un rato.** |
| Return. | **Regrese.**<br>rreh-GREH-seh |
| Return to your house. | **Regrese a su casa.** |

☞ *See also* Return/**Vuelva** *on p. 210.*

| | |
|---|---|
| Roll down. | **Baje. ~ Bájese.**<br>BAH-heh ~ BAH-heh-seh |
| Roll down the car window. | **Baje la ventanilla del carro.** |
| Save yourself. | **Sálvese.**<br>SAHL-beh-seh |
| Save yourself if you can. | **Sálvese quien pueda.** |
| Separate. | **Separe.**<br>seh-PAH-reh |
| Shoot. | **Dispare. ~ Tire.**<br>dee-SPAH-reh ~ TEE-reh |
| Don't shoot. | **No dispare. ~ No tire.** |

| | |
|---|---|
| Shout. | **Grite.** GREE-teh |
| Don't shout. | **No grite.** |
| Show. | **Enseñe. ~ Muestre.** ehn-SEH-nyeh ~ MWEH-streh |
| Show me your license. | **Enséñeme su licencia. ~ Muéstreme su licencia.** |
| Show me where it is. | **Enséñeme donde está. ~ Muéstreme donde está.** |
| Shut. | **Cierre.** SYEH-rreh |
| Shut the door with your foot. | **Cierre la puerta con un pie.** |
| Shut your eyes. | **Cierre los ojos.** |
| Shut your mouth. | **Cierre la boca.** |
| Shut up. | **Cállese.** KAH-yeh-seh |
| Shut up and get out of here. | **Cállese y váyase.** |
| Shut your mouth. | **Cállese la boca.** |
| Sign. | **Firme.** FEER-meh |
| Sign here for your belongings. | **Firme aquí por sus pertenencias.** |
| Sit down. | **Siéntese.** SYEHN-teh-seh |
| Sit down here. | **Siéntese aquí.** |
| Smoke. | **Fume.** FOO-meh |
| Don't smoke. | **No fume.** |
| Don't smoke in bed. | **No fume en la cama.** |
| Speak. | **Hable.** AH-bleh |
| Speak clearly. | **Hable claro.** |
| Speak English, please. | **Hable inglés, por favor.** |

| | |
|---|---|
| Speak louder. | **Hable más alto. ~ Hable más fuerte.** |
| Speak slower. | **Hable más despacio.** |
| Speak slowly. | **Hable despacio.** |
| Spread. | **Separe.** seh-PAH-reh |
| Spread your knees. | **Separe las rodillas.** |

☞ *See also* Spread/**Abra** *on p. 210.*

| | |
|---|---|
| Squeeze. | **Apriete.** ah-pree-EH-teh |
| Squeeze hard. | **Apriete fuerte.** |
| Squeeze my hand. | **Apriete mi mano.** |
| Stand. | **Párese.** PAH-reh-seh |
| Stand up facing away from me and put your hands behind your head. | **Párese con su espalda hacia mí y ponga las manos detrás de la cabeza.** |
| Don't stand between the cars. | **No se pare entre los carros.** |
| Stand back. | **Échese para atrás. ~ Retírese.** EH-cheh-seh PAH-rah ah-TRAHS ~ reh-TEE-reh-seh |

☞ *See also* Stand back/**Póngase atrás** *on p. 210.*

| | |
|---|---|
| Stand up. | **Levántese.** leh-BAHN-teh-seh |
| Start. (an engine) | **Arranque.** ah-RRAHN-keh |
| Start your (car's) engine. | **Arranque el motor (de su carro).** |
| Stay. | **Quédese.** KEH-theh-seh |
| Stay behind the barricades. | **Quédese detrás de las barricadas.** |
| Stay in the car. | **Quédese en el carro.** |
| Stay in the street. | **Quédese en la calle.** |

| | |
|---|---|
| Step out. | **Baje. ~ Bájese.**<br>BAH-heh ~ BAH-heh-seh |
| Step out of the car. | **Baje del carro. ~ Bájese del carro.** |
| Stop. | **Pare. ~ Párese.**<br>PAH-reh ~ PAH-reh-seh |
| Stop the car. | **Pare el carro.** |
| Stop or we'll shoot. | **Párese o disparamos.** |

☞ *See also* Stop/**Detenga** *on p. 210.*

| | |
|---|---|
| Surrender. | **Dése.**<br>DEH-seh |
| Take. | **Tome.**<br>TOH-meh |
| Take a seat. | **Tome asiento.** |
| Don't drink and drive. | **No tome y maneje.** |
| Take care. | **Cuídese.**<br>KWEE-deh-seh |
| Take off. | **Quítese.**<br>KEE-teh-seh |
| Take off your cap. | **Quítese la gorra.** |
| Take off your shoes. | **Quítese los zapatos.** |
| Take out. | **Saque.**<br>SAH-keh |
| Take your license out of your wallet. | **Saque la licencia de la cartera. ~ Saque la licencia de la billetera.** |
| Tell. | **Cuente.**<br>KWEHN-teh |
| Tell me exactly what happened. | **Cuénteme exactamente lo que pasó.** |

☞ *See also* Tell/**Diga** *on p. 210.*

| | |
|---|---|
| Threaten. | **Amenace.**<br>ah-meh-NAH-seh |
| Don't threaten me. | **No me amenace.** |

| | |
|---|---|
| Throw. | **Tire. ~ Lance.**<br>TEE-reh ~ LAHN-seh |
| Throw the keys in the street. | **Tire las llaves a la calle. ~ Lance las llaves a la calle.** |
| Touch. | **Toque.**<br>TOH-keh |
| Touch the tip of your nose. | **Toque la punta de la nariz.** |
| Try. | **Trate.**<br>TRAH-teh |
| Don't try to get up. | **No trate de levantarse. ~ No trate de pararse.** |
| Turn. | **Vire. ~ Dé (la) vuelta. ~ Doble.**<br>BEE-reh ~ deh (lah) BWEHL-tah ~ DOH-bleh |
| Turn right. | **Vire a la derecha. ~ Dé (la) vuelta a la derecha.** |
| Turn left. | **Doble a la izquierda.** |
| Turn around. | **Voltéese. ~ Dése vuelta.**<br>bohl-TEH-eh-seh ~ DEH-seh BWEHL-tah |
| Turn around slowly. | **Voltéese despacio. ~ Dése vuelta despacio.** |
| Turn off _____. (something running) | **Apague _____.**<br>ah-PAH-geh |
| Turn off the lights. | **Apague las luces.** |
| Turn off the motor. | **Apague el motor.** |
| Wait. | **Espere.**<br>eh-SPEH-reh |
| Wait here. | **Espere aquí.** |
| Wait in the car. | **Espere en el carro.** |
| Wait outside. | **Espere afuera.** |
| Wait there. | **Espere allí.** |

| | |
|---|---|
| Walk. | **Camine. ~ Ande.** kah-MEE-neh ~ AHN-deh |
| Walk, please. Don't run. | **Camine, por favor. No corra. ~ Ande, por favor. No corra.** |
| Walk straight ahead. | **Camine derecho. ~ Ande derecho.** |
| Watch. | **Mire.** MEE-reh |
| Watch where you step. | **Mire donde pisa.** |
| worry | |
| Don't worry. | **No se preocupe.** noh seh preh-oh-KOO-peh |

## A Commands

### Los mandatos con A

To form A commands, remove the **-er** or **-ir** ending from the dictionary form (infinitive): **vend*er*** ("to sell") → **vend**- or **sub*ir*** ("to get in") → **sub**-. Then add **-a**: **vend**- + **-a** → **Venda** ("Sell") or **sub-** + **-a** → **Suba** ("Get in"). When addressing two or more persons, add **-an**: **Vendan** ("(You all) sell") or **Suban** ("(You all) get in"). To say "don't," add **no**: **No venda** ("Don't sell") or **No suba** ("Don't get in").

| | |
|---|---|
| afraid | |
| Don't be afraid. | **No tenga miedo.** noh TEHN-gah MYEH-thoh |
| Answer. | **Responda.** rreh-SPOHN-dah |
| Answer my question. | **Responda a mi pregunta.** |

☞ *See also* Answer/**Conteste** *on p. 189.*

| | |
|---|---|
| Ask for. | **Pida.** PEE-thah |
| Ask for help. | **Pida ayuda. ~ Pida auxilio.** |
| Be careful. | **Tenga cuidado.** TEHN-gah kwee-THAH-thoh |
| Break. | **Rompa.** RROHM-pah |

| | |
|---|---|
| Break the windowpane. | **Rompa el cristal.** |
| Bring. | **Traiga.**<br>TRAY-gah |
| Bring it to me. | **Tráigamelo.** |
| Climb. | **Suba. ~ Súbase.**<br>SOO-bah ~ SOO-bah-seh |
| Climb onto the roof. | **Suba al techo.** |
| Climb the ladder. | **Suba la escalera.** |
| Come. | **Venga.**<br>BEHN-gah |
| Come here. | **Venga aquí.** |
| Come with me. | **Venga conmigo.** |
| Cover. | **Cubra.**<br>KOO-brah |
| Cover your mouth and nose. | **Cúbrase la boca y la nariz.** |
| Cover yourself. | **Cúbrase.** |
| Cover yourself with a blanket. | **Cúbrase con una manta. ~ Cúbrase con una cobija.** |

☞ *See also* Cover/**Tape** *on p. 191.*

| | |
|---|---|
| Describe. | **Describa.**<br>deh-SKREE-bah |
| Describe the accident. | **Describa el accidente.** |
| Describe the man. | **Describa al hombre.** |
| Describe the woman. | **Describa a la mujer.** |
| Do. | **Haga.**<br>AH-gah |
| Do it (right) now. | **Hágalo ya.** |
| Don't do anything. | **No haga nada.** |
| Don't do that. | **No haga eso.** |
| Drink. | **Beba.**<br>BEH-bah |
| Drink water. | **Beba agua.** |

☞ *See also* Drink/**Tome** *on p. 192.*

| | |
|---|---|
| Extend. | **Extienda.**<br>ehks-TYEHN-dah |
| Extend your arms like this. | **Extienda los brazos así.** |
| fall | |
| Don't fall. | **No se caiga.**<br>noh seh KAY-gah |
| Follow. | **Siga.**<br>SEE-gah |
| Follow me. | **Sígame.** |
| Get. (become) | **Póngase.**<br>POHN-gah-seh |
| Don't get nervous. | **No se ponga nervioso[a].** |
| Get. (obtain) | **Consiga. ~ Obtenga.**<br>kohn-SEE-gah ~ ohb-TEHN-gah |
| Get an arrest warrant from the judge. | **Consiga una orden de arresto del juez.** |
| Get the money. | **Consiga el dinero. ~ Obtenga el dinero.** |
| Get back. | **Póngase atrás.**<br>POHN-gah-seh ah-TRAHS |

☞ *See also* Get back/**Échese** *on p. 192.*

| | |
|---|---|
| Get into. | **Suba. ~ Súbase.**<br>SOO-bah ~ SOO-bah-seh |
| Get into the police car. | **Suba al carro de policía.** |
| Get out. (leave) | **Salga. ~ Sálgase.**<br>SAHL-gah ~ SAHL-gah-seh |
| Get out of the car. | **Sálgase del carro.** |
| Get out quickly. | **Sálgase rápido.** |

☞ *See also* Get out/**Quite** *on p. 193.*

| | |
|---|---|
| Give _____ back. | **Devuelva _____.**<br>deh-BWEHL-bah |
| Give me back my money. | **Devuelva mi dinero.** |

☞ *See also* Give back/**Regrese** *on p. 193.*

| | |
|---|---|
| Go. | **Vaya.**<br>BAH-yah |
| Go home. | **Vaya a casa.** |
| Go to court. | **Vaya a la corte.** |
| Let's go, fast. | **Vamos, rápido.** |
| Go away. | **Váyase.**<br>BAH-yah-seh |
| Go away. It's an emergency. | **Váyase. Es una emergencia.** |

☞ *See also* Go away/**Márchese** *on p. 194.*

| | |
|---|---|
| Go back. | **Vuelva.**<br>BWEHL-bah |
| Go back home. | **Vuelva a casa.** |

☞ *See also* Go back/**Regrese** *on p. 194.*

| | |
|---|---|
| Have … | **Tenga…**<br>TEHN-gah |
| Have emergency phone numbers near. | **Tenga números de emergencia cerca.** |
| interfere | |
| Don't interfere. | **No se entremeta.**<br>noh seh ehn-treh-MEH-tah |
| Keep. | **Mantenga.**<br>mahn-TEHN-gah |
| Keep your arms at your side. | **Mantenga los brazos al lado.** |
| Keep your hands where I can see them. | **Mantenga las manos donde las pueda ver.** |

☞ *See also* Keep/**Guarde** *on p. 195.*

| | |
|---|---|
| Keep on … (doing something). | **Siga…**<br>SEE-gah |
| Keep on walking. | **Siga caminando.** |
| Leave. | **Salga. ~ Sálgase.**<br>SAHL-gah ~ SAHL-gah-seh |
| Leave quickly. | **Sálgase rápido.** |

| | |
|---|---|
| Let. (permit) | **Permita.**<br>pehr-MEE-tah |
| Let me help. | **Permítame ayudar.** |

☞ *See also* Let/**Deje** *on p. 195.*

| | |
|---|---|
| Listen. | **Oiga.**<br>OY-gah |
| Listen to me. | **Óigame.** |
| Make a fist. | **Haga un puño.**<br>AH-gah oon POO-nyoh |
| Move./Move on. | **Mueva. ~ Muévase.**<br>MWEH-bah ~ MWEH-bah-seh |
| Move back. | **Muévase hacia atrás.** |
| Don't move. | **No mueva. ~ No se mueva.** |
| Don't move your neck. | **No mueva el cuello.** |
| Don't move until you hear the words "Do it now." | **No se muevan hasta oír las palabras: Hágalo ya.** |
| Hold still. | **No se mueva.** |
| Obey. | **Obedezca.**<br>oh-beh-THEH-skah |
| Obey our orders very carefully. | **Obedezcan nuestras órdenes con mucho cuidado.** |
| Open. | **Abra.**<br>AH-brah |
| Open your hands. | **Abra las manos.** |
| Open your mouth. | **Abra la boca.** |
| Pick up. | **Recoja.**<br>rreh-KOH-hah |
| Pick up that coin. | **Recoja la moneda.** |
| Press 9-1-1. | **Oprima nueve-uno-uno.**<br>oh-PREE-mah NWEH-beh OO-noh OO-noh |
| Prevent accidents. | **Prevenga los accidentes.**<br>preh-BEHN-gah lohs ahk-see-THEHN-tehs |

| | |
|---|---|
| Protect. | **Proteja. ~ Protéjase.**<br>proh-TEH-hah ~<br>proh-TEH-hah-seh |
| Protect the children. | **Proteja a los niños.** |
| Protect yourself. | **Protéjase.** |
| Pull over. | **Hágase a un lado.**<br>AH-gah-seh ah oon LAH-thoh |
| Pull over to the curb. | **Hágase a la orilla de la calle. ~ Hágase al borde de la calle.** |
| Pull over to the side. | **Hágase al lado.** |

☞ *See also* Pull over/**Arrime** *on p. 197.*

| | |
|---|---|
| Put. (place) | **Ponga.**<br>POHN-gah |
| Put both hands out of the window. | **Ponga las dos manos afuera de la ventana.** |
| Put it here. | **Póngalo aquí.** |
| Put your weapon on the ground slowly. | **Ponga su arma en el suelo despacio.** |

☞ *See also* Put/**Coloque** *on p. 197.*

| | |
|---|---|
| Put in. | **Meta. ~ Métase.**<br>MEH-tah ~ MEH-tah-seh |
| Don't put your hands in your pockets. | **No meta las manos en los bolsillos. ~**<br>**No se meta las manos en los bolsillos.** |
| Put on. | **Póngase.**<br>POHN-gah-seh |
| Put on your clothes. | **Póngase la ropa.** |
| Read. | **Lea.**<br>LEH-ah |
| Read the Spanish. | **Lea el español.** |
| Read and sign here. | **Lea y firme aquí.** |
| Repeat, please. | **Repita, por favor.**<br>rreh-PEE-tah pohr fah-BOHR |

| | |
|---|---|
| Resist. | **Resista.** rreh-SEE-stah |
| Don't resist. | **No resista.** |
| Return. | **Vuelva.** BWEHL-bah |
| Return home. | **Vuelva a casa.** |

☞ *See also* Return/**Regrese** *on p. 199.*

| | |
|---|---|
| Run. | **Corra.** KOH-rrah |
| Run fast. | **Corra rápido.** |
| Don't run. | **No corra.** |
| Spread. | **Abra.** AH-brah |
| Spread your legs and your feet. | **Abra las piernas y los pies.** |

☞ *See also* Spread/**Separe** *on p. 201.*

| | |
|---|---|
| Stand back. | **Póngase atrás.** POHN-gah-seh ah-TRAHS |

☞ *See also* Stand back/**Échese para atrás** *on p. 201.*

| | |
|---|---|
| Stop. | **Detenga. ~ Deténgase.** deh-TEHN-gah ~ deh-TEHN-gah-seh |
| Stop or I'll shoot. | **Deténgase o disparo.** |
| Stop the car. | **Detenga el carro.** |

☞ *See also* Stop/**Pare** *on p. 202.*

| | |
|---|---|
| Stretch. | **Extienda.** ehks-TYEHN-dah |
| Tell. | **Diga.** DEE-gah |
| Tell me everything. | **Dígame todo.** |
| Tell me the truth. | **Dígame la verdad.** |
| Tell me what happened. | **Dígame lo que pasó.** |

☞ *See also* Tell/**Cuente** *on p. 202.*

| | |
|---|---|
| Turn on. | **Prenda. ~ Encienda.** PREHN-dah ~ ehn-SYEHN-dah |
| Turn on your lights. | **Prenda las luces. ~ Encienda las luces.** |
| Write. | **Escriba.** eh-SKREE-bah |
| Write your name and address. | **Escriba su nombre y su dirección.** |

## KEY QUESTIONS AND STATEMENTS
### Las preguntas y las declaraciones claves

This section has key questions and statements dealing with important law enforcement activities, emergency professions, objects, weapons, vehicles, injuries, and on-scene tools. Like with commands, you can get quick answers by reading many high-level key questions and statements to victims, suspects, and witnesses directly from this book. Once you familiarize yourself with this list, you will be able to find personalized questions and statements fast.

| | |
|---|---|
| accident | **el accidente** ahk-see-THEHN-teh |
| Have you had an accident? | **¿Ha tenido un accidente?** |
| When and where did the accident happen? | **¿Cuándo y dónde pasó el accidente?** |
| alarm | **la alarma** ah-LAHR-mah |
| false alarm | **la falsa alarma** |
| fire alarm | **la alarma de fuego** |
| alcohol | **el alcohol** ahl-koh-OHL |
| Do you have an alcohol or drug problem? | **¿Tiene problemas con alcohol o drogas?** |
| Have you been drinking alcohol? | **¿Ha estado tomando alcohol?** |

| | |
|---|---|
| ambulance | **la ambulancia**<br>ahm-boo-LAHN-syah |
| Do you need an ambulance? | **¿Necesita una ambulancia?** |
| Do you want an ambulance? | **¿Quiere una ambulancia?** |
| answer | **la respuesta**<br>rreh-SPWEH-stah |
| I need answers to my questions. | **Necesito respuestas a mis preguntas.** |
| I need short and simple answers. | **Necesito respuestas cortas y sencillas.** |
| arrest | **el arresto**<br>ah-RREH-stoh |
| I have an arrest warrant. | **Tengo una orden de arresto.** |
| You're under arrest. | **Está arrestado[a]. ~ Dése preso[a].** |
| bleeding | **la hemorragia ~ sangrando**<br>eh-moh-RRAH-hee-ah ~ sahn-GRAHN-doh |
| Are you bleeding? | **¿Está sangrando?** |
| internal bleeding | **la hemorragia** |
| bottle | **la botella**<br>boh-TEH-yah |
| Where's the (bottle) label? | **¿Dónde está la etiqueta (de la botella)?** |
| medicine bottle | **la botella de medicina** |
| broken | **roto[a] ~ quebrado[a]**<br>RROH-toh[-tah] ~ keh-BRAH-thoh[-thah] |
| I think you have a broken bone. | **Pienso que tiene un hueso roto. ~ Pienso que tiene un hueso quebrado.** |
| bruise | **el moretón**<br>moh-reh-TOHN |
| Do you have any bruises? | **¿Tiene moretones?** |

There are several words for car: **el carro, el auto, el automóvil,** and **el coche**.

| | |
|---|---|
| burn | **la quemadura**<br>keh-mah-THOO-rah |
| You have a serious burn. | **Tiene una quemadura seria.** |
| burned | **quemado[a]** |
| Is it burned?/Are you burned? | **¿Está quemado[a]?** |
| car | **el carro**<br>KAH-rroh |
| car accident | **el accidente de carro** |
| car crash | **el choque de carro** |
| police car | **el carro de policía** |
| care | **el cuidado**<br>kwee-THAH-thoh |
| You need medical care. | **Necesita cuidado médico.** |
| citation | **el tíquete ~ el tiquete**<br>TEE-keh-teh ~ tee-KEH-teh |
| Do you have any citations? | **¿Tiene tíquetes?** |
| I'm giving you a citation. | **Le doy un tíquete.** |
| clinic | **la clínica**<br>KLEE-nee-kah |
| Do you need to go to a clinic? | **¿Necesita ir a una clínica?** |
| Do you want to go to a clinic? | **¿Quiere ir a una clínica?** |

¡Ojo!

Rural areas in Latin America have **las clínicas** ("clinics"). **Los hospitales** ("hospitals") are found in larger cities.

| | |
|---|---|
| collision | **el choque**<br>CHOH-keh |
| a car collision | **un choque de carro** |
| court | **la corte ~ el tribunal**<br>KOHR-teh ~ tree-boo-NAHL |
| You have to go to court. | **Usted tiene que ir a la corte. ~ Usted tiene que ir al tribunal.** |
| court order/warrant | **la orden de la corte** |
| crash | **el choque**<br>CHOH-keh |
| a car crash | **un choque de carro** |
| cut | **la cortada**<br>kohr-TAH-thah |
| You have a deep cut. | **Usted tiene una cortada profunda.** |
| cut | **cortado[a]** |
| Are you cut? | **¿Está cortado[a]?** |
| danger | **el peligro**<br>peh-LEE-groh |
| Out of danger. | **Fuera de peligro.** |
| There's danger of death. | **Hay peligro de muerte.** |
| dangerous | **peligroso[a]** |
| It's very dangerous. | **Es muy peligroso.** |
| description | **la descripción**<br>deh-skreep-SYOHN |
| I want a description of the suspect. (*male*) | **Quiero una descripción del sospechoso.** |
| I want a description of the suspect. (*female*) | **Quiero una descripción de la sospechosa.** |
| detective | **el / la detective**<br>deh-tehk-TEE-beh |
| I'm a detective from the police department. | **Soy detective del departamento de policía.** |
| I'm a detective from the sheriff's department. | **Soy detective del departamento del sheriff.** |
| We're detectives. | **Somos detectives.** |

A male detective is **el detective**.
A female detective is **la detective**.

A male dispatcher is **el despachador**.
A female dispatcher is **la despachadora**.

| | |
|---|---|
| detective bureau | **el despacho de detectives ~ la oficina de detectives** |
| diabetes | **la diabetes**<br>dee-ah-BEH-tehs |
| Do you have diabetes? | **¿Tiene diabetes?** |
| diabetic | **diabético[a]** |
| Are you (a) diabetic? | **¿Es diabético[a]?** |
| dispatch | **el despacho**<br>deh-SPAH-choh |
| dispatch center | **el centro de despacho** |
| dispatcher | **el despachador / la despachadora**<br>deh-spah-chah-THOHR / deh-spah-chah-THOH-rah |
| I'm a dispatcher. | **Soy despachador. / Soy despachadora.** |
| doctor | **el médico / la médica**<br>MEH-thee-koh / MEH-thee-kah<br>**el doctor / la doctora**<br>dohk-TOHR / dohk-TOH-rah |
| You should see a doctor. | **Usted debe ver un médico.** |
| Do you need a doctor? | **¿Necesita un médico?** |
| driver | **el conductor ~ el chofer**<br>kohn-dook-TOHR ~ choh-FEHR |
| Are you the driver of the vehicle? | **¿Es usted el conductor del vehículo?** |
| ambulance driver | **el conductor de ambulancia** |
| bus driver | **el conductor de autobús** |

|  |  |
|---|---|
| drown | |
| He/She drowned in the water. | **Se ahogó en el agua.**<br>seh ah-oh-GOH ehn ehl AH-gwah |
| He/She is drowning. | **Se está ahogando.** |
| drug | **la droga**<br>DROH-gah |
| Do you take drugs? | **¿Toma drogas?** |
| drugged | **drogado[a]** |
| Are you on drugs? | **¿Está drogado[a]?** |
| emergency | **la emergencia**<br>eh-mehr-HEHN-syah |
| It's an emergency. | **Es una emergencia.** |
| emergency exit | **la salida de emergencia** |
| English | **el inglés**<br>een-GLEHS |
| I speak English. | **Hablo inglés.** |
| I understand English. | **Comprendo inglés. ~ Entiendo inglés.** |
| Do you speak English? | **¿Habla inglés?** |
| Do you understand English? | **¿Comprende inglés? ~ ¿Entiende inglés?** |
| escape | **el escape**<br>eh-SKAH-peh |
| fire escape (stairs) | **la escalera de escape** |
| a jail escape | **un escape de la cárcel** |
| evacuation | **la evacuación**<br>eh-bah-kwah-SYOHN |
| evacuation routes | **las rutas de evacuación** |
| fire | **el fuego**<br>FWEH-goh |
| Is there a fire here? | **¿Hay un fuego aquí?** |
| The building is on fire. | **El edificio está ardiendo. ~ El edificio está en llamas.** |

**Fuego** is the general word for "fire."
**Incendio** means a destructive fire, especially one that may involve arson.

**El bombero** is a male firefighter.
**La bombera** is a female firefighter.

| | |
|---|---|
| fire (destructive) | **el incendio** |
| It's arson. | **Es un incendio premeditado.** |
| firefighter | **el bombero / la bombera**<br>bohm-BEH-roh/<br>bohm-BEH-rah |
| Who called the firefighters? | **¿Quién llamó a los bomberos?** |
| first aid | **los primeros auxilios**<br>pree-MEH-rohs<br>ah-ook-SEE-lee-ohs |
| Do you need first aid? | **¿Necesita los primeros auxilios?** |
| I'm giving you first aid. | **Le doy los primeros auxilios.** |
| gang | **la pandilla ~ la ganga**<br>pahn-DEE-yah ~ GAHN-gah |
| Are you a gang member? | **¿Es miembro de una pandilla? ~**<br>**¿Es miembro de una ganga?** |
| gang associate | **el asociado de la pandilla** |
| gang member | **el miembro de una pandilla ~ el pandillero / la pandillera** |
| gang name | **el nombre de pandilla** |
| gas | **el gas**<br>gahs |
| It smells of gas. | **Huele a gas.** |
| gas leak | **una fuga de gas** |

Don't confuse bottled gas (**el gas en botella ~ el gas en bombona**) with gasoline (**la gasolina**).

| | |
|---|---|
| gasoline | **la gasolina**<br>gah-soh-LEE-nah |
| gas tank (car) | **el tanque de gasolina** |
| gun/pistol | **la pistola**<br>pee-STOH-lah |
| Is it your gun? | **¿Es su pistola?** |
| Whose gun is it? | **¿De quién es la pistola?** |
| heart | **el corazón**<br>koh-rah-SOHN |
| Do you have a heart condition? | **¿Sufre del corazón?** |
| Do you have heart problems? | **¿Tiene problemas del corazón?** |
| Have you had a heart attack? | **¿Ha tenido un ataque cardíaco? ~ ¿Ha tenido un ataque al corazón?** |
| help | **el auxilio ~ la ayuda**<br>ah-ook-SEE-lee-oh ~ ah-YOO-thah |
| Do you want (any) help? | **¿Quiere ayuda? ~ ¿Quiere auxilio?** |

**Socorro, auxilio**, and **ayuda** all mean "help."

Rural areas in Latin America have **las clínicas** ("clinics"). **Los hospitales** ("hospitals") are found in larger cities.

| | |
|---|---|
| hospital | **el hospital**<br>oh-spee-TAHL |
| Do you need to go to a hospital? | **¿Necesita ir a un hospital?** |
| Do you want to go to a hospital? | **¿Quiere ir a un hospital?** |
| hurt | **herido[a] ~ lastimado[a]**<br>eh-REE-thoh[-thah] ~ lah-stee-MAH-thoh[-thah] |
| Are you hurt? | **¿Está herido[a]? ~ ¿Está lastimado[a]?** |
| identification/ID | **la identificación**<br>ee-dehn-tee-fee-kah-SYOHN |
| Do you have an ID card? | **¿Tiene una tarjeta de identificación?** |
| I need your identification. | **Necesito su identificación.** |
| illness | **la enfermedad**<br>ehn-fehr-meh-THAHTH |
| Do you have any illnesses? | **¿Tiene enfermedades?** |
| ill/sick | **enfermo[a]** |
| Are you sick? | **¿Está enfermo[a]? ~ ¿Está malo[a]?** |
| injury | **la herida**<br>heh-REE-thah |
| Do you have an injury? | **¿Tiene una herida?** |
| injured | **herido[a] ~ lastimado[a]** |
| Are you injured? | **¿Está herido[a]? ~ ¿Está lastimado[a]?** |
| insurance | **el seguro ~ la aseguranza**<br>seh-GOO-roh ~ ah-seh-goo-RAHN-sah |
| Do you have insurance? | **¿Tiene seguro? ~ ¿Tiene aseguranza?** |
| Do you have proof of insurance? | **¿Tiene prueba de seguro?** |

A male interpreter is **el intérprete**.
A female interpreter is **la intérprete**.

Don't confuse "interpreter," who translates the spoken word, and "translator," who translates the written word.

interpreter — **el / la intérprete**
een-TEHR-preh-teh

Do you want an interpreter? — **¿Quiere intérprete?**

jail — **la cárcel**
KAHR-sehl

I'm taking you/him/her to jail. — **Lo / La llevo a la cárcel.**

We're going to jail. — **Vamos a la cárcel.**

label — **la etiqueta**
eh-tee-KEH-tah

Where's the label? — **¿Dónde está la etiqueta?**

license — **la licencia**
lee-SEHN-syah

Driver's license, insurance, and registration, please. — **Licencia de manejar, seguro y registro, por favor.**

medical help — **la ayuda médica ~ la asistencia médica**
ah-YOO-thah MEH-thee-kah ~ ah-see-STEHN-syah MEH-thee-kah

Do you need medical help? — **¿Necesita ayuda médica?**

medication — **la medicamento**
meh-thee-kah-MEHN-toh

medicine — **la medicina**
meh-thee-SEE-nah

Are you allergic to any medicine? — **¿Es alérgico[a] a alguna medicina?**

Don't confuse the Spanish word for "name" (**el nombre**) with "number" (**el número**).

**La orden** is a legal request or order. Alphabetical order is **el orden alfabético.**

| | |
|---|---|
| Are you taking medicine now? | **¿Está tomando medicina ahora?** |
| number | **el número** NOO-meh-roh |
| What is your telephone number? | **¿Cual es su número de teléfono?** |
| What is your street number? | **¿Cual es su número de calle?** |
| officer | **el / la oficial** oh-fee-SYAHL |
| I am a police officer. | **Soy policía.** |
| I'm Officer Jones. | **Soy Oficial Jones.** |
| peace officer | **el / la oficial de orden público** |
| probation officer | **el / la oficial de probación** |
| order | **la orden** OHR-thehn |
| an arrest warrant | **una orden de arresto** |
| a court order | **una orden de la corte** |
| a restraining order | **una orden de retiro y restricción** |
| a search warrant | **una orden de registro** |

☞ *See also entries under* Court *on p. 214.*

A police officer is **un oficial de policía**. Identify yourself as **Oficial Jones, un policía** ("Officer Jones, a police officer").

Don't confuse **dolor** ("pain") with **dólar** ("dollar").
See "False Friends" on pp. 277–278.

| | |
|---|---|
| pain | **el dolor**<br>doh-LOHR |
| Where do you have pain? | **¿Dónde tiene dolor?** |
| paramedic | **el paramédico / la paramédica**<br>pah-rah-MEH-thee-koh / pah-rah-MEH-thee-kah |
| Do you need a paramedic? | **¿Necesita un paramédico?** |
| Do you want a paramedic? | **¿Quiere un paramédico?** |
| parole | **el parole**<br>pah-ROH-leh |
| Are you on parole? | **¿Está en parole?** |
| What's your parole officer's name? | **¿Cómo se llama su oficial de parole?** |
| passenger | **el pasajero / la pasajera**<br>pah-sah-HEH-roh / pah-sah-HEH-rah |
| passenger in back | **el pasajero de atrás / la pasajera de atrás** |
| passenger in front | **el pasajero de enfrente / la pasajera de enfrente** |
| passenger side | **el lado del pasajero** |
| patrol | **la patrulla**<br>pah-TROO-yah |
| police patrol car | **el carro de (la) patrulla** |
| patrol officer | **el patrullero / la patrullera**<br>pah-troo-YEH-roh / pah-troo-YEH-rah |
| I'm a patrol officer. | **Soy patrullero. / Soy patrullera.** |

A male paramedic is **el paramédico.**
A female paramedic is **la paramédica.**

A male patrol officer is **el patrullero.**
A female patrol officer is **la patrullera.**

A male police officer is **el policía.**
A female police officer is **la policía.**

A male sheriff's deputy is **el oficial del sheriff.**
A female sheriff's deputy is **la oficial del sheriff.**

| | |
|---|---|
| pills | **las pastillas**<br>pah-STEE-yahs |
| What pills do you take? | **¿Cuáles pastillas toma?** |
| How many pills are you taking? | **¿Cuántas pastillas toma?** |
| sleeping pills | **las pastillas para dormir** |
| poison | **el veneno**<br>beh-NEH-noh |
| Have you swallowed poison? | **¿Ha tomado veneno?** |
| Poison Control | **el Control de Envenenamiento** |
| poisoning | **el envenenamiento** |
| police (general) | **la policía**<br>poh-lee-SEE-ah |
| Do you need the police? | **¿Necesita la policía?** |
| Who called the police? | **¿Quién llamó a la policía?** |
| police officer | **el / la policía**<br>poh-lee-SEE-ah |
| We're police officers. | **Somos policías.** |
| police station | **la estación de policía**<br>eh-stah-SYOHN deh poh-lee-SEE-ah |
| You have to go to the police station. | **Tiene que ir a la estación de policía.** |

Even though **problema** ends in **-a**, it is masculine: **el problema** ("the problem"), **los problemas** ("the problems").

| | |
|---|---|
| pregnancy | **el embarazo**<br>ehm-bah-RAH-soh |
| pregnant | **embarazada** |
| Are you pregnant? | **¿Está embarazada?** |
| probation | **la probación**<br>proh-bah-SYOHN |
| Are you on probation? | **¿Está en probación?** |
| What's your probation officer's name? | **¿Cómo se llama su oficial de probación?** |
| problem | **el problema**<br>proh-BLEH-mah |
| Do you have a problem? | **¿Tiene (usted) un problema?** |
| What's the problem here? | **¿Cuál es el problema aquí?** |
| question | **la pregunta**<br>preh-GOON-tah |
| I have some questions for you. | **Tengo algunas preguntas para usted.** |
| Do you have any questions? | **¿Tiene preguntas?** |
| registration | **el registro**<br>rreh-HEE-stroh |
| You have an expired registration. | **Tiene el registro expirado.** |
| Where's the car's registration? | **¿Dónde está el registro para el carro?** |
| safety | **la seguridad**<br>seh-goo-ree-THAHTH |
| We're worried about your safety. | **Estamos preocupados por su seguridad.** |

| | |
|---|---|
| safe | **seguro[a]** |
| Everybody's safe. | **Todos están seguros.** |
| You're safe. | **Está seguro[a].** |
| seizure(s)/convulsions | **las convulsiones**<br>kohn-bool-SYOH-nehs |
| Are you having a seizure now? | **¿Tiene convulsiones ahora?** |
| sheriff | **sheriff**<br>SHEH-reef |
| I'm from the sheriff's department. | **Soy del departamento del sheriff.** |
| I'm a sheriff's deputy. | **Soy oficial del sheriff.** |
| sheriff's station | **la estación del sheriff** |
| shooting | **el disparo ~ el tiro ~ el tiroteo**<br>dee-SPAH-roh ~ TEE-roh ~ tee-roh-TEH-oh |
| drive-by shooting | **el tiroteo de un carro en marcha** |
| shot | **el disparo ~ el tiro ~ el tiroteo** |
| sick | **enfermo[a] ~ malo[a]**<br>ehn-FEHR-moh[-mah] ~ MAH-loh[-lah] |
| Are you sick? | **¿Está enfermo[a]? ~ ¿Está malo[a]?** |
| smoke | **el humo**<br>OO-moh |
| Where there's smoke, there's fire. | **Donde hay humo, hay fuego.** |
| smoke alarm | **la alarma de humo** |
| Spanish | **el español**<br>eh-spah-NYOHL |
| I speak very little Spanish. | **Yo hablo muy poco español.** |
| Do you speak Spanish? | **¿Habla usted español?** |

| | |
|---|---|
| suspect | **el sospechoso / la sospechosa**<br>soh-speh-CHOH-soh / soh-speh-CHOH-sah |
| You are a crime suspect. | **Usted es un[-a] sospechoso[a] del crimen.** |
| armed suspect | **el sospechoso armado** |
| suspicious | **sospechoso[a]** |
| a suspicious fire | **un fuego sospechoso** |
| ticket | **el tíquete ~ el tiquete**<br>TEE-keh-teh ~ tee-KEH-teh |
| I'm giving you a ticket. | **Le doy un tíquete.** |
| Do you have any tickets? | **¿Tiene tíquetes?** |
| translator | **el traductor / la traductora**<br>trah-thook-TOHR / trah-thook-TOH-rah |
| Do you need a translator? | **¿Necesita un traductor?** |
| under arrest | **arrestado[a]**<br>ah-rreh-STAH-thoh[-thah] |
| You're under arrest. | **Está arrestado[a].**<br>**Dése preso[a].** |

☞ *See also entries under* Arrest *on p. 212.*

| | |
|---|---|
| victim | **la víctima**<br>BEEK-tee-mah |
| Where's the victim? | **¿Dónde está la víctima?** |
| Any victims? | **¿Hay víctimas?** |

Don't confuse "translator," who translates the written word, and "interpreter," who translates the spoken word.

**La víctima** is used for both male and female victims.

|  |  |
|---|---|
| warning | **el aviso ~ la advertencia** ah-BEE-soh ~ ahd-behr-TEHN-syah |
| I'm giving you a warning. | **Le doy un aviso. ~ Le doy una advertencia.** |
| emergency warning light | **la luz de aviso para emergencias** |
| warrant (from the court) | **la orden de la corte** OHR-thehn deh lah KOHR-teh |
| an arrest warrant | **una orden de arresto** |
| an entry and search warrant | **una orden para entrar y esculcar** |
| a search warrant | **una orden de registro ~ una orden de esculque** |

☞ *See also entries under* Order *on p. 221.*

|  |  |
|---|---|
| weapon | **el arma** AHR-mah |
| Do you/Does he/she have a weapon? | **¿Tiene un arma?** |
| a firearm | **un arma de fuego** |
| witness | **el / la testigo** teh-STEE-goh |
| Is there a witness here? | **¿Hay un[-a] testigo aquí?** |
| Are you a witness of the crime? | **¿Es usted un[-a] testigo del crimen?** |
| eyewitness | **el / la testigo ocular** |

"The weapon" is **el arma.** "A weapon" is **un arma.** "The weapons," **las armas**. All forms are feminine.

A male witness is **el testigo**.
A female witness is **la testigo**.

# Law Enforcement Scenarios

These scenarios put the vocabulary of previous chapters into a real-life context. Here, the focus is more on what *you* would say rather than victims, suspects, or witnesses. The scenarios have been reviewed by peace officers, and we have them organized in three groups: General Law Enforcement, Patrol Officers/Deputies, and Detectives/Investigators.

Use these scenarios as models that you can adapt to your specific job responsibilities. Read through them and consider what words you would use in particular situations. The scenarios begin with simple, short questions requiring bottom-line answers in field interviews and basic emergencies. More-involved crimes require more description, so the second part of each scenario includes much more description. In addition, past-tense verbs must be used to describe the scenarios.

Realistically, you should not attempt more complicated scenarios without further language training and experience. Most cases would be insufficiently documented and thrown out of court. These scenarios are given here as reference material and as basic orientation in specific situations.

## GENERAL LAW ENFORCEMENT
El cumplimiento de la ley en general

### Scenario · REASSURING TERMS
Términos de confianza

| | |
|---|---|
| Calm down. | **Cálmese.** |
| You're all right. | **Usted está bien.** |
| It's okay. | **Está bien.** |
| Everything's okay. | **Todo está bien.** |
| Don't worry. | **No se preocupe.** |
| Don't be afraid. | **No tenga miedo.** |
| Don't be frightened. | **No se asuste.** |
| Everyone is safe. | **Todos están a salvo. ~ Todos están seguros.** |
| It's not serious. | **No es grave. ~ No es serio.** |
| (*to a male*) We're here to help you. | **Estamos aquí para ayudarlo.** |
| (*to a female*) We're here to help you. | **Estamos aquí para ayudarla.** |
| We're taking care of you. | **Lo / La estamos cuidando.** |

"You" can be expressed as **Lo** in Spanish when you're speaking to a male. "You" can be expressed as **La** when you're speaking to a female.

| | |
|---|---|
| I'm arresting you for ... | **Lo / La arresto por...** |

| | |
|---|---|
| Take care of yourself. | **Cuídese.** |
| Do you feel any better? | **¿Se siente algo mejor?** |
| I'm very sorry. | **Lo siento mucho.** |
| What a pity! | **Qué lástima.** |

## Scenario · CROWD CONTROL
### El control de la muchedumbre

In crowd control, take charge. The following commands address a group of people. When addressing only one person, omit **-n** in the action word (verb). To tell a crowd to disperse, say: **Dispérsense**. To tell one person, omit **-n**: **Dispérsese**.

Expressions of courtesy like **por favor** ("please") and **gracias** ("thanks") get you more public cooperation.

| | |
|---|---|
| Attention, please. | **Atención, por favor.** |
| Break it up. | **Dispérsense.** |
| Don't congregate. | **No formen grupos.** |
| Get in line. | **Formen una fila.** |
| Listen up, please. | **Oigan, por favor.** |
| Listen to me. | **Escúchenme.** |
| Let me get through. | **Déjenme pasar.** |
| Leave the building. | **Sálganse del edificio.** |
| Everyone, please leave. | **Márchense todos, por favor.** |
| Go home, please. | **Márchense a casa, por favor. ~ Váyanse a casa, por favor.** |
| There's nothing to see here. | **No hay nada que ver aquí.** |
| Stand back. | **Pónganse atrás. ~ Échense para atrás.** |

| | |
|---|---|
| Vacate the premises now. | **Abandonen el lugar ahora.** |
| Get back, please. | **Retrocedan, por favor. ~ Retírense, por favor.** |
| Get out now, and quickly. | **Sálganse ahorita y rápido.** |
| Walk, don't push. | **Anden, no empujen. ~ Caminen, no empujen.** |
| Follow my orders. | **Sigan mis órdenes.** |
| Go back to your cars. | **Regresen a sus carros.** |
| Go back to your houses. | **Regresen a sus casas.** |
| You need to leave the area. | **Necesitan irse del área.** |

## Scenario · ICEBREAKERS
### Empezando una conversación

Project a positive image. The following icebreakers, or conversation starters, serve to introduce you to victims, suspects, or witnesses, get their attention, and win over their confidence.

| | |
|---|---|
| Good morning, sir. | **Hola, buenos días, señor.** |
| Good morning, ma'am. | **Hola, buenos días, señora.** |
| Good morning, miss. | **Hola, buenos días, señorita.** |
| Good afternoon. What's happening? | **Hola, buenas tardes. ¿Qué pasa?** |
| Good evening. How are you? | **Hola, buenas noches. ¿Cómo está?** |
| Do you speak English? | **¿Habla inglés?** |
| Do you speak Spanish? | **¿Habla español?** |

First, ask *in English* if the person speaks English. Then, ask *en español* if the person speaks Spanish (in case you've misidentified his or her nationality).

Chapter 5 contains additional icebreaker terms in useful words and expressions, as well as everyday conversation.

| | |
|---|---|
| I speak a little Spanish. | **Hablo un poquito de español.** |
| (Does) anyone here speak English? | **¿Alguien aquí habla inglés?** |
| Listen, please. I'm Officer Tim Hagel from the police department. (I'm Deputy Tim Hagel from the sheriff's department.) | **Oiga, por favor. Soy Oficial Tim Hagel del departamento de policía. (Soy Oficial Tim Hagel del departamento del sheriff.)** |
| Come here, please. | **Venga aquí, por favor.** |
| Wait a moment, please. | **Espere un momento, por favor.** |
| May I speak with you? | **¿Puedo hablar con usted?** |
| I have some questions for you. | **Tengo algunas preguntas para usted.** |

## Warrants

Las órdenes (de la corte)

The following search and arrest warrant scenarios involve high risk and are typically used with crimes of violence involving gangbangers and violators of parole/probation.

## Scenario · HIGH-RISK SEARCH WARRANT

La orden de registro de alto riesgo

| | |
|---|---|
| Police. | **Policía.** |
| We have a search warrant. | **Tenemos una orden de registro.** |
| We'd like permission to search your house. | **Nos gustaría tener permiso para registrar su casa.** |
| You're surrounded. | **Están rodeados.** |
| You can't escape. | **No pueden escaparse.** |
| Everybody on the floor, with your hands out. | **Todos en el piso con las manos extendidas.** |
| Freeze. Don't move. | **Quietos. No se muevan.** |
| Hands in sight. | **Manos en vista.** |
| You're under arrest. | **Están arrestados.** |

We'll explain later. **Les vamos a explicar más tarde.**

## Scenario · ARREST WARRANT
La orden de arresto

In this scenario, you serve an arrest warrant to a felon.

I'm Detective P.J. Dain from the Ventura County Sheriff's Department. **Soy Detective P.J. Dain del Departamento del Sheriff del Condado de Ventura.**

I have an arrest warrant for you for … **Tengo una orden de arresto contra usted por…**

stealing cars. **robar carros.**

shooting someone. **disparar contra alguien.**

You're under arrest. **Está arrestado[a].**

We're going to jail. **Vamos a la cárcel.**

## Scenario · MIRANDA ADVISEMENT AND WAIVER
La advertencia y la renuncia Miranda

Mirandizing suspects keeps you in line with the D.A. You don't have to memorize this; just put it on a cheat sheet and read it off! It can also be found on p. 287.

**ADVISEMENT** La advertencia

You have the right to remain silent. Do you understand? **Usted tiene el derecho de guardar silencio. ¿Entiende?**

Anything you say may be used against you in a court of law. Do you understand? **Cualquier cosa que usted diga puede ser usada en su contra en una corte de justicia. ¿Entiende?**

You have the right to talk to an attorney and have one present with you before and while being questioned. Do you understand? **Usted tiene el derecho de hablar con un abogado y tenerlo presente con usted antes de y durante el interrogatorio. ¿Entiende?**

| | |
|---|---|
| If you cannot afford an attorney, one will be appointed for you, free of charge, before any questioning, if you wish. Do you understand? | **Si no tiene dinero para contratar un abogado, uno será nombrado para representarlo/representarla sin costo alguno, antes del interrogatorio, si desea. ¿Entiende?** |
| **EXPRESS WAIVER** | La renuncia |
| Please answer with a "yes" or "no." | **Por favor, conteste con "sí" o "no".** |
| Do you want to talk about what happened? | **¿Quiere hablar de lo que pasó?** |
| Do you want to tell your side of the story? | **¿Quiere contar su versión de lo que pasó?** |
| Do you want to talk with me (with us) now? | **¿Quiere hablar conmigo (con nosotros) ahora?** |

## PATROL OFFICERS / DEPUTIES
Patrulleros/oficiales del sheriff

In the following scenarios, you're on patrol. You're stopping suspects for questioning and getting personal information.

### Scenario · FIELD INTERVIEW
La entrevista

As a patrol officer, ask the following one-liner questions—or show them this book and point to this section. You'll gain confidence with experience.

| | |
|---|---|
| Last and first name. | **Apellido y nombre.** |
| What is your name? | **¿Cómo se llama?** |
| What is your full name? | **¿Cuál es su nombre completo?** |
| Nickname./A.K.A. | **Otros nombres. ~ Apodo. ~ Sobrenombre.** |
| Do you have other names? | **¿Tiene otros nombres?** |
| Driver's license and state. | **Licencia de manejar y estado.** |

Most descriptive words (adjectives) that describe males or masculine things end in **-o**. You change the **-o** to **-a** when you're describing females or things that are feminine.

| | |
|---|---|
| He's white. | **(Él) es blanco.** |
| She's white. | **(Ella) es blanca.** |
| The coat is red. | **El abrigo es rojo.** |
| The jacket is red. | **La chaqueta es roja.** |

| | |
|---|---|
| Home address. | **Dirección.** |
| Number. | **Número.** |
| Street. | **Calle.** |
| City. | **Ciudad.** |
| Zip code. | **Zona postal.** |
| State. | **Estado.** |
| What is your complete address? | **¿Cuál es su dirección completa?** |
| Phone number. | **Número de teléfono.** |
| What's your home phone number? | **¿Cuál es su número de teléfono de casa?** |
| What's your work phone number? | **¿Cuál es su número de teléfono de trabajo?** |
| Parents' first and last names. | **Nombres y apellidos de padres.** |
| School. | **Escuela.** |
| Work. | **Trabajo.** |
| Business. | **Negocio.** |
| What's your profession? | **¿Cuál es su profesión?** |
| Date of birth—month, day, year. | **Fecha de nacimiento—mes, día, año.** |
| When were you born? | **¿Cuándo nació?** |
| Where were you born? | **¿Dónde nació?** |
| Man or woman. | **Hombre o mujer.** |
| Height and weight. | **Estatura y peso.** |

| | |
|---|---|
| Race. | **Raza.** |
| Your/His/Her race? | **¿Cuál es su raza?** |
| white | **blanco[a]** |
| Hispanic/Latin | **hispano[a] ~ latino[a]** |
| black | **negro[a]** |
| Oriental/Asian | **oriental ~ asiático[a]** |
| other race | **otra raza** |
| Hair. | **Pelo. ~ Cabello.** |
| What color is your/his/her hair? | **¿De qué color es su pelo? ~ ¿De qué color es su cabello?** |
| black | **negro** |
| blond | **rubio** |
| brown | **café** |
| gray | **gris ~ canoso** |
| red | **rojo** |
| redhead | **pelirrojo** |
| What's your/his/her hair like? | **¿Cómo es su pelo? ~ ¿Cómo es su cabello?** |
| short | **corto** |
| medium | **mediano** |
| long | **largo** |
| bald | **calvo ~ pelón** |
| shaved | **afeitado** |
| Eyes. | **Ojos.** |
| What color are your/his/her eyes? | **¿De qué color son sus ojos?** |
| blue | **azules** |
| brown | **cafés** |
| green | **verdes** |
| Facial hair. | **Pelo de cara.** |
| Do you/Does he have facial hair? | **¿Tiene pelo de cara?** |
| full beard | **barba llena ~ barba completa** |

| | |
|---|---|
| goatee | **barba de chivo** |
| mustache | **bigote** |
| other | **otro** |
| none | **nada** |
| Glasses. | **Lentes. ~ Anteojos.** |
| Do you/Does he/she wear glasses? | **¿Lleva lentes?** |
| Scars, marks, tattoos. | **Cicatrices, marcas, tatuajes.** |
| Do you/Does he/she have scars, marks, tattoos? | **¿Tiene cicatrices, marcas, tatuajes?** |
| Clothes. | **La ropa.** |
| What clothes are you/ is he/she wearing? | **¿Qué ropa lleva?** |
| hat | **sombrero** |
| jacket | **chaqueta** |
| shirt | **camisa** |
| blouse | **blusa** |
| skirt | **falda** |
| pants | **pantalones** |
| dress | **vestido** |
| shoes | **zapatos** |
| Gang. | **Pandilla. ~ Ganga.** |
| Associate. | **Asociado. / Asociada.** |
| Are you/Is he/she a gang member? | **¿Es miembro de una pandilla? ~ ¿Es pandillero? / ¿Es pandillera?** |
| Gang name. | **Nombre de pandilla. ~ Nombre de ganga.** |
| What's its name? | **¿Cuál es su nombre?** |
| What's the gang called? | **¿Cómo se llama la pandilla?** |
| What's the name of the gang? | **¿Cuál es el nombre de la pandilla?** |
| Are you on probation? | **¿Está en probación?** |

| | |
|---|---|
| Probation officer's name. | **Nombre y apellido del oficial de probación.** |
| What's the name of the probation officer? | **¿Cómo se llama el oficial de probación?** |

## Scenario · PEDESTRIAN STOP
### La detención de un peatón

In this scenario, a suspected gang member is hanging out in a park. You suspect him of drinking alcohol in public or possessing drugs and need his personal information. You've already filled out your department's FI (Field Interview) card in the last scenario.

| | |
|---|---|
| Do you have a photo ID? | **¿Tiene identificación con foto?** |
| Show it to me. | **Enséñemela.** |
| Is the information here correct? | **¿La información aquí es correcta?** |
| Is it correct? | **¿Es correcto?** |
| I'm speaking to you because ... | **Le hablo porque...** |
| you seem to be a gang member. | **parece ser miembro de una pandilla. ~ parece ser pandillero[a].** |
| I'm citing you for ... | **Lo / La cito por...** |
| drinking alcohol in public. | **tomar alcohol en público.** |
| You're under arrest. | **Está arrestado[a].** |
| I'm arresting you for ... | **Lo / La arresto por...** |
| possessing drugs. | **tener drogas.** |
| I'm giving you a warning. | **Le doy un aviso. ~ Le doy una advertencia.** |
| You can leave now. | **Puede irse ahora.** |
| Go home, please. | **Vaya a casa, por favor.** |
| The park is closed. | **El parque está cerrado.** |
| Have a nice day. | **Que pase un buen día.** |
| Have a good evening. | **Que pase una buena noche.** |
| Good-bye and good evening. | **Adiós y buenas noches.** |

"You" can be expressed as **Lo** in Spanish when you're speaking to a male. "You" can be expressed as **La** when you're speaking to a female.

| | |
|---|---|
| I'm arresting you for … | **Lo / La arresto por…** |

## Scenario · LOW-RISK VEHICLE STOP

### Una detención de un vehículo de bajo riesgo

In this patrol scenario, identify yourself, give your reason for stopping the vehicle, and get driver documentation.

| | |
|---|---|
| I'm stopping you for … | **Lo / La paro por…** |
| driving carelessly. | **manejar con descuido.** |
| driving very fast. | **manejar muy rápido.** |
| Your license, registration, and insurance, please. | **Su licencia, registro y seguro, por favor.** |
| Do you still live there? | **¿Todavía vive allí?** |
| Is the information here correct? | **¿La información aquí es correcta?** |
| Is it correct? | **¿Es correcto?** |
| Wait here. | **Espere aquí.** |
| One moment, please. | **Un momento, por favor.** |
| I'm citing you for … | **Lo / La cito por…** |
| I'm giving you a ticket for … | **Le doy un tíquete por…** |
| driving very fast. | **manejar muy rápido.** |
| not stopping at a red light. | **no parar en una luz roja.** |

To determine which language to use, first ask the driver *in English* if he or she speaks English. If not, make sure that he or she speaks Spanish. Then continue in Spanish.

| | |
|---|---|
| You've got to ... | **Tiene que...** |
| go to court in the city of Ventura ... | **ir a la corte en la ciudad de Ventura...** |
| on May 3rd at 9 A.M. | **el 3 de mayo, a las 9 de la mañana.** |
| on June 1st at 2 P.M. | **el primero de junio, a las 2 de la tarde.** |
| Signing this ticket is not an admission of guilt. | **Firmar este tíquete no es una admisión de su culpa.** |
| Sign here, please. | **Firme aquí, por favor.** |
| Get out of the car slowly. | **Sálgase del carro despacio.** |
| I have an arrest warrant. | **Tengo una orden de arresto.** |
| I'm arresting you for ... | **Lo / La arresto por...** |
| driving a stolen car. | **manejar un carro robado.** |
| driving under the influence. | **manejar bajo la influencia.** |
| Hands behind you. | **Manos detrás de usted.** |
| You're under arrest. | **Está arrestado[a].** |
| We're going to jail now. | **Vamos a la cárcel ahora.** |
| I'm giving you a warning. | **Le doy un aviso. ~ Le doy una advertencia.** |
| You've got to ... | **Tiene que...** |
| fix the taillight. | **reparar la luz trasera.** |
| get your registration and insurance in order. | **arreglar el registro y el seguro.** |
| Have a nice day. | **Que pase un buen día. ~ Que tenga un buen día.** |

## Scenario · HIGH-RISK VEHICLE STOP
### Una detención de un vehículo de alto riesgo

In this high-risk scenario, you stop some gangbangers and exit them from the vehicle one at a time, cuffing and placing each one in custody.

| | |
|---|---|
| Stop—police. | **Alto—policía.** |
| Hands behind your heads. | **Manos atrás de la cabeza.** |

| | |
|---|---|
| Don't move. | **No se muevan.** |
| Do exactly what we order. | **Hagan exactamente lo que mandamos.** |
| Do exactly what we say. | **Hagan exactamente lo que decimos.** |
| If you take out a weapon, we're going to shoot. | **Si sacan un arma, vamos a disparar.** |
| Don't move until you hear the words "Do it now." | **No se muevan hasta oír las palabras: Hágalo ya.** |
| Obey our orders very carefully. | **Obedezcan nuestras órdenes con mucho cuidado.** |

Up to this point, you have been using commands for two or more persons (plural) (for example, **No se muevan**). For the remainder of the scenario, you switch to commands for one person (singular) by omitting **-n** in the action word (verb) (for example, **No se mueva**).

| | |
|---|---|
| Driver, roll down the car window. | **Conductor, baje la ventana del carro.** |
| Take out the keys and throw them in the street. | **Saque las llaves y tírelas a la calle.** |
| Place both hands out of the window. | **Ponga las dos manos afuera de la ventana.** |
| Open the door from the outside. | **Abra la puerta desde fuera.** |
| Stand up, facing away from me, and put your hands behind your head. | **Párese con su espalda hacia mí y ponga las manos detrás de la cabeza.** |
| Take two steps to your left. | **Tome dos pasos a la izquierda.** |
| Close the door with your foot. | **Cierre la puerta con un pie.** |
| With your left hand, pull up your shirt from the back of your collar. | **Con la mano izquierda, agarre el cuello de su camisa y levántela.** |

Take off your cap slowly. **Quítese la gorra despacio.**

Turn slowly in a circle. **Voltéese despacio en un círculo.**

Stop now, with your back toward me. **Alto ahora con su espalda a mí.**

Back up five steps. Stop. **Camine cinco pasos para atrás. Alto.**

Walk to the left. **Camine para la izquierda.**

Walk to the right. **Camine para la derecha.**

Get on your knees. **De rodillas.**

Hands behind you. Palms together. **Manos atrás de usted. Palmas juntas.**

Now, passenger in front. **Ahora, pasajero de enfrente.**

You, hiding in the car, hands up. **Usted, escondido[a] en el carro, manos arriba.**

## Scenario · DEAD BODY CALL
### Una persona muerta

In this patrol scenario, you take an incident report for the coroner and ask family members or friends about the medical history of the deceased. More vocabulary on illnesses can be found on p. 150.

Who was present at the time of death? **¿Quién estaba presente en el momento de la muerte?**

I need your personal information. **Necesito su información personal.**

(At) what exact time did he/she die? **¿A qué hora en punto murió?**

Are you family members? **¿Son familiares?**

Are you friends? **¿Son amigos?**

What were his/her recent illnesses? **¿Cuáles eran sus enfermedades recientes?**

Was it an unexpected death? **¿Fue una muerte inesperada?**

I'm going to examine the body. **Voy a examinar el cadáver.**

| | |
|---|---|
| We're going to call the coroner. | **Vamos a llamar al médico forense.** |
| Did he/she have medical problems? | **¿Tenía problemas médicos?** |
| When was his/her last doctor's visit? | **¿Cuando fue su última visita con el médico?** |
| (What) medicine (was he/she taking)? | **¿(Qué) medicina (tomaba)?** |
| How long was he/she ill? | **¿Desde cuándo estaba enfermo[a]?** |
| Please answer with a yes or no. | **Favor de responder con un sí o no.** |
| Did he/she have a history of ...? | **¿Tenía una historia médica de...?** |
| AIDS | **SIDA** |
| cancer | **cáncer** |
| diabetes | **diabetes** |
| heart attack | **ataque al corazón** |
| hepatitis | **hepatitis** |
| stroke | **embolia ~ ataque del cerebro** |
| tuberculosis | **tuberculosis** |

## Scenario · NARCOTICS BUST
### Un arresto de narcóticos

In this scenario, you arrest drug traffickers in a narcotics bust. Drug vocabulary can be found on pp. 141–147.

| | |
|---|---|
| What are you doing here? | **¿Qué hace aquí?** |
| Are you a drug dealer? | **¿Es usted narcotraficante?** |
| Why do you have a beeper? | **¿Por qué tiene un beeper?** |
| How much money do you have? | **¿Cuánto dinero tiene?** |
| Are you a drug addict? | **¿Es usted drogadicto[a]?** |
| What's the name of your contact? | **¿Cómo se llama su conexión?** |

| | |
|---|---|
| What are you selling? | **¿Qué vende?** |
| What are you taking? | **¿Qué toma?** |
| What are you buying? | **¿Qué compra?** |
| What (Which) drugs? | **¿Cuáles drogas?** |
| Where are the drugs? | **¿Dónde están las drogas?** |
| When did you buy them? | **¿Cuándo las compró?** |
| Where did you buy them? | **¿Dónde las compró?** |
| From whom did you buy them? | **¿De quién las compró?** |
| What color and shape? | **¿El color y la forma?** |
| How many times a day? | **¿Cuántas veces al día?** |
| What time? | **¿A qué hora?** |
| How much does it (do they) cost? | **¿Cuánto cuesta(n)?** |
| The price? | **¿El precio?** |
| Do you inhale drugs? | **¿Inhala drogas?** |
| Do you smoke drugs? | **¿Fuma drogas?** |
| Do you take drugs? | **¿Toma drogas?** |
| Do you have any marks or scars? | **¿Tiene marcas o cicatrices?** |
| The sale of illegal drugs is against the law. | **La venta de drogas ilegales es contra la ley.** |
| The buying of illegal drugs is against the law. | **La compra de drogas ilegales es contra la ley.** |
| The possession of illegal drugs is against the law. | **La posesión de drogas ilegales es contra la ley.** |
| I'm going to arrest you. | **Lo / La voy a arrestar.** |
| I'm going to search you. | **Lo / La voy a esculcar.** |
| I'm going to handcuff you. | **Lo / La voy a esposar.** |
| Have you been arrested before? | **¿Ha estado arrestado[a] antes?** |
| We're going to jail. | **Vamos a la cárcel.** |
| Get in my car. | **Suba a mi carro.** |

## Scenario · PRELIMINARY DUI INTERVIEW

La entrevista preliminar de un DUI

Here, you get the driver's medical and drug/alcohol background.

| | |
|---|---|
| Are you under the influence of drugs or alcohol? | **¿Está bajo la influencia de drogas o de alcohol?** |
| Are you drunk? | **¿Está borracho[a]?** |
| Does your car have any mechanical problems? | **¿Tiene defectos mecánicos su vehículo?** |
| Are you diabetic or epileptic? | **¿Es diabético[a] o epiléptico[a]?** |
| Do you take insulin? | **¿Está tomando insulina?** |
| Are you sick or injured? | **¿Está enfermo[a] o herido[a]?** |
| Do you have any physical or mental defects? | **¿Tiene defectos físicos o mentales?** |
| Are you seeing a doctor or dentist? Why? | **¿Está viendo un doctor o dentista? ¿Por qué?** |
| When was your last appointment? | **¿Cuándo fue su última cita?** |
| What's the name of your doctor? | **¿Cómo se llama su doctor?** |
| What's the name of your dentist? | **¿Cómo se llama su dentista?** |
| (When did you) last sleep? | **¿(Cuándo fue) la última vez que durmió?** |
| How long did you sleep? | **¿Cuánto tiempo durmió?** |
| (When did you) last eat? | **¿(Cuándo fue) la última vez que comió?** |
| Describe what and how much (you ate). | **Describa qué y cuánto (comió).** |
| What have you been drinking? | **¿Qué ha estado tomando?** |
| What brand? | **¿Qué marca?** |
| How much? | **¿Cuánto?** |

| | |
|---|---|
| When did you start (drinking)? | **¿Cuándo empezó (a tomar)?** |
| When did you stop (drinking)? | **¿Cuándo terminó (a tomar)?** |
| Where were you drinking? | **¿Dónde estaba tomando?** |
| With whom were you drinking? | **¿Con quién estaba tomando?** |
| Do you feel the effects of the drinks? | **¿Siente los efectos de las bebidas?** |
| Have you been drinking since the accident? | **¿Ha estado tomando desde el accidente?** |
| If so, what (did you drink)? | **Si es así, ¿qué (tomó usted)?** |
| How much? | **¿Cuánto?** |
| Are you taking medicine or drugs? | **¿Está tomando medicina o drogas?** |
| Have you taken any medicine or drugs? | **¿Ha tomado medicina o drogas?** |
| What? | **¿Qué?** |
| What doctor? | **¿Cuál doctor?** |
| How much? | **¿Cuánto?** |
| Time of last dosage? | **¿Última vez que tomó medicina?** |
| Do you feel the effects of the drugs? | **¿Siente los efectos de las drogas?** |
| Were you driving the vehicle? | **¿Estaba usted manejando el vehículo?** |
| If not, who? | **Si no, ¿quién?** |
| Who was driving the vehicle? | **¿Quién estaba manejando el vehículo?** |
| Where were you driving the vehicle? | **¿Adónde estaba manejando el vehículo?** |
| Where did you start driving? | **¿Dónde comenzó a manejar?** |
| Where were you going? | **¿Adónde iba usted?** |
| Where are you (right) now? | **¿Dónde está ahorita?** |

More information on food and drink is in Chapter 1, pp. 58–62. For information on alcohol and drugs, see pp. 141–147.

| | |
|---|---|
| Do you understand? | **¿Comprende?** |
| Don't move your head. | **No mueva la cabeza.** |
| Focus on the tip of my pen. | **Enfoque en la punta de mi pluma.** |
| Follow the movement of the pen with your eyes only. | **Siga los movimientos de la pluma con los ojos solamente.** |

## Scenario · SOBRIETY TEST/ DIVIDED ATTENTION EXERCISES

La prueba de sobriedad

Now you give the suspect a sobriety test or divided attention exercises. You tell him or her to move specific body parts. Most of the commands are given without action words (verbs), for example, "heel to toe" and "straight line." My officer students say the sobriety test is tricky, so be sure you have this scenario down pat! Defense attorneys will likely try to punch holes in your Spanish.

| | |
|---|---|
| I'm going to give you some tests. | **Le voy a hacer unas pruebas.** |
| I'll show you. Look at me. | **Le muestro. Míreme.** |
| Heel of your right foot to toe of your left foot. | **Tacón del pie derecho enfrente del pie izquierdo.** |
| Straight line, hands at sides. | **Línea derecha, manos al lado del cuerpo.** |
| Count from 1 to 30 slowly. | **Cuente de uno a treinta despacio.** |

| | |
|---|---|
| Raise one leg six inches (15 centimeters) off the ground. | **Levante una pierna enfrente seis pulgadas (quince centímetros) del suelo. ~ Levante una pierna enfrente seis pulgadas (quince centímetros) del piso.** |
| Hands at sides. | **Manos al lado del cuerpo.** |
| Count from 1 to 30 slowly. | **Cuente de uno a treinta despacio.** |
| Hands at sides, feet together. | **Manos al lado del cuerpo, pies juntos.** |
| Head tilted back, eyes closed. | **Cabeza para atrás, ojos cerrados.** |
| Count from 1 to 30 slowly. | **Cuente de uno a treinta despacio.** |
| Count backward from 99 to 79. | **Cuente para atrás de noventa y nueve hasta setenta y nueve.** |
| The alphabet from A to Z. | **El alfabeto de A hasta zeta.** |
| Arm extended to forehead. | **Brazo extendido a la frente.** |
| Index finger up. | **Dedo índice para arriba.** |
| With the tip of your finger, touch the tip of your nose with the hand that I tell you. | **Con la punta del dedo, toque la punta de su nariz con la mano que le diga.** |
| Put your hand down each time. | **Baje la mano cada vez.** |
| Eyes closed, head back. | **Ojos cerrados, cabeza para atrás.** |
| You're under arrest for driving under the influence (of alcohol/drugs). | **Está arrestado[a] por manejar bajo la influencia (de alcohol/drogas).** |

## Scenario · DOMESTIC VIOLENCE

La violencia doméstica

In this spousal abuse scenario, you investigate the victim's injuries, gather evidence, and interview the victim, witness(es), and suspect. Then you take the suspect to jail.

| | |
|---|---|
| Is this the Lopez residence? | **¿Es ésta la casa de la familia López?** |
| Who here called the police? | **¿Quién aquí llamó a la policía?** |
| (Is there) anyone hurt? | **¿(Hay) alguien herido?** |
| I understand there's a family problem here. What happened? | **Comprendo que hay un problema familiar aquí. ¿Qué pasó?** |
| We need to document the incident. | **Necesitamos documentar el incidente.** |
| Who, when, how, and with what did he hit you? | **¿Quién, cuándo, cómo y con qué la golpeó?** |
| (Are there any) weapons inside? | **¿(Hay) armas adentro?** |
| (Are there any) firearms inside? | **¿(Hay) armas de fuego adentro?** |
| Is he violent? | **¿Es una persona violenta?** |
| Are you married, divorced, or living together? | **¿Están casados, divorciados o viviendo juntos?** |
| Where's your husband now? | **¿Dónde está su marido ahora?** |
| Is he armed? | **¿Está armado?** |
| Is he drunk? | **¿Está borracho?** |
| Is he on drugs? | **¿Está drogado?** |
| Do you have a bruise, burn, or wound? | **¿Tiene moretón, quemadura o herida?** |
| Where is it? | **¿Dónde está?** |
| You need medical attention. I'm going to call an ambulance. | **Necesita ayuda médica. Voy a llamar una ambulancia.** |

| | |
|---|---|
| Do you want me to arrest him? A court order? | **¿Quiere que lo arreste? ¿Una orden de la corte?** |
| I'm going to arrest him. | **Lo voy a arrestar.** |
| I'm going to take him to jail. | **Lo voy a llevar a la cárcel.** |
| Here's a pamphlet on domestic violence. | **Aquí está un folleto sobre la violencia doméstica.** |
| You should contact a clinic. | **Debe comunicarse con una clínica.** |
| Do you need any more help? | **¿Necesita más ayuda?** |

## Scenario · CHILDBIRTH
### El parto

In this scenario, you help deliver a child. Here are a few pointers to help out with the delivery.

| | |
|---|---|
| Are you pregnant? | **¿Está embarazada?** |
| Do you have any ...? | **¿Tiene...?** |
| bleeding | **sangre** |
| discharge | **descarga** |
| contractions | **contracciones** |
| cramps | **calambres** |
| labor pains | **dolores de parto** |
| pain | **dolor** |
| Have you had pregnancy problems before? | **¿Ha tenido algunas complicaciones de embarazo antes?** |
| How long are the pains? | **¿Cuánto tiempo duran los dolores?** |
| How close together are they? | **¿Cada cuándo le vienen?** |
| How long do they last? | **¿Cuánto tiempo le duran?** |
| days | **días** |
| hours | **horas** |
| minutes | **minutos** |
| seconds | **segundos** |

| | |
|---|---|
| Lie back and breathe deeply. | **Acuéstese y respire profundamente.** |
| Spread your legs and bend your knees. | **Separe las piernas y doble las rodillas.** |
| Grab my hand and push hard. | **Agarre mi mano y empuje fuerte.** |
| Don't push. | **No empuje.** |
| It's coming now. | **Ya viene.** |
| It's a boy. | **Es un niño.** |
| It's a girl. | **Es una niña.** |
| Congratulations. | **La felicito.** |

## DETECTIVES / INVESTIGATORS
Los detectives / los investigadores

We present five scenarios: an initial phone contact, and investigations of welfare fraud, a jewelry store robbery, a home invasion robbery, and a rape. See the burglary investigation, pp. 94–96.

### Scenario · INITIAL PHONE CONTACT
Hablando por teléfono por primera vez

As a detective or investigator, you make an initial contact on the phone.

| | |
|---|---|
| I'm Detective Joe Friday from the sheriff's (police) department. | **Soy Detective Joe Friday del departamento del sheriff (de policía).** |
| I need to speak with José García. | **Necesito hablar con José García.** |
| Relax! He's not in trouble with the law. | **Tranquilo[a]. No tiene problemas con la ley.** |
| I only need to speak with him about a police matter. | **Solo necesito hablar con él sobre un asunto de policía.** |
| Where is he? | **¿Dónde está?** |
| Where does he work? | **¿Dónde trabaja?** |
| What time is he coming home? | **¿A qué hora regresa a casa?** |

He needs to come to the station to speak with us. **Él necesita venir a la estación para hablar con nosotros.**

Please tell him to come. **Por favor, dígale que venga.**

Please tell him to call me at 890-123-4567. **Por favor, dígale que me llame al 890-123-4567.**

## Scenario · WELFARE FRAUD
### El fraude de bienestar

In this scenario, you're a welfare fraud investigator. You try to track down a welfare recipient's husband or boyfriend.

I'm an investigator from Ventura County. (*male*) **Soy investigador del Condado de Ventura.**

I'm an investigator from Ventura County. (*female*) **Soy investigadora del Condado de Ventura.**

Do you have a phone? **¿Tiene teléfono?**

Can/May I use your phone? **¿Puedo usar su teléfono?**

Can/May I come in? **¿Puedo entrar?**

I have an entry and search warrant. **Tengo una orden para entrar y esculcar.**

Are you married? **¿Está usted casada?**

Where and when? **¿Dónde y cuándo?**

Do you live together? **¿Viven juntos?**

Can/May I see your closet? **¿Puedo ver su armario? ~ ¿Puedo ver su ropero?**

Is your husband the father of all your children? **¿Es su marido el padre de todos sus hijos?**

Is your boyfriend the father of all your children? **¿Es su novio el padre de todos sus hijos?**

How many children do you have? **¿Cuántos hijos tiene usted?**

How old are your children? **¿Cuántos años tienen sus hijos?**

Where is your husband now? **¿Dónde está su marido ahora?**

Where are your children now? **¿Dónde están sus hijos ahora?**

| | |
|---|---|
| What school do your children go to? | **¿A qué escuela van sus hijos?** |
| Where does your husband work? | **¿Dónde trabaja su marido?** |
| Where does your boyfriend work? | **¿Dónde trabaja su novio?** |
| I need to see some documents. Show me … | **Necesito ver algunos documentos. Enséñeme…** |
| a photo ID | **su identificación con foto** |
| your driver's license | **su licencia de manejar** |
| your green (resident) card | **la mica** (*slang*) |
| your Social Security card | **su tarjeta de seguro social** |
| the rental agreement | **el convenio de renta ~ el convenio de alquiler** |
| check stubs | **talones de cheques** |
| the car registration | **el registro de carro** |
| Do you receive child support? | **¿Recibe sostenimiento para sus hijos?** |
| Do you receive other financial help? | **¿Recibe otra ayuda financiera?** |
| From what agency? | **¿De cuál agencia?** |
| From the Welfare Agency? | **¿De la Agencia de Bienestar?** |
| Here's my card. | **Aquí está mi tarjeta.** |
| Call me later, please. | **Llámeme más tarde, por favor.** |

## Scenario · JEWELRY STORE ROBBERY

### Un robo de una joyería

In this scenario, you're investigating a jewelry store robbery. The action words (verbs) are in the past. Further study is needed before attempting this scenario.

| | |
|---|---|
| You said that the thieves were young people. Can you describe them? | **Ustedes dijeron que los ladrones eran jóvenes. ¿Los pueden describir?** |
| And the other? | **¿Y el otro?** |

| | |
|---|---|
| Were they armed? | **¿Tenían armas?** |
| What type of weapons? | **¿Qué tipo de armas?** |
| When did the robbery occur? | **¿Cuándo ocurrió el robo?** |
| How did they get in? | **¿Cómo entraron?** |
| How did it happen? | **¿Cómo pasó?** |
| What did they steal from you? | **¿Qué les robaron?** |
| I need a list of the stolen property. | **Necesito una lista de la propiedad robada.** |
| Do you have the serial numbers of the objects? | **¿Tienen los números de serie de los objetos?** |
| And how much money did they take? | **¿Y cuánto dinero tomaron?** |
| Were there any other witnesses present? | **¿Había otros testigos presentes?** |
| Did you see their car? | **¿Vieron su coche?** |
| What make and model? | **¿Qué marca y modelo?** |
| What direction were they heading in? | **¿En qué dirección iban?** |
| Thanks a lot. Here's my card. | **Muchas gracias. Aquí está mi tarjeta.** |
| If you remember anything else, call us. | **Si recuerdan algo más, llámenos.** |
| We're going to try to catch them. | **Vamos a tratar de pescarlos.** |
| We'll keep you informed about what we find out. | **Los vamos a mantener al tanto de lo que averiguamos.** |

## Scenario · HOME INVASION ROBBERY

Un robo en el hogar

In this scenario, you investigate a home invasion robbery. Like the last scenario, the action words (verbs) are in the past.

| | |
|---|---|
| Did you call the police? | **¿Llamó a la policía?** |
| How many suspects entered the house? | **¿Cuántos sospechosos entraron la casa?** |
| What clothing were they wearing? | **¿Qué ropa llevaban?** |
| What were the (two) suspects like? | **¿Cómo eran los (dos) sospechosos?** |
| Tell me, please, what happened and when was it? | **Dígame, por favor, ¿qué pasó y cuándo fue?** |
| How did they enter your home? | **¿Cómo entraron en su casa?** |
| Were you alone in the house at the time? | **¿Estaba sola en la casa en el momento?** |
| Where were you hiding? | **¿Dónde estaba escondida?** |
| Did they find you? | **¿La encontraron?** |
| Then what happened? | **Entonces, ¿qué pasó?** |
| And then? | **¿Y luego?** |
| What did they steal from you? | **¿Qué le robaron?** |
| Do you have the serial numbers? | **¿Tiene los números de serie?** |
| How did they leave? | **¿Cómo salieron?** |
| Did they have a vehicle? | **¿Tenían un vehículo?** |
| Make and model? | **¿Marca y modelo?** |
| Could you see what direction they were going in? | **¿Podían ver en que dirección iban?** |
| We're going to try to catch them. | **Vamos a tratar de pescarlos.** |

| | |
|---|---|
| I'll be back later to finish the robbery report. Excuse me. | **Luego, voy a regresar para terminar el reporte de robo. Con permiso.** |

## Scenario · RAPE

### Una violación

When investigating a rape, you need to be sensitive to the victim's situation and needs. The action words (verbs) are mainly in the past.

| | |
|---|---|
| I'm Detective Jeff Miller from the Oxnard Police Department. | **Soy Detective Jeff Miller del Departamento de Policía de Oxnard.** |
| I know that rape is a horrible crime. | **Sé que la violación es un crimen horrible.** |
| I understand it's very difficult for you. | **Comprendo que es muy difícil para usted.** |
| To find the man who raped you, I need information and I have some difficult questions for you. | **Para encontrar al hombre que la violó, necesito información y tengo algunas preguntas difíciles para usted.** |
| Did you know the man who attacked you? | **¿Conocía al hombre que la atacó?** |
| What's his name? | **¿Cómo se llama?** |
| Could you recognize him? | **¿Podría reconocerlo?** |
| Please give me a complete physical description of the suspect. | **Por favor, déme una descripción completa del sospechoso.** |
| Did you change clothes? | **¿Se cambió de ropa?** |
| I need the clothes. | **Necesito la ropa.** |
| A doctor should examine you. | **Un médico debe revisarla.** |
| Tell me, please, what happened and when was it? | **Dígame, por favor, ¿qué pasó y cuándo fue?** |

| | |
|---|---|
| Did the man actually rape you? That is to say, was there vaginal or rectal penetration? | **¿El hombre llegó a violarla? Es decir, ¿hubo penetración vaginal o rectal?** |
| Did he force you to perform any abnormal sexual act? | **¿La obligó a hacer algún acto sexual anormal?** |
| Did he force you to use foreign objects? | **¿La obligó a usar objetos extranjeros?** |
| What did he threaten you with? | **¿Con qué la amenazó?** |
| Did he have an accent? | **¿Tenía un acento?** |
| What language was he speaking? | **¿Qué idioma hablaba?** |
| I'll ask you to identify the suspect at the police station. | **Le voy a pedir que identifique a este sospechoso en la estación de policía.** |
| When did you last menstruate? | **¿Cuándo fue la última vez que tuvo la menstruación? ~ ¿Cuándo fue la última vez que tuvo su regla?** |
| When did you last have sexual relations? | **¿Cuándo fue la última vez que tuvo relaciones sexuales?** |
| Do you want to go to a Rape Crisis Center? | **¿Quiere ir a un "Rape Crisis Center"?** |
| Do you want me to call anybody? | **¿Quiere que llame a alguien?** |
| You're safe now. | **Usted está segura ahora.** |
| I'll be in touch with you. | **Voy a estar en contacto con usted.** |

# Culture and Survival Tips

Don't be zapped by culture shock! The following tips include communication shortcuts, useful words and expressions, basic conversation, a list of countries/continents and nationalities, Spanglish, street Spanish and "dirty words," and **falsos amigos** ("false friends") and deceptive words.

## COMMUNICATION SHORTCUTS

### Cómo mejorar la comunicación

The following tips will help you to improve your Spanish and communicate more effectively with Spanish speakers.

- Improve your pronunciation by stretching the muscles of your mouth. Exaggerate your pronunciation of Spanish vowels (**a**, **e**, **i**, **o**, and **u**).
- Establish eye contact with the person you're speaking with.
- Speak louder than normal and project your voice. Speak as clearly as you can. Repeat yourself when necessary. Use hand gestures for pointing and touching. Latinos use nonverbal "hand jive" and facial expressions, touching, close face-to-face speaking, and hand signals to communicate.
- When giving commands, be polite by adding expressions like **por favor** ("please") and **perdón** ("excuse me"). Use titles of respect like **señor** ("sir") and **señora** ("ma'am"). Courtesy and friendly greetings establish trust with Latinos.
- Be sure you're speaking to Spanish speakers. Don't assume that all victims, suspects, or witnesses who have dark features or "look foreign" are Latinos. Speak English during your initial contact.
- Make sure there is communication in Spanish. First, establish that you understand each other.

| | |
|---|---|
| Do you understand me okay? | **¿Me comprende bien?** |
| I don't understand anything. | **No comprendo nada.** |

Then, ask them how you can help.

| | |
|---|---|
| What's the matter? | **¿Qué pasa?** |
| How can I help you? | **¿En qué puedo servirle?** |
| What do you want me to do? | **¿Qué quiere que (yo) haga?** |

- Try first to discuss a problem with the oldest male—the most respected person in a family—to defuse a potentially explosive situation.
- In many situations, you may ask English-speaking children to serve as interpreters for their parents. You may also ask for an interpreter on scene.
- If necessary, ask Spanish speakers to slow down (**más despacio**) or repeat (**repita**).
- Don't be shy when you speak Spanish, even if you feel a bit awkward at first. Latinos appreciate your effort. What's important is what you say, not how you say it. Ask Spanish-speaking co-workers to correct your Spanish.
- Take charge of the conversation. Victims need your help, and they must communicate with you in any way possible. Tell them you're trying to understand them so that you can help them.
- Don't confuse languages with nationalities. Spaniards speak Spanish and eat Spanish food. Mexicans speak Spanish, but they eat Mexican food. Spaniards don't know beans about tacos and burritos!
- Request numbers one by one (**los números uno por uno**) to avoid mistakes. Better yet, have them write numbers down on your notepad.
- Avoid the metric system if possible. You don't need to use complicated charts to convert weights and distances. Just ask for weight in pounds (**peso en libras**) and height in feet and inches (**estatura en pies y pulgadas**).
- When writing dates, Latinos usually put the day before the month. For example, January 12, 2006 may be written 12/01/2006, and June 28, 2007 may be written 28/06/07.

- Use "we" instead of "I" when reassuring victims: **Somos policías** ("We're police officers") and **Estamos aquí para ayudarle** ("We're here to help you").
- Many Latinos from rural areas pay little attention to numbers and precise facts. Don't be surprised if they are unclear about a street address, age, or date of birth. In many cases, they simply don't know the information.
- Use rising intonation at the end of a question. Use falling intonation at the end of sentences and commands.
- Latinos have no middle names. Instead, they have two last names: The first is the father's family name, and the second is the mother's family name. Ask for both family names: the father's (**apellido paterno**) and the mother's (**apellido materno**). It is important to get the full name for official records. Also, do not translate Spanish names of cities or streets into English.
- Carry a "cheat sheet" of essential words and phrases, as well as expressions useful in scenarios.
- Learn to recognize profanity and street slang for your own protection, but don't use it in public!
- Saying "hello" on the phone varies among Spanish-speaking countries. You may hear **bueno**, **diga**, **oiga**, or **aló**.
- If some tough guys are harassing you, be direct and say, **Déjenme en paz** ("Bug off") or **No es asunto suyo** ("None of your business").

## USEFUL WORDS AND EXPRESSIONS
### Las palabras y las expresiones útiles

| | |
|---|---|
| agree | |
| I agree. | **De acuerdo.** |
| already | **ya** |
| also | **también** |
| bother | |
| Don't bother. | **No se moleste.** |
| Can I have ...? | **¿Puedo tener...?** |
| depend | |
| That depends. | **Depende.** |

| | |
|---|---|
| enough | **basta** |
| That's enough. | **Es bastante.** |
| Excuse me. | **Perdón. ~ Con permiso.** |
| go | |
| Let's go. | **Vámonos. ~ Vamos.** |
| good | **bueno** |
| Good idea. | **Buena idea.** |
| Good luck. | **Buena suerte.** |
| Great! | **Qué bueno.** |
| here | **aquí** |
| home | |
| at home | **en casa** |
| (to) home | **a casa** |
| hope | |
| I hope so. | **Ojalá.** |
| How do you say …? | **¿Cómo se dice…?** |
| How do you spell …? | **¿Cómo se escribe…?** |
| Listen, please. | **Oiga, por favor.** |
| lot | |
| a lot | **mucho** |
| maybe | **quizás** |
| Me neither. | **Yo tampoco.** |
| Me too. | **Yo también.** |
| more or less | **más o menos** |
| need | |
| I need … | **Necesito…** |
| not yet | **todavía no** |
| now | **ahora** |
| right now | **ya** |
| of course | **por supuesto** |
| okay | **bueno** |
| pardon | |
| I beg your pardon. | **¿Cómo? ~ ¿Mande?** |
| Really? | **¿Verdad?** |
| right away | **en seguida** |
| right now | **ya** |
| see | |
| I see. | **Ya veo.** |

| | |
|---|---|
| sorry | |
| I'm very sorry. | **Lo siento mucho.** |
| Tell me, please. | **Dígame, por favor.** |
| Thanks a lot. | **Muchas gracias.** |
| then | **entonces** |
| there | **allí** |
| There is .../There are ... | **Hay...** |
| therefore | **por eso** |
| think | |
| I think so. | **Creo que sí.** |
| want | |
| I want ... | **Quiero...** |
| Well ... | **Pues... ~ Vaya...** |
| with much pleasure | **con mucho gusto** |
| yes | **sí ~ claro ~ cómo no** |
| yet | |
| not yet | **todavía no** |
| You're welcome. | **De nada.** |

## BASIC CONVERSATION
La conversación básica

| | |
|---|---|
| Good morning. | **Buenos días.** |
| Good afternoon. | **Buenas tardes.** |
| Good evening. | **Buenas noches.** |
| Hi. | **Hola.** |
| How are you? | **¿Cómo está?** |
| How's it going? | **¿Qué tal?** |
| Fine. | **Bien.** |
| So-so. | **Así así.** |
| Lousy./Badly. | **Mal.** |
| Very badly. | **Muy mal.** |
| What's up? | **¿Qué hay?** |
| Nothing. | **Nada.** |
| What's your name? | **¿Cómo se llama?** |
| My name's Juan. | **Me llamo Juan.** |
| And you? | **¿Y tú?** (*familiar*) ~ **¿Y usted?** (*formal*) |

| | |
|---|---|
| I'm José. | **Soy José.** |
| Glad to meet you. | **Mucho gusto.** |
| Same here. | **Igualmente.** |
| Do you speak Spanish? | **¿Habla español?** |
| No, I don't speak Spanish. | **No, no hablo español.** |
| Yes, I speak a little. | **Sí, hablo un poco.** |
| I speak a little Spanish. | **Hablo un poco de español.** |
| I speak very little Spanish. | **Hablo un poquito de español.** |
| I speak English. | **Hablo inglés.** |
| Are you studying Spanish? | **¿Estudia español?** |
| Yes, Spanish is very important. | **Sí, el español es muy importante.** |
| I need Spanish for my work. | **Necesito español para mi trabajo.** |
| Do you understand? | **¿Comprende?** |
| Yes, I understand. | **Sí, comprendo.** |
| Speak more slowly. | **Hable más despacio.** |
| Repeat, please. | **Repita, por favor.** |
| Good-bye. | **Adiós.** |
| So long. | **Hasta luego.** |
| Until tomorrow. | **Hasta mañana.** |
| See you later. | **Hasta la vista.** |

## COUNTRIES/CONTINENTS AND NATIONALITIES

### Los países/los continentes y las nacionalidades

| COUNTRY/CONTINENT | | NATIONALITY |
|---|---|---|
| Africa | **África** | **africano[a]** |
| Argentina | **Argentina, la** | **argentino[a]** |
| Asia | **Asia** | **asiático[a]** |
| Australia | **Australia** | **australiano[a]** |
| Bolivia | **Bolivia** | **boliviano[a]** |
| Brazil | **Brasil, el** | **brasileño[a]** |
| Canada | **Canadá, el** | **canadiense** |
| Chile | **Chile** | **chileno[a]** |
| China | **China** | **chino[a]** |

| COUNTRY/CONTINENT | | NATIONALITY |
|---|---|---|
| Colombia | **Colombia** | **colombiano[a]** |
| Costa Rica | **Costa Rica** | **costarricense** |
| Cuba | **Cuba** | **cubano[a]** |
| Dominican Republic | **República Dominicana, la** | **dominicano[a]** |
| Ecuador | **Ecuador, el** | **ecuatoriano[a]** |
| El Salvador | **El Salvador** | **salvadoreño[a]** |
| England | **Inglaterra** | **inglés / inglesa** |
| France | **Francia** | **francés / francesa** |
| Germany | **Alemania** | **alemán / alemana** |
| Guatemala | **Guatemala** | **guatemalteco[a]** |
| Honduras | **Honduras** | **hondureño[a]** |
| India | **India, la** | **indio[a] ~ hindú** |
| Iran | **Irán** | **iraní** |
| Ireland | **Irlanda** | **irlandés / irlandesa** |
| Italy | **Italia** | **italiano[a]** |
| Japan | **Japón, el** | **japonés / japonesa** |
| Mexico | **México** | **mexicano[a]** |
| Nicaragua | **Nicaragua** | **nicaragüense** |
| North America | **Norteamérica** | **norteamericano[a] ~ estadounidense** |
| Panama | **Panamá, el** | **panameño[a]** |
| Paraguay | **Paraguay, el** | **paraguayo[a]** |
| Peru | **Perú, el** | **peruano[a]** |
| Philippines | **Filipinas, las** | **filipino[a]** |
| Poland | **Polonia** | **polaco[a]** |
| Portugal | **Portugal** | **portugués / portuguesa** |
| Puerto Rico | **Puerto Rico** | **puertorriqueño[a]** |
| Russia | **Rusia** | **ruso[a]** |
| South America | **Sudamérica** | **sudamericano[a]** |
| Spain | **España** | **español / española** |
| Sweden | **Suecia** | **sueco[a]** |
| Switzerland | **Suiza** | **suizo[a]** |
| United States | **Estados Unidos, los** | **norteamericano[a] ~ estadounidense** |
| Uruguay | **Uruguay, el** | **uruguayo[a]** |
| Venezuela | **Venezuela** | **venezolano[a]** |
| Vietnam | **Vietnám** | **vietnamita** |

## DO YOU SPEAK SPANGLISH?
¿Habla espanglish?

Spanglish is an evolving blend of Spanish and English. Most Spanish speakers use it to adapt non-translatable English words. Spanglish is no longer considered "border slang," "Tex Mex," or "street language" from East L.A. or El Paso. Spanglish has become an unofficial dialect spoken throughout North America. It's used everywhere Latinos migrate! It has worked its way from Los Angeles to Vancouver, from Houston to Chicago, from Atlanta to Montreal. Most teachers and language purists hate it, but you will almost certainly hear it a lot on your beat.

Here's a list of some common Spanglish words and expressions.

### Law Enforcement

**el cherife** ~ **el cherifato** ~ **el shérif** (sheriff)
**el crack**
**el daime** (dime bag)
**el dispatch**
**la ganga** (gang)
**el ID** (identification (card))
**el LSD**
**el nicle** (nickel bag)
**el parole**
**la probación** (probation)
**el ranger**
**el tatú** (tattoo)
**el tíquete** ~ **el tiquete** ~ **el ticket** (ticket/citation)

### Vehicles

**las brekas** (brakes)
**el garach** (garage)
**el jip** (jeep)
**el mofle** (muffler)
**el pickup**
**el station wagon**
**el taxi**
**el trailer**
**la troca** ~ **el troque** (truck)
**el ven** ~ **el van** (van)

## Sports

**el béisbol** (baseball)
**el fútbol** (football)
**el jogging**
**el jonrón** (home run)
**el knockout**
**el match**
**el pitcher**

## Food and Drink

**el Big Mac**
**el bistec** (beef steak)
**el cóctel** (cocktail)
**las donas** (donuts)
**la hamburguesa** (hamburger)
**el lonche** (lunch)
**Pisa Ho** (Pizza Hut)
**la pizza**
**el rosbif** (roast beef)
**el sandwich**
**Sebenileben** (7-Eleven)
**el six-pack**
**la soda**

## Medicine

**el CPR**
**el EKG**
**el EMT**
**el estrés** (stress)
**el IV**
**el kit**
**la nurse**

## Technology

**el computer**
**el DVD**
**el fax**
**el modem**
**el pager**
**el VCR**

## Clothes

**el brazier** (bra)
**los chorts** (shorts)
**el suéter** (sweater)
**el t-shirt**

## House

**el closet**
**el driway** (driveway)
**el hall**
**el yard sale**
**la yarda** (yard)

## Miscellaneous

**bloke** (block)
**la cama twin** (twin bed)
**culísimo** (very cool)
**el dry-wall**
**el estore** (store)
**la honi** (honey)
**la mecha** (match)
**el mercato** (market)
**okey** (okay)
**la washitería** (laundromat)

## Spanglish Action Words (Verbs)

**bleachear** (to bleach)
**blofear en poker** (to bluff in poker)
**cachar** (to catch)
**chequear** (to check)
**chopear un carro** (to "chop" a car)
**cuquear** (to cook)
**dompear** (to dump)
**drinquear** (to drink)
**eskipear** (to skip a class)
**flipar** (to flip out)
**llamar para atrás** (to call back)
**lonchar** (to have lunch)
**mopear** (to mop)
**parquear** (to park)

**signear** (to sign)
**surfar** (to surf)
**sweepear** (to sweep)
**taipear** (to type)
**watchear** (to watch)
**yogear** (to jog)

## STREET SPANISH AND "DIRTY WORDS"
### El español de la calle y las palabras groseras

This section includes slang and filthy street terms. Don't use these terms yourself. Just be informed when you're being insulted. These "dirty words" and expressions are provided here so that you can recognize them and understand their meanings. Literal English translations of the Spanish are in parentheses. The worst are listed as vulgar.

| | |
|---|---|
| alert | |
| Be alert! | **Aguas.** |
| | **Awas.** |
| | **Fíjate.** |
| | **Ojo.** |
| | **Trucha.** |
| | **Wacha.** (watch out) |
| anglo | **el gavacho** |
| | **el gringo** |
| | **el huero / la huera** (blond) |
| arrest (*verb*) | **agarrar** (to grab) |
| | **rodar** (to roll) |
| | **torcer** (to twist) |
| ass | **el culo** (*vulgar*) |
| big woman | **la nalgona** (from **nalgas**, buttocks) |
| asshole | **el culero** (*vulgar*) |
| Bad scene! / Bummer! | **Qué cacho.** |
| | **Qué cachondeo.** |
| | **Qué gacho.** |
| bag, small | **el borrego** (sheep) |
| bald (head) | **el pelón** |
| balls | **los cojones** (*vulgar*) |
| | **los huevos** (eggs) |

| | |
|---|---|
| You don't have any balls. | **No tienes huevos.** |
| bastard | **el cabrón** (*vulgar*) |
| | **el pinchi** (*vulgar*) |
| beer | **la birria** |
| | **el chupé** |
| | **el pisto** |
| | **unas frías** (some cold ones) |
| big deal | |
| It's no big deal. | **No hay pedo.** (There's no fart.) |
| big woman | **la nalgona** (from **nalgas**, buttocks) |
| bitch | **la chingona** (*vulgar*) |
| | **la perrona** (from **perra**, dog) |
| black | **chanate** |
| | **mayate** |
| | **negrito[a]** |
| | **prieto[a]** |
| | **tinto[a]** (tinted) |
| boy | **el vato** |
| boyfriend | **el chavo** (kid) |
| | **el chico** (boy) |
| wife's boyfriend | **el sancho** (from Sancho Panza in *Don Quijote*) |
| break | |
| Give me a break. | **Dame una chanza.** |
| broad | **la chava** |
| | **la ruca** (*vulgar*) |
| bug | |
| Don't bug me. | **No me friegues.** (from **fregar**, to wash) |
| bullshit | **las macanas** (*vulgar*) |
| busted | **chingo[a]** |
| | **torcido[a]** (twisted) |
| cap | **la cachucha** (*slang*) |
| car | **la carga** |
| | **la carrucha** |
| | **la ramfla** |
| jalopy | **la carcancha** |

| | |
|---|---|
| change (money) | **la feria** (fair) |
| | **la lana** (wool) |
| cigarette(s) | **los frajos** |
| | **el humo** (smoke) |
| clothing | **las garas** |
| | **la pistola** (gun) |
| | **la riata** |
| cocaine | **la coca** |
| | **el talco** |
| Cool! | **Ese.** |
| | **Órale.** |
| cop | **el cerdo** (pig) |
| | **la chota** |
| | **el cochi** (pig) |
| | **el garfil** |
| | **la jura** (oath) |
| | **la ley** (law) |
| | **el marrano** (pig) |
| | **la placa** (badge) |
| | **el puerco** (pig) |
| | **el zorrillo** (skunk) |
| cop on the take | **el mordelón** |
| | **la mordida** (bite) |
| county jail | **el condado** (county) |
| crazy | **chiflado[a]** |
| | **clavó** |
| | **deschavetado[a]** |
| crazy dude | **el vato loco** |
| dick | **el detective** (*vulgar*) |
| | **el polizonte** (*vulgar*) |
| | **la verga** (*vulgar*) |
| drugs | **la caca** (baby poop) |
| drunk | |
| to get drunk | **agarrarse un pedo** (fart) |
| dude | **el vato** |
| crazy dude | **el vato loco** |

| | |
|---|---|
| dummy | **el buey** (ox) |
| | **el idiota** |
| | **el menso** |
| | **el nopal** (cactus) |
| ex-con | **el pinto** |
| fag (male homosexual) | **la florecita** (little flower) |
| | **el joto** |
| | **el maricón** |
| | **la mariposa** (butterfly) |
| fart (*verb*) | **echarse el pedo** (fart) |
| | **ponerse el pedo** (fart) |
| fat guy | **el panzón** (from Sancho Panza in *Don Quijote*) |
| fight | **el chingazo** (*vulgar*) |
| finger | |
| to finger (to inform on) | **el dedo** (finger) ~ **chivar** |
| to give the finger to | **hacer el dedo** |
| food | **el pipirín** |
| | **el refín** |
| | **el tragazón** |
| friend | **el / la camarada** |
| good friend | **el carnal** |
| | **el compadre** |
| | **el compra** |
| fuck/fucking | **chingar** (*vulgar*) |
| | **coger** (*vulgar*) |
| | **joder** (*vulgar*) |
| Don't fuck with me. | **No chingues conmigo.** (*vulgar*) |
| Fuck your mother. | **Chinga tu madre.** (*vulgar*) |
| fucking asshole | **el pinchi cabrón** (*vulgar*) |
| It's fucked up. | **Está chingado[a].** (*vulgar*) |
| | **Está jodido[a].** (*vulgar*) |
| motherfucker | **la puta madre** (*vulgar*) |
| gang chick | **la chava** |
| | **la ruca** (*vulgar*) |
| gangbangers | **los cholos** |
| Get ready. | **Ponte abusado[a].** |

| | |
|---|---|
| Get the hell out of here. | **Vete a la chinga.** (*vulgar*) |
| Let's get the hell out of here. | **Vamos en chinga.** (*vulgar*) |
| girl | |
| tough girl | **la chavala** |
| | **la morra** |
| | **la tipa** |
| Go to hell. | **Vete a la chingada.** (*vulgar*) |
| | **Vete a la mierda.** (*vulgar*) |
| good friend | **el carnal** |
| | **el compadre** |
| | **el compra** |
| gun | **el quette** |
| Grab his/her gun. | **Agárrale la pistola.** |
| half-breed | **el cholo / la chola** |
| hashish | **el achi** |
| | **la dura concentrada** |
| | **la mota** |
| Heads up! | **Aguas.** |
| | **Awas.** |
| | **Fíjate.** |
| | **Ojo.** |
| | **Trucha.** |
| | **Wacha.** (watch out) |
| heroin | **la carga** |
| | **la chiva** |
| Hey! | **Ese.** |
| | **Órale.** |
| Hide it. | **Escóndelo. / Escóndela.** |
| Hit him/her. | **Pégalo. / Pégala.** |
| Let's hit him/her. | **Lo / La pegamos.** |
| home/house | **el cantón** |
| | **el chante** |
| homeboy/homie | **el camarada** |
| | **el homeboy** |
| | **el homie** |
| homosexual (*male*) | **la florecita** (little flower) |
| | **el joto** |
| | **el maricón** |
| | **la mariposa** (butterfly) |

| | |
|---|---|
| Hurry up. | **Ándale.** |
| | **En chingada.** (*vulgar*) |
| idiot | **el buey** (ox) |
| | **el idiota** |
| | **el menso** |
| | **el nopal** (cactus) |
| drooling idiot | **la baba** |
| | **el baboso / la babosa** |
| immigration | **la migra** |
| | **la verde** |
| jail | **el bote** (tin can) |
| | **la pinche cárcel** (fucking jail, *vulgar*) |
| | **el tanque** (tank) |
| county jail | **el condado** (county) |
| penitentiary | **la pinta** |
| prison | **la peni** |
| | **la pinta** |
| jerk | **el pendejo** (*vulgar*) |
| jump | |
| Let's jump him/her. | **Lo / La brincamos.** |
| Kill him/her. | **Chíngaselo. / Chíngasela.** (Fuck it to him/her., *vulgar*) |
| | **Dale guante.** (Give him/her the glove.) |
| | **Échaselo. / Échasela.** (Toss it to him/her.) |
| | **Friégaselo. / Friégasela.** (Rub him/her out.) |
| | **Jódeselo. / Jódesela.** (Fuck it to him/her., *vulgar*) |
| | **Madreáselo. / Madreásela.** (Mother it to him/her.) |
| | **Mándaselo a San Pedro. / Mándasela a San Pedro.** (Send him/her to Saint Peter.) |
| | **Mátalo. / Mátala.** |
| knife | **la fila** (file) |
| | **el filero** |

| | |
|---|---|
| lady | **la chava** |
| | **la ruca** (*vulgar*) |
| Latino | **la raza** (race) |
| man | **el vato** |
| marijuana | **la grifa** |
| | **la yerba** (grass) |
| | **la yesca** (tinder) |
| | **el zacate** (fodder) |
| money | **la feria** (fair) |
| | **la lana** (wool) |
| motherfucker | **la puta madre** (*vulgar*) |
| Move it. / Move ass. | **Arre.** |
| needle | **el clavo** (nail) |
| | **la punta** |
| new | **el novato** |
| | **el novatón** |
| | **verde** (green) |
| No! / No way! | **Chale.** |
| | **Nel.** |
| now | |
| Do it now. | **Órale.** |
| Okay! | **Ese.** |
| | **Órale.** |
| outfit | **las garas** |
| | **la pistola** (gun) |
| | **la riata** |
| over | |
| It's over with. | **Ya estuvo.** |
| paddy wagon | **la julia** |
| parent | **el viejo / la vieja** |
| penitentiary | **la pinta** |
| pest | **la mosca** (fly) |
| piss (*verb*) | **mear** (*vulgar*) |
| prick | **el detective** (*vulgar*) |
| | **el polizonte** (*vulgar*) |
| | **la verga** (*vulgar*) |
| prison | **la peni** |
| | **la pinta** |

| | |
|---|---|
| prostitute (*male*) | **la mariposa** (butterfly) |
| | **el puto** (*vulgar*) |
| punk | |
| street punk | **el cholo / la chola** |
| pussy | **la panocha** (*vulgar*) |
| queer | **la mariposa** (butterfly) |
| | **el puto** (*vulgar*) |
| ready | |
| Get ready. | **Ponte abusado[a].** |
| rookie | **el novato** |
| | **el novatón** |
| | **verde** (green) |
| shaved head | **el pelón** |
| shit | **la mierda** (*vulgar*) |
| | **la regué** (*vulgar*) |
| shit (*verb*) | **cagar** (*vulgar*) |
| | **zurrar** (*vulgar*) |
| sister | **la carnala** |
| slang | **el caló** |
| snitch | **el metiche** |
| | **la rata** (rat) |
| | **el relaje** (relax) |
| | **el soplón** (blower) |
| | **el vendido** (sold out) |
| son of a bitch | **el hijo de la chingada** (*vulgar*) |
| | **el hijo de puta** (*vulgar*) |
| spouse | **el viejo / la vieja** |
| squeal (*verb*) | **soplar** (to blow) ~ **chivar** |
| steal (*verb*) | **bajar** (to lower) |
| | **pegar** (to hit) |
| straight person | **el / la firme** (firm) |
| stupid person | **el buey** (ox) |
| | **el idiota** |
| | **el menso** |
| | **el nopal** (cactus) |
| thieves | **las uñas** (fingernails) |

| | |
|---|---|
| turncoat | **el metiche** |
| | **la rata** (rat) |
| | **el relaje** (relax) |
| | **el soplón** (blower) |
| | **el vendido** (sold out) |
| underwear | **los chones** |
| veteran | **el chuco** |
| | **el veterano** |
| Watch out! | **Aguas.** |
| | **Awas.** |
| | **Fíjate.** |
| | **Ojo.** |
| | **Trucha.** |
| | **Wacha.** (watch out) |
| weed | **la grifa** |
| | **la yerba** (grass) |
| | **la yesca** (tinder) |
| | **el zacate** (fodder) |
| wetback | **la espalda mojada** |
| | **el chuntaro / la chuntara** |
| | **el mojado / la mojada** (wet) |
| What's up? | **¿Qué onda?** (wave, ripple) |
| whore | **la prito** |
| | **la pros** |
| | **la puta** (*vulgar*) |
| | **la vieja de la calle** (old lady of the street) |
| whorehouse | **la casa de putas** (*vulgar*) |
| wife's boyfriend | **el sancho** (from Sancho Panza in *Don Quijote*) |
| Wow! | **Híjole.** |
| yes | **simón** |

## "FALSE FRIENDS" AND DECEPTIVE WORDS

### Los falsos amigos y las palabras engañosas

"False friends" are words that are similar in English and Spanish but have different meanings. For example, a dispatcher hears **choque** and thinks of choking—but it's really a crash or shock. **Bomba** can mean "bomb," but it can also mean "fuel pump."

Confusion can also result from a slight change in a word. Instead of saying **Tengo hambre** ("I'm hungry"), you may say **Tengo hombre** ("I have man"). The following list can help you avoid putting your foot in your mouth.

| | | | |
|---|---|---|---|
| a lot | **mucho[a]** | very | **muy** |
| bargain | **la ganga** | gang | **la ganga** |
| between | **entre** | Enter. | **Entre.** |
| bill/invoice | **la factura** | fracture | **la fractura** |
| bomb | **la bomba** | fuel pump | **la bomba de gasolina** |
| book | **el libro** | pound | **la libra** |
| bother, to | **molestar** | molest, to | **abusar** |
| but | **pero** | dog | **el perro** |
| crash/shock | **el choque** | choke, to | **asfixiarse** |
| cut | **el corte** | court | **la corte** |
| door | **la puerta** | port | **el puerto** |
| expensive | **caro** | car | **el carro** |
| expensive | **cara** | face | **la cara** |
| facing | **frente a** | in front of | **enfrente de** |
| female dog | **la perra** | pear | **la pera** |
| fifteen | **quince** | fifty | **cincuenta** |
| fifteen | **quince** | five hundred | **quinientos** |
| four | **cuatro** | fourth | **cuarto** |
| gas (bottled) | **el gas** | gasoline | **la gasolina** |
| good | **bueno[a]** | well | **bien** |
| hair | **el cabello** | horse | **el caballo** |
| hill | **el cerro** | zero | **cero** |
| house | **la casa** | case | **el caso** |
| late | **tarde** | afternoon | **la tarde** |
| little (bit) | **poco[a]** | small | **pequeño[a]** |

| | | | |
|---|---|---|---|
| man | **el hombre** | hunger | **la hambre** |
| man | **el hombre** | shoulder | **el hombro** |
| married | **casado[a]** | tired | **cansado[a]** |
| name | **el nombre** | number | **el número** |
| nine | **nueve** | new | **nuevo[a]** |
| pain/ache | **el dolor** | dollar | **el dólar** |
| pregnant | **embarazada** | embarrassed | **molesto[a]** |
| relatives | **los parientes** | parents | **los padres** |
| right, to the | **a la derecha** | straight ahead | **derecho** |
| room | **el cuarto** | fourth | **cuarto** |
| salt | **la sal** | sun | **el sol** |
| sick | **enfermo[a]** | nurse | **el enfermero / la enfermera** |
| sidewalk | **la banqueta** | banquet | **el banquete** |
| sixty | **sesenta** | seventy | **setenta** |
| stupid | **tonto[a]** | so much | **tanto[a]** |
| tomorrow | **mañana** | morning | **la mañana** |
| Turkey (country) | **Turquía** | turkey (animal) | **el pavo** |
| very | **muy** | much | **mucho** |
| when | **cuando** | how much | **cuanto[a]** |

# Quick Reference

Our quick reference section includes a list of commands and terms from the key questions and statements section in Chapter 3.

| | |
|---|---|
| Abandon. | **Abandone.** |
| accident | **el accidente** |
| afraid | |
| Don't be afraid. | **No tenga miedo.** |
| alarm | **la alarma** |
| alcohol | **el alcohol** |
| ambulance | **la ambulancia** |
| answer | **la respuesta** |
| Answer. | **Conteste. ~ Responda.** |
| arrest | **el arresto** |
| Ask for. | **Pida.** |
| attack | **el ataque** |
| Back. | **Atrás.** |
| Back up. | **Regrese.** |
| Be alert. | **Esté alerta.** |
| Be ready. | **Esté listo[a].** |
| Bend. | **Doble.** |
| Bend over. | **Agáchese.** |
| bleeding | **la hemorragia ~ sangrando** |
| bottle | **la botella** |
| Break. | **Rompa.** |
| Break it up. | **Dispérsese.** |
| Breathe. | **Respire.** |
| Bring. | **Traiga.** |
| broken | **roto[a] ~ quebrado[a]** |
| bruise | **el moretón** |

| | |
|---|---|
| burn | **la quemadura** |
| burned | **quemado[a]** |
| Call./Call off. | **Llame.** |
| Calm down. | **Cálmese.** |
| car | **el carro** |
| care | **el cuidado** |
| Take care. | **Cuídese.** |
| Careful. | **Cuidado.** |
| Check. (inspect) | **Revise.** |
| Check. (test) | **Compruebe. ~ Pruebe.** |
| Check. (verify) | **Verifique.** |
| citation | **el tiquete ~ el tíquete** |
| Clean. | **Limpie. ~ Límpiese.** |
| Climb. | **Suba. ~ Súbase.** |
| clinic | **la clínica** |
| Close. | **Cierre.** |
| collision (car) | **el choque** |
| Come. | **Venga.** |
| Count. | **Cuente.** |
| court | **la corte ~ el tribunal** |
| court order/warrant | **la orden de la corte** |
| Cover yourself. | **Cúbrase. ~ Tápese.** |
| crash (car) | **el choque** |
| Cross. | **Cruce.** |
| cut | **la cortada** |
| cut | **cortado[a]** |
| danger | **el peligro** |
| dangerous | **peligroso[a]** |
| Describe. | **Describa.** |
| detective | **el / la detective** |
| diabetes | **la diabetes** |
| diabetic | **diabético[a]** |
| Dial 9-1-1. | **Marque nueve-uno-uno.** |
| dispatch | **el despacho** |
| dispatcher | **el despachador / la despachadora** |
| Disperse. | **Dispérsese.** |
| Do. | **Haga.** |

| | |
|---|---|
| doctor | **el médico / la médica ~ el doctor / la doctora** |
| Down. | **Abajo.** |
| Drink. | **Beba. ~ Tome.** |
| Drive. | **Maneje.** |
| driver | **el conductor / la conductora ~ el / la chofer** |
| Drop. | **Suelte. ~ Deje caer.** |
| drown | |
| He/She drowned. | **Se ahogó.** |
| He/She is drowning. | **Se está ahogando.** |
| drug | **la droga** |
| drugged | **drogado[a]** |
| emergency | **la emergencia** |
| Empty. | **Vacíe.** |
| English | **el inglés** |
| Enter. | **Entre.** |
| escape | **el escape** |
| Escape. | **Escápese.** |
| evacuation | **la evacuación** |
| Evacuate. | **Evacue.** |
| Extend. | **Extienda.** |
| fall | |
| Don't fall. | **No se caiga.** |
| Fast. | **Rápido. ~ Pronto.** |
| finger | |
| Index finger up. | **Dedo índice para arriba.** |
| fire | **el fuego** |
| fire (destructive) | **el incendio** |
| firefighter | **el bombero / la bombera** |
| first aid | **los primeros auxilios** |
| Follow. | **Siga.** |
| foot | |
| Feet together. | **Pies juntos.** |
| On your feet. | **De pie.** |
| Forward. | **Adelante.** |
| Freeze. | **Quieto. / Quieta.** |
| gang | **la pandilla ~ la ganga** |
| gas | **el gas** |

| | |
|---|---|
| gasoline | **la gasolina** |
| Get. (become) | **Póngase.** |
| Get. (obtain) | **Consiga. ~ Obtenga.** |
| Get back. | **Échese para atrás. ~ Retírese. ~ Póngase atrás.** |
| Get down. | **Baje. ~ Bájese. ~ Arrástrese. ~ Tírese.** |
| Get going. | **Ándele. ~ Ándenle.** |
| Get into. | **Suba. ~ Súbase.** |
| Get out. (leave) | **Quite. ~ Quítese ~ Salga. ~ Sálgase.** |
| Get out (of). | **Baje. ~ Bájese.** |
| Get up. | **Levántese.** |
| Give. | **Dé.** |
| Give back. | **Devuelva. ~ Regrese.** |
| Give up. | **Dése.** |
| Go. | **Vaya.** |
| Go away. | **Márchese. ~ Váyase.** |
| Go back. | **Regrese. ~ Vuelva.** |
| Grab. | **Agarre.** |
| gun | **la pistola** |
| Hand(s) down. | **Mano(s) abajo.** |
| Hands up. | **Manos arriba.** |
| Hang./Hang up the phone. | **Cuelgue.** |
| Have. | **Tenga.** |
| Head (tilted) back. | **Cabeza para atrás.** |
| heart | **el corazón** |
| help | **la ayuda ~ el auxilio** |
| Help. | **Ayude.** |
| Hold on (to). | **Agarre.** |
| hospital | **el hospital** |
| Hurry up. | **Apúrese.** |
| hurt | **herido[a] ~ lastimado[a]** |
| illness | **la enfermedad** |
| ill/sick | **enfermo[a]** |
| Immediately. | **De inmediato. ~ Inmediatamente.** |
| injury | **la herida** |
| injured | **herido[a] ~ lastimado[a]** |

| | |
|---|---|
| Inside. | **Adentro.** |
| Inspect. | **Revise.** |
| insurance | **el seguro ~ la aseguranza** |
| interfere | |
| Don't interfere. | **No se entremeta.** |
| Interlace your fingers. | **Entrelace los dedos.** |
| interpreter | **el / la intérprete** |
| jail | **la cárcel** |
| Join. | **Junte.** |
| Jump. | **Brinque. ~ Salte.** |
| Keep. | **Guarde. ~ Conserve. ~ Mantenga.** |
| Keep on. | **Siga.** |
| Kneel down. | **Hínquese. ~ Arrodíllese.** |
| label | **la etiqueta** |
| Lean. | **Inclínese.** |
| Leave. | **Salga. ~ Sálgase.** |
| Let. (allow/permit) | **Deje. ~ Permita.** |
| Lie back. | **Acuéstese.** |
| Lie down. | **Acuéstese.** |
| Lift. | **Levante. ~ Alce.** |
| Listen. | **Escuche. ~ Oiga.** |
| Look (at). | **Mire.** |
| Look (for). | **Busque.** |
| Look out! | **Ojo.** |
| Make. | **Haga.** |
| medication | **el medicamento** |
| medicine | **la medicina** |
| medical help | **la ayuda médica ~ la asistencia médica** |
| Move./Move on. | **Mueva. ~ Muévase.** |
| number | **el número** |
| Obey. | **Obedezca.** |
| Open. | **Abra.** |
| Outside. | **Fuera. ~ Afuera.** |
| pain | **el dolor** |
| Palms in sight. | **Palmas a la vista.** |
| paramedic | **el paramédico / la paramédica** |

| | |
|---|---|
| parole | **el parole** |
| Pass. | **Rebase. ~ Pase.** |
| passenger | **el pasajero / la pasajera** |
| patrol | **la patrulla** |
| Pick up. | **Descuelgue. ~ Recoja.** |
| pills | **las pastillas** |
| Place. | **Ponga. ~ Coloque.** |
| poison | **el veneno** |
|   poisoning | **el envenenamiento** |
| police | **la policía** |
|   police officer | **el / la policía** |
| pregnancy | **el embarazo** |
|   pregnant | **embarazada** |
| Press. | **Oprima.** |
| Prevent. | **Prevenga.** |
| probation | **la probación** |
| problem | **el problema** |
| Protect. | **Proteja. ~ Protéjase.** |
| Pull. | **Tire. ~ Jale.** |
| Pull over. | **Arrime. ~ Hágase.** |
| Pull up. | **Agarre.** |
| Push. | **Empuje.** |
| Push down. | **Pise.** |
| Put. (place) | **Ponga. ~ Coloque.** |
| Put down. | **Baje. ~ Bájese.** |
| Put in. | **Meta. ~ Métase.** |
| Put on. | **Póngase.** |
| Put out. (a burning object) | **Apague.** |
| Put together. | **Junte.** |
| Quick. | **Rápido. ~ Pronto.** |
| Raise. | **Levante. ~ Alce.** |
| Read. | **Lea.** |
| registration | **el registro** |
| Relax. | **Esté tranquilo[a]. ~ Relájese.** |
| Release. | **Suelte. ~ Deje caer.** |
| Remain. | **Quédese.** |
| Remove. | **Quite. ~ Quítese.** |
| Repair. | **Repare.** |
|   Get repaired. | **Haga reparar.** |

| | |
|---|---|
| Repeat. | **Repita.** |
| Report. | **Reporte.** |
| Resist. | **Resista.** |
| Rest. | **Descanse.** |
| Return. | **Regrese. ~ Vuelva.** |
| Right now. | **Ahora mismo. ~ Ahorita. ~ Ya.** |
| Roll down. | **Baje. ~ Bájese.** |
| Run. | **Corra.** |
| Don't run. | **No corra.** |
| safety | **la seguridad** |
| safe | **seguro[a]** |
| Save yourself. | **Sálvese.** |
| Say. | **Diga.** |
| seizure | **las convulsiones** |
| Separate. | **Separe.** |
| Shoot. | **Dispare. ~ Tire.** |
| shooting/shot (gun) | **el disparo ~ el tiro ~ el tiroteo** |
| Shout. | **Grite.** |
| Show. | **Enseñe. ~ Muestre.** |
| Shut. | **Cierre.** |
| Shut up. | **Cállese.** |
| sick | **enfermo[a]** |
| Sign. | **Firme.** |
| Sit down. | **Siéntese.** |
| Slow./Slowly. | **Despacio. ~ Lentamente.** |
| smoke | **el humo** |
| Don't smoke. | **No fume.** |
| Spanish | **el español** |
| Speak. | **Hable.** |
| Spread. | **Abra. ~ Separe.** |
| Squeeze. | **Apriete.** |
| Stand. | **Pare. ~ Párese.** |
| Stand back. | **Póngase atrás. ~ Échese para atrás. ~ Retírese.** |
| Stand up. | **Levántese.** |
| Start. | **Arranque.** |
| Stay. | **Quédese.** |

| | |
|---|---|
| Step out. | **Baje. ~ Bájese.** |
| Stop. | **Alto.** |
| Stop. | **Detenga. ~ Deténgase ~ Pare. ~ Párese.** |
| Stretch. | **Extienda.** |
| Surrender. | **Dése.** |
| suspect | **el sospechoso / la sospechosa** |
| Take. | **Tome.** |
| Don't drink and drive. | **No tome y maneje.** |
| Take off. (clothes) | **Quítese.** |
| Take out. | **Saque.** |
| Tell. | **Cuente. ~ Diga.** |
| Threaten. | **Amenace.** |
| Don't threaten me. | **No me amenace.** |
| Throw. | **Tire. ~ Lance.** |
| ticket | **el tíquete ~ el tiquete** |
| Touch. | **Toque.** |
| translator | **el traductor / la traductora** |
| Try. | **Trate.** |
| Turn. | **Vire. ~ Dé (la) vuelta. ~ Doble.** |
| Turn around. | **Voltéese. ~ Dése vuelta.** |
| Turn off. (something running) | **Apague.** |
| Turn on. (switch on) | **Prenda. ~ Encienda.** |
| victim | **la víctima** |
| Wait. | **Espere.** |
| Walk. | **Camine. ~ Ande.** |
| warning | **el aviso ~ la advertencia** |
| warrant | **la orden** |
| Watch. | **Mire.** |
| weapon | **el arma** |
| witness | **el / la testigo** |
| worry | |
| Don't worry. | **No se preocupe.** |
| Write. | **Escriba.** |

# MIRANDA ADVISEMENT AND WAIVER

La advertencia y la renuncia Miranda

**ADVISEMENT** — La advertencia

You have the right to remain silent. Do you understand?
**Usted tiene el derecho de guardar silencio. ¿Entiende?**

Anything you say may be used against you in a court of law. Do you understand?
**Cualquier cosa que usted diga puede ser usada en su contra en una corte de justicia. ¿Entiende?**

You have the right to talk to an attorney and have one present with you before and while being questioned. Do you understand?
**Usted tiene el derecho de hablar con un abogado y tenerlo presente con usted antes de y durante el interrogatorio. ¿Entiende?**

If you cannot afford an attorney, one will be appointed for you, free of charge, before any questioning, if you wish. Do you understand?
**Si no tiene dinero para contratar un abogado, uno será nombrado para representarlo/representarla sin costo alguno, antes del interrogatorio, si desea. ¿Entiende?**

**EXPRESS WAIVER** — La renuncia

Please answer with a "yes" or "no."
**Por favor, conteste con "sí" o "no".**

Do you want to talk about what happened?
**¿Quiere hablar de lo que pasó?**

Do you want to tell your side of the story?
**¿Quiere contar su versión de lo que pasó?**

Do you want to talk with me (with us) now?
**¿Quiere hablar conmigo (con nosotros) ahora?**